CONGRESSIONAL POWER: CONGRESS and SOCIAL CHANGE

Gary Orfield

The Brookings Institution

Under the General Editorship of
James David Barber, Duke University

HEU

HARCOURT BRACE JOVANOVICH, INC.
New York Chicago San Francisco Atlanta

Cover illustration by Carol Robson

ISBN: 0-15-513081-1

Library of Congress Catalog Card Number: 74-23945

Printed in the United States of America

PREFACE

The Watergate scandal made us realize that we need Congress, but it did little to help us understand the role Congress plays in the development of national policy. Commentators who had ignored Congress for years, or discounted it as a weak and obstructionist organization, began to recognize its ability to serve as the ultimate check on the abuse of executive authority. For a time people stopped talking about Congressional junkets and log-rolling political deals and observed with surprise that the members of the House Judiciary Committee struggling with impeachment were intelligent and visibly concerned both with moral issues and Constitutional questions. Perhaps if the impeachment process had run its full course a basically new understanding of Congress would have emerged.

The resignation of President Nixon and the beginning of the Ford Administration shifted the center of attention and the focus of public hopes. As soon as Congress had done its part in saving the nation from a desperate situation, press and public attention quickly reverted to the Presidency. Once again it was assumed that Congress would play only a secondary role in the shaping of national policy. I believe that assumption is mistaken and that it rests on a widely shared but erroneous perception of Congress's role in the recent past.

Congress is powerful, and it has regularly exercised considerable power in the shaping of domestic policy. Contrary to the
perception of Congress as an obstacle to progressive social
policy proposed by the President, recent performance has shown
Congress to be the initiator and the President the obstacle on
a number of important issues. Both the real power of Congress
and the direction of its influence can be discerned with unusual
clarity through close study of the pre-Watergate years of the
Nixon Presidency, the period most closely examined in the case
studies included in this book. The particularly revealing quality
of the Nixon years stems from the clear partisan division between Congress and the President throughout that period and
from the fact that President Nixon continually tested the limits
of executive authority through confrontations with Congress.

Not only was Nixon the first President in more than a century
to take office without carrying either house of Congress, but he
was also the most disdainful and disrespectful of Congress's
role in policy-making. In many areas where in normal circumstances the interplay of legislative and executive authority would
have been expressed in quiet compromises, anticipated reactions, and negotiations, the Nixon years brought visible, unambiguous contests. The openness of the clashes and the President's frequent refusal to compromise, even when defeat was
very likely, provided a rare opportunity to measure the relative
contemporary strength of the institutions. It will probably be a
long time before the country has, or can afford, another such
test.

As a representative body of 535 members who are chosen
from widely different state and local political parties and who
define their roles in Washington in a confusing variety of ways,
Congress is an exceedingly complicated political institution. An
enormous range of concerns reach Congress; its members are
preoccupied with problems ranging from the Department of
Agriculture's classification system for black-eyed peas to consequences of nuclear proliferation for the future of humanity.
Merely reading the *Congressional Record* for a few days reveals
the vast array of issues and perspectives that must be worked
into the Congressional process. Consequently, any attempt to
describe Congress must abstract a certain set of issues from the
millions of words and thousands of actions that emerge from
Capitol Hill each year. This book concentrates not on the details of the inner functioning of committees or on the great
public spectacles of Vietnam or the battle over impeachment
but on the development of domestic social policy. It is con-

cerned basically with two questions—Congress's contemporary capacity to initiate policy and the evolutionary change in the ideological complexion of Congress in recent years. I have made these my central concerns because I believe they respond to misconceptions so widespread that they seriously distort thinking about such important issues as the internal reform of Congress, the appropriate political strategies for liberals and conservatives, and the need for changes in the distribution of power between the executive and legislative branches.

Congressional Power: Congress and Social Change argues that Congress is more important and less conservative than is generally believed. It should not be read, however, as a defense of the status quo. While most members of Congress are honest and a good number are remarkably talented, there are lazy and incompetent legislators, members with no hesitation about financing their campaigns with money from interests they have directly aided, and even a few old-fashioned demagogues. Although Congress may be more progressive than conservative Presidents like Nixon and Ford, it rarely provides powerful new leadership on controversial social issues. This book does not deny that we need massive new social reforms, but it does argue that we cannot blame our difficulties on Congress as an institution. If we are to achieve basic change we must change not the rules of Congress but the outcomes of elections. The evidence strongly suggests that Congress will change if the public really wants change and sends to Washington new members committed to legislating that change. It is a fundamental and self-defeating mistake to think that there is an easier route.

Although a great many Americans, including many students, become actively involved in Presidential campaigns, few show much concern over races for the House or Senate. In many areas of the country these elections are fought with small groups of workers and relatively little money. Volunteers can have more impact on these races than on massive Presidential contests, particularly in closely divided districts or where the incumbent is retiring. Primaries without incumbents usually have low turnouts and are particularly easy to affect. On the single occasion in recent history when large numbers of students did enter primary campaigns, after the 1970 Cambodian invasion, they helped challengers defeat powerful incumbents in several important contests. Two of the new members who prevailed in those 1970 battles, Representatives Sarbanes (D-Md.) and Drinan (D-Mass.), played significant roles in the House impeachment proceedings just four years later.

Progressive and conservative forces have been so narrowly divided in the House in recent years that major issues frequently have been decided by a handful of votes. Thus a small number of election victories can have a real policy impact, and, given the very high rate of reelection for new incumbents, that impact is likely to last. If Congress is much more important than commonly believed, so too are Congressional elections.

I have attempted throughout the book to avoid jargon and to use the results of contemporary statistical studies of Congress without carrying along the methodological apparatus. The book relies more heavily on Congressional publications than do most recent studies of Congress. These choices reflect my judgments about the appropriate methods for answering the particular questions central to the book. I don't rely much on scales of roll call votes or *Congressional Quarterly*'s "Presidential support scores," for example, because I think that the results are often meaningless or even misleading. I see Congressional publications, on the other hand, as a vast and largely unexploited body of data on how policy is shaped and on the major ideological justifications for policy decisions.

Some of the best writers on Congress, from Woodrow Wilson to Ralph Huitt, have based their writings largely on sensitive reading of records that Congress makes easily available to anyone. While questionnaires, interviews, and sociological studies of groupings within Congress are very useful in answering certain questions, my own intensive research on some bills and my personal involvement in the shaping of other legislative issues have given me great respect for the value of the printed records, in spite of the possibilities of manipulating them. Frequently members of Congress and their top staff people are so involved with a vast array of constantly changing issues that they cannot recount the development of a particular policy as accurately as a careful reader of all the relevant materials. Students of Congress who are concerned primarily with policy issues rather than internal institutional developments should give serious consideration to Congressional documents.

Many people have helped directly or indirectly in the development of this book. I greatly appreciate the tolerance and the insights of a number of students at the University of Virginia and Princeton on whom I first tried out various versions of the ideas expressed here. Many conversations on Capitol Hill have helped me greatly. I would like to thank Professors James David Barber of Duke University and Benjamin I. Page of the University of Chicago for useful comments on an earlier draft and express my appreciation to the extremely helpful staff at Harcourt Brace Jovanovich, especially Harrison Griffin, Tom Williamson, Clifford Browder, and Peter Kaldheim. Writing a book is, of course, a major strain on the entire family, and I am very thankful for the patience and help of my wife, Antonia, and my daughters, Amy and Sonia. I wish that I could promise that they would no longer have to endure endless stacks of *Congressional Records*, but I'm afraid I'm incurably fascinated.

Like many of my fellow political scientists, I am an activist liberal Democrat, but I cannot share the common disposition to blame Congress as an institution for continual governmental failure to face urgent social and economic problems. My research has given me deepening respect for the existing and potential power of Congress and for its reasonably representative character in most areas of national policy. The real obstacles to significant reform lie not in the structure of Congress but in the party structure that selects members, in our system of public beliefs, and, recently, in the White House.

Gary Orfield

TO MY MOTHER AND FATHER
with thanks for their love and understanding

CONTENTS

part three   CONGRESS AND THE SCHOOLS:
MONEY, RACE, AND CHANGE

part four   CONGRESS AND JOBS

part one
OBSOLETE IMAGES, CHANGING REALITIES

INTRODUCTION

Popular Stereotypes of Congress

Americans continually proclaim their pragmatic flexibility and realism. Yet they maintain the oldest set of stable political institutions in the world and repeatedly describe the operations of that structure in terms of seldom challenged myths. These myths include a view of Congress as a declining and hopelessly fragmented body trying with little success to cope with the expansive and even dangerous power of a stronger institution, the Presidency.

Even in early 1974, when, with the deepening of the Watergate crisis, respect for Presidential authority approached its modern low point Congress was seen in an even more intensely unfavorable light. While the polls showed that only a fourth of the public approved of the job President Nixon was doing, they also showed that Congress had the respect and approval of only one American in five.[1] Even Congress's impressive performance in the impeachment proceedings, which forced President Nixon's resignation, has produced little confidence that Congress can play a major positive role in the formation of national policy.

The assumptions about the sorry state of Congress have often been so pervasive that observers don't even bother to look at the evidence. This book will argue that the popular stereotype is fundamentally wrong. Congress is alive and well, at least in the field of domestic policy. If it is not progressive, it is usually reasonably representative and responsive. As public opinion changes, as Presidents define their constituency in different ways, and political circumstances gradually alter the membership of the House and Senate, Congress has been moving away from its traditional conservative or passive role in the development of national policy. This change became quite apparent with the beginning of the Nixon Administration. As the President moved sharply to the right on social policy, and the Supreme Court was largely neutralized by a series of four conservative appointments, Congress often remained the most progressive of the three branches in dealing with social policy issues.

The early 1970s did not see Congress become a seedbed for liberal activism. Although the legislative branch was now often *more* responsive to new social needs than the other principal institutions of government, there were still very broad and important areas of inaction and stalemate in domestic policy. This analysis will show that there is nothing in the institutional structure of Congress which renders the legislative branch either weak or conservative. In fact, Congress regularly exercises more power than it is credited with, and the ideological impact of its participation shifts from issue to issue and from political circumstance to political circumstance.

Our political system's lack of responsiveness to some of the very real social crises that preoccupy many intellectuals is not inherent in the Congressional process. Congressional reformers are simply wrong when they claim that institutional changes will produce "good" responses to the environmental problem, to inequitable taxation, irrational urban policies, and other major difficulties. The basic problem is more fundamental, and arises from the fact that the major progressive political force in this society, the activist liberal wing of the Democratic Party, is almost always a minority. Reformers spread the illusion that different procedures within Congress would produce answers to problems most Americans simply don't want to face. So long as Congress is a representative body, it is highly unlikely to produce decisive answers to controversial questions before public opinion accepts the necessity of action.

This study will try to correct mistaken perceptions of Congressional impotence and inherent conservatism both through a new examination of the available evidence on Congress's general role in the political system, and through an intensive

4

analysis of the impact of Congressional action in several significant areas of domestic policy. The investigation draws on elements of continuing value in each of the two major streams of political science writing on Congress: the traditional group of scholars preoccupied with the need to reform Congress's role in the political system, and the behaviorists of the present generation who have produced detailed studies of how various segments of the Congressional process actually work. This study will attempt to answer some of the central questions about Congress's role in shaping national policy while drawing on the data collected by the behaviorists. It will try to avoid both the traditionalist fallacy that Congress as an institution is to blame for the more basic problems of our political structure and public ideologies, and the tendency of the behaviorists to ignore policy issues.

The Changing Presidency in the Nixon Era

The policy analysis of this book will deal at length with the Congressional-Presidential struggles of the Nixon Administration. This period is particularly revealing because it provides an almost unique test case of clashing institutional objectives. Nixon was the first President in 120 years to be elected to a first term without carrying either house of Congress. Even his massive 1972 reelection victory left Congress solidly Democratic.

The results of the 1968 election meant that, for the first time since political science emerged as a discipline, the normal political incentive to obscure White House-Capitol Hill conflicts so as to maintain at least a façade of party unity, was absent from the outset of the Administration. In fact, the close partisan division in the 1968 election, and the contentious nature of President Nixon's personal political record, tended to encourage relatively open battles from the beginning. Mr. Nixon's repeated decisions to force issues to divisive votes, rather than to quietly seek accommodations, made the struggles all the more visible. When Mr. Nixon acted as if all the popular clichés about vast Presidential power were true, the results were highly instructive.

In another important respect the Nixon period provides a valuable corrective. Scholars steeped in the memory of the New Deal, the Fair Deal, the New Frontier, and the Great Society have often implicitly or explicitly concluded that the Presidency

5

has become the dominant progressive institution in American politics. The modern institutionalized Presidency, we are often told, serves as the only real source of major new advances in social policy. Unless the President draws on the inherently superior capacity of the executive branch to devise answers to new social needs, it is said, Congress is virtually incapable of action.

During the Nixon years, however, the President proposed comparatively little substantive legislation, and his rate of success with the measures he supported was very low. Congress, on the other hand, initiated major new programs, frequently provoking Presidential vetoes.

The Presidency, political scientists have often said, is inherently progressive because the Presidential election system has a built-in liberal bias, while Congressional power grows out of an electoral structure that magnifies local concerns. A number of Presidential campaigns during the past several decades have been organized around competition for the big blocks of electoral votes in the large urbanized states. At the same time Congressional malapportionment overrepresented rural areas in the House, while the lightly populated nonindustrial states have always been greatly overrepresented in the Senate.

Most political scientists have argued that the great importance of the big, closely divided states in Presidential elections has magnified the political influence of the urban minorities concentrated in these states. The political situation, analysts argued, made the President the natural spokesman for minority and urban needs. This very argument was used by some Congressional liberals in 1969 against adoption of a Constitutional amendment for direct election of the President.

Whatever the historical validity of these assertions, they no longer hold. In the 1964, 1968, and 1972 Presidential campaigns the GOP candidates wrote off the black vote and operated on the assumption that the real swing vote was in the suburbs. The Republican nominees saw the black vote, not as a swing vote, but as an integral locked-in element of the Democratic Party base. Turning their backs on the declining central-city electorate, they looked to the suburbs. In dramatic contrast to previous elections, the GOP adamantly refused to concede the South to the Democrats. By following a strategy that ignored the urban ghettos and put primary importance on the Southern and Border states, the Republicans were altering the Presidential political base from a source of liberal leverage to a collection of forces desiring to slow and reverse social changes al-

6

ready underway. The important thing about this strategy is that it was accepted at the top levels of three successive campaigns, two of which succeeded in winning the Presidency.

Not only Republican political writers but also some widely publicized Democratic experts saw a vast change occurring in the Presidential constituency. On the GOP side, 1968 campaign advisor Kevin Phillips spelled out the new electoral situation in his book *The Emerging Republican Majority*, which emphasized the political importance of the South and West. On the other side, moderate Democrats Scammon and Wattenberg attracted wide attention with *The Real Majority*, their 1970 analysis of the need for Democratic candidates to downplay sensitive social issues and emphasize a broadly based political appeal to the "unpoor" and the "unyoung" white voters.[2] All candidates were affected by the growing racial polarization which was fanned and exploited by the candidacies of George Wallace and Richard Nixon.

The Decline of Conservative Power in Congress

While a new interpretation of the Presidential constituency was taking hold in the minds of many, something quite the opposite was beginning to become evident in Congress. As the 1970s began, the big cities enjoyed reasonable representation and growing seniority power within Congress. As political competition in the South spread and produced real challenges in former one-party districts, a growing proportion of the safe, stable, one-party districts that remained were located in the central cities, where Democratic voters frequently constitute overwhelming majorities. Given the continuing decline in central-city population and the ten-year time lag before a new reapportionment, the relatively liberal central-city constituencies were destined to have increasing overrepresentation in the House as the 1970s advanced. At the same time, the continued emigration of central-city liberal voters would affect the nature of suburban districts.

The future consequences of the changing distribution of safe seats were dramatically illustrated in January 1973, when Rules Committee Chairman William Colmer was replaced by Representative Ray Madden of Indiana. The rural Southern Democrat from Pascagoula, Mississippi, was succeeded by a liberal urban Congressman representing Gary, Indiana. Furthermore, the next three ranking members of the committee were Northern urban Democrats.[3] This was not, of course, a characteristic pattern in the House yet, but it was a sign of the breakdown of the old order.

The liberalization of the Senate began much earlier, partly because of a very important set of historic circumstances. Although political scientists tend to look at changing patterns within Congress, external political circumstances can often be decisive influences. Democratic control of the Senate was consolidated in the 1958 election, when, in the most dramatic Democratic Congressional victory since the 1936 New Deal landslide, the Senate gained fifteen additional Democratic members. Democrats carried such conservative states as Maine, Utah, West Virginia, Indiana, Wyoming, and Nevada.[4] Most of the new members voted solidly with the party's liberal bloc, eventually tipping the balance against the old Senate establishment.

Thanks to the most important change instituted in Senate operations in the 1950s, the "Johnson rule," which provided a major committee assignment for each new Senator, the new members began to accumulate seniority on important committees at once. Normally much of this liberal seniority would have been wiped out when the GOP recaptured seats from some of the vulnerable liberals. The 1964 Goldwater fiasco, however, preserved the group intact. In 1970, when President Nixon directed a harsh ideological campaign against liberal Democratic incumbents and strongly appealed for a conservative Senate, the liberals held their own, actually scoring gains outside the South. This election virtually assured Democratic control of the Senate until 1977, and domination of Senate Democrats by the party's Northern and Western wing.

The GOP membership in the Senate began to change character also, perhaps in response to the demands of their increasingly urbanized constituencies for improved governmental services. The tendency was apparent in the 1966 election, when the strong midterm GOP comeback from the Johnson landslide produced strikingly different new groups of Republicans in the House and Senate. In the House the new members tended to be staunch conservatives, committed to rolling back some of the Great Society programs. In the Senate, on the other hand, five of the six new GOP members identified with the moderate wing of the party. Among the new members, Senators Charles Percy (R-Ill.), Mark Hatfield (R-Ore.), and Edward Brooke (R-Mass.) were soon to emerge as national spokesmen for progressive Republicans.

8

The growing strength of the GOP moderate faction was evident in the 1969 vote that named Hugh Scott (R-Pa.) successor to Everett Dirksen (R-Ill.) as the party's Senate Leader. The replacement of the conservative leader from Pekin, Illinois, with the moderate Philadelphian was to have significant impact on domestic policy. The Senate was now seldom in the control of the old, rigidly conservative coalition of Southern Democrats and Republicans. On a number of issues it was now possible to form a moderate-liberal majority in support of social policy proposals.

The Unchanging Criticism of Congress

Congress was changing, but perceptions of Congress remained largely fixed. Denunciations of Congressional ineptitude and legislative stalemate continued to proliferate. Inside and outside of Congress, critics said that only basic reforms could preserve Congress's intended role as a major force in American government. Even while they were sending their local incumbents back to Washington in great numbers, the American people expressed extremely low regard for Congress as an institution.

Characteristically, both the criticisms of Congress and the proposed cures are usually stated in institutional terms. We are told that the Congressional structure is inefficient or unresponsive, or that the rules screen out the competent and stifle innovation. Implicitly, however, the criticisms are political. When a critic says that Congress is not responsive, he obviously has in mind some set of national needs he believes Congress should respond to. Often these are the needs of an oppressed social group or of important decaying public institutions like the central cities and their school systems. The reform proposals often implicitly assume that procedural changes would release a suppressed progressive majority, likely to take a far more activist role in the provision of governmental services. This assumption may well be incorrect.

While the claim that certain major institutional features of Congress imposed a conservative bias on the legislative process has considerable historic validity, the recent picture is unclear. With a few notable exceptions, which run in both liberal and conservative directions, recent Congresses have rather accurately reflected the values and the confusion of the public in dealing with major issues of social change.

If the interpretation offered here is correct, liberals are un-   9 likely to accomplish much by reforming Congressional procedures. The sobering reality is that the real obstacles are not so much on Capitol Hill as in the society as a whole. While tinkering with legislative arrangements may permit some minor improvements, basic social reforms probably require a political movement able to change public values.

Most of the time, we have the Congress we really want and the Congress we deserve. We send the same members back to Washington time after time. Congress is inherently neither liberal nor conservative. Its political tendencies change with the times, with political circumstances, with the delayed responses of the seniority system, and with tides of public opinion. In social policy battles of the early 1970s, Congress became relatively more progressive and activist than the Presidency.

Recent Areas of Confrontation

The interplay of Presidential and Congressional influences can be examined by closely looking at the development of policy in three broad areas—civil rights, education, and employment—during the period from the late Johnson Administration through the early portion of President Nixon's second term. These issues, analyzed in the central portion of this study, and others discussed in less detail thereafter, obviously cannot adequately represent the whole sweep of domestic social policy. Each, however, is a prominent and long-standing political question on which there were relatively clear progressive and conservative positions. By looking at the development of several issues through a large number of legislative battles spanning several years, one obtains a more realistic portrait of the policy process than by merely examining the legislative history of one or a few bills.

The civil rights section will underline the limits of Presidential authority and the power of the Congressional veto when the President tries to reverse reforms that are already part of established law. Though he invested considerable time and prestige and intensely pressured his Congressional supporters, the President met a series of costly defeats. Even though he drew on his leadership role to deepen and exploit racial polarization, the President encountered successive frustrations.

In education policy the President's main objectives were to reduce the federal support for education and to renounce most of the existing federal leverage on state and local school systems. Congress, on the other hand, pressed each year for higher funding and retention of the federal requirements in the Great Society legislation. It was Congress that prevailed—only modestly in the financial struggle, but much more clearly in the protection of the legislative framework.

While the civil rights and school policy battles often involved legislative vetoes of conservative White House initiatives, the development of a new jobs policy is best seen as an important Democratic Party effort to initiate a new domestic policy from a Congressional base, in the face of strong Presidential opposition. Study of this effort provides an opportunity to reflect on both the possibilities and the limitations of Congressional policy initiation during a period of executive hostility.

The Need for Reassessment of Congress

Although this book argues that Congress is more important and less rigidly conservative than many critics claim, it is not intended as a defense of the status quo in Congress, and disputes the conclusions of naive reformers. Liberals who believe that fundamental problems in our society require drastic changes in social and economic policy should not cherish the illusion that good, progressive policies will emerge from Congress if only a few procedures can be changed. The inadequacies of our policies will never be corrected in the caucus rooms on Capitol Hill. Basic change will come only if the supporters of new policies do the hard local political work to elect members who will expand the liberal minorities in each house.

While this study is intended to deflate inaccurate descriptions of the political effects of the seniority system, the Rules Committee, and other often criticized aspects of the political process, it is certainly not intended to recommend these practices and institutions. While the latter no longer play the powerful negative role they once did, they are still not good or sensible ways to run an extremely important legislative body.

The fact that Congress was often more progressive than the Nixon Administration does not, of course, mean that Congress is inherently progressive, or that it has been a great force for rapid and effective repair of chronic social inequities. It would be tragic if we replaced the idealization of the Presidency, now vastly deflated by the Watergate fiasco, with the idealization of Congress. This book merely argues that there is nothing *inherent* in the structure of Congress that makes it the more

11

conservative branch, and that evidence indicates the liberal minority is accumulating increasing power.

We must stop thinking in terms of institutional stereotypes and unexamined assumptions. Both scholars and activists need to devote more attention to reassessing the contemporary reality and future possibilities of Congressional policy initiatives. They need to think less in terms of a handful of visible new bills, and more in terms of the whole array of Congressional influences that help shape policy in a given area. It is time for critics to rethink their wildly overoptimistic promises about Congressional reform, and to recognize that Congress often only reflects the indecision or contradictory desires of the local publics and the local political structures.

It is a delusion for liberals to think that there is a hidden majority for basic social reform somewhere inside Congress that could be liberated by a few institutional reforms. Activist liberals must begin with the realization that they have only a minority in Congress, particularly in the House. On some issues, in fact, a more democratic House might be an even less progressive House. If strong progressive programs are to prevail in Congress, their supporters must first prevail in elections.

NOTES

[1] Harris Survey in *Washington Post*, February 12, 1974.

[2] The two books cited are the most widely read descriptions of the changing nature of the Presidential constituency: Kevin P. Phillips, *The Emerging Republican Majority* (New Rochelle, N.Y.: Arlington House, 1969); and Richard W. Scammon and Ben J. Wattenberg, *The Real Majority* (New York: Coward, McCann, 1970). While both books oversimplify the facts and underestimate the continuing political power of minority groups and poor people, they do contain valuable data.

[3] The data on committee membership comes from the *Congressional Directory*, 92d Cong., 1st Sess., 1971, p. 275.

[4] Congressional Quarterly, *Congress and the Nation*, Vol. 1 (Washington: Congressional Quarterly, Inc., 1965), p. 30.

2

TRADITIONAL
INTERPRETATIONS

The Reformers' Fear of Congress

Until the recent past, political scientists have been among the worst offenders in spreading inaccurate clichés about the role of Congress. The discipline of political science emerged in the late nineteenth and early twentieth centuries, and was deeply influenced by a series of reform movements that struggled against massive corruption of all levels of government. (The reputation of Congress had perhaps reached its nadir when many members, including the Speaker, were implicated in the Crédit Mobilier case in the 1870s.) The dominant scholarly influences on the early study of Congress were, on the one hand, the legalistic tradition, and on the other hand, the continued force of an idealized model of the English parliamentary system, which was used as a standard of comparison. Early political scientists, like the reformers, thought corruption could be cured by restructuring faulty institutions.

The reformers fought to defeat the corrupt bosses by crushing the institutions they used—institutions ranging from local party organizations to the leadership of the House of Representatives. Less concentrated power and more "democracy," they believed, would permit reasonable men to agree on good answers to public problems.

Early political scientists shared the fear of excessive concentration of power in Congress—a fear that went all the way back to the Founding Fathers. James Madison, principal author of the Constitution and a political theorist of decisive importance in shaping American views of the governmental system, was deeply preoccupied with the danger of excessive legislative power, warning the people to "exhaust all their precautions" to prevent Congressional domination of the other branches.[1]

The concentration of power within Congress early in this century was built on the broad authority given to the legislative branch by the Constitution. In striking contrast to the brief description of executive power, Congress was given most of the basic sources of domestic governmental authority. Every national law must come from Congress, and the power of the purse is firmly anchored on Capitol Hill. Even the exercise of the President's major powers in defense, diplomatic relations, and administration of the executive branch required Congressional approval. The lower federal court system was left very largely within the sphere of Congressional regulation, and Senate confirmation was required for all judicial appointments. Congress had firm possession, under the Constitution, of the great historic bases of legislative power—taxation and spending. Congress's Constitutional authority over domestic policy was and is so extensive that the President must often play a subordinate role when Congress is able to effectively exercise its power. Most Presidents, even most strong Presidents, have appreciated this reality.

Congress not only has a broad base of Constitutional powers, but also has been perhaps the most successful of all national legislative assemblies in developing internal adaptations that permit it to retain great power as governmental functions expand vastly in scale and complexity. Unlike most declining parliamentary bodies, it has created strong permanent standing committees and reasonably strong institutions of political party leadership—leadership independent of the President or the national party organizations. As government became specialized and administrative agencies proliferated, Congress had to embrace one of two alternatives: internal specialization, or delegation of authority. Very early it chose to specialize through the creation of permanent standing committees. Within Congress there also developed a powerful national party leader, the Speaker of the House, who combined broad procedural authority as presiding officer with the political influence accruing to the majority party's chief spokesman. By the late nineteenth century, the Speaker had acquired vast control over the management of the House's business and the allocation of power within the House.

When political scientists began to look at Congress, they worked within a system where the Presidency had still not recovered from the brutal fight over Reconstruction policy and the impeachment of President Andrew Johnson. Congress was often the dominant element in the development of national policy, and critics were increasingly worried about the negative uses of committee and leadership power.

Professor Woodrow Wilson's classic study, *Congressional Government*, outlined criticisms of the committee system which have reverberated in studies of Congress ever since. To Wilson, Congress was an "aggressive spirit" that had "virtually taken into its own hands all the substantial powers of government."[2] National policy, he charged, was worked out in closed committee meetings, where neither the President nor the national party organizations had much influence and where the public was excluded.[3]

> I know not how better to describe our form of government in a single phrase than by calling it a government by the Standing Committees of Congress. This disintegrate ministry, as it figures on the floor of the House of Representatives, has many peculiarities. In the first place it is made up of the elders of the assembly . . . ; in the second place, it is constituted of selfish and warring elements . . . ; in the third place, instead of being composed of the associated leaders of Congress, it consists of the dissociated heads of forty-eight "little legislatures."[4]

Congressional government, said the future President, meant "division of authority and concealment of responsibility" resulting in "very distressing paralysis in moments of emergency."[5] The President was often reduced to "mere obedience of directions from the masters of policy, the Standing Committees."[6]

The Attack on the Speaker of the House

Congressional committee power and the success of a series of Speakers in consolidating power over both the legislative process and the House committee system made the Speakers

15

major rivals of the Presidents in the early 1900s. The Speaker controlled the Rules Committee and thus the management of legislation, made all major committee appointments, shaped debates through his function of recognizing speakers, and dealt in national politics as an acknowledged power. Sometimes he could challenge the President and dominate the House, even in the face of a determined and popular Executive like Theodore Roosevelt.

Boss Cannon, the Speaker from 1903 to 1911, so angered the progressive wing of his own Republican Party, that they joined the Democrats in a sweeping revolt in 1909–10. Afraid of the arbitrary use of great power, the reformers removed not the man who abused the Speaker's power, but the possibility of power. The result, of course, was not to abolish power but to fragment it. In trying to avoid bad leadership, they made effective positive leadership almost impossible. When the revolt was over, the Speaker could no longer make committee assignments, had lost his seat on the Rules Committee, and found his procedural control of the House severely weakened. The seniority system was greatly strengthened.

The reformers failed to provide any alternative focus of leadership, and their reforms had the result of actually strengthening committee chairmen, a group far less representative and responsive to the party that elected House leaders. The reformers viewed the institutional reforms as ends in themselves; having maimed the office of Speaker, they had no further political program and even permitted Cannon's reelection as Speaker. The impact of the reform movement was to render the whole idea of leadership suspect. The House was left without leadership, and its influence in national politics rapidly receded.[7]

The Modern Presidency and the Legislative Process

Not long after the destruction of the House leadership structure, the modern Presidency began to emerge as a major element in the legislative process. Woodrow Wilson became the first President to openly introduce and fight for a legislative program—something that became routine in the 1930s. In the end, however, Wilson's paramount effort, the quest for ratification of the League of Nations treaty, was defeated by Senate resistance.

Not until the Great Depression did the contemporary image of Presidential government become commonplace. In the early days of President Franklin Roosevelt's New Deal, it seemed as if Congress had simply abdicated. Major laws dealing with the terrible economic crisis were drafted by White House brain trusters and overwhelmingly enacted before most members even had a chance to read them. FDR bypassed Congress, taking his program directly to the people with his "fireside chats," using the radio to create a communications advantage for the Presidency that Congress has yet to overcome. The New Deal also saw the emergence of the institutionalized Presidency with its group of isolated White House aides, responsible only to the President.

Actually, the extent of the change under Roosevelt is often overstated. While the reality of impending economic calamity did produce a rare period of Congressional acquiescence, the period was brief and some of the measures adopted had originally been developed through years of effort by Congressional progressives. Congress's decisive defeat of Roosevelt's effort to enlarge the Supreme Court destroyed much of the political momentum created by FDR's 1936 landslide victory. The President was defeated on much of his second-term legislative package, and his domestic innovation virtually ended during his third term.

Strong and successful Presidential leadership on social legislation has been rare between the late 1930s and the present. Most Presidents have had to content themselves with ambiguous outcomes on secondary issues. Only during the first part of the Johnson Administration did the White House approach a dominant role in the shaping of domestic policy. Even at the height of the Johnson period, major bills were usually drafted with care to minimize conflict and often incorporated Congressional proposals. Legislation frequently emerged from Congress so altered that a new program had actually been designed under the title of the initial Administration bill.

The Responsibility for Legislative Impasse

Looking at the past three decades, one is struck by the continuing inability of the national government to act on a variety of issues with major social consequences. The impasse, however, cannot fairly be blamed on Congress. It reflects both the   17 built-in difficulties of achieving decisive action from a Constitutional system designed to prevent excessive governmental activity, and the close and indecisive ideological division of the country. One could fairly say the institutions of government have failed only if it is possible to show that they have failed repeatedly to respond to clear majority support for major policies. This is difficult to demonstrate.

It is possible, in fact, to develop an argument almost in direct contradiction to the popular view of Congress. It can be argued that the few times the public has provided a clear liberal majority in the House and Senate, Congress has been more than willing to support far-reaching changes in domestic policy.

A recent study of two Congresses where a political landslide gave large numbers of seats normally controlled by one party to its adversaries showed that the new members provided a very high degree of support for new policies. In both cases the newly elected party members from opposition districts were far more likely than other party members, or even other new party members from safe seats, to support new programs. Another intensive analysis of the impact of the new Democratic members elected to the House from normally Republican districts in the 1964 landslide supports this conclusion. Although they came from conservative districts, these members were unusually strong supporters of liberal programs.[8] These studies suggest that when the public is sufficiently dissatisfied with the status quo to send new members to Washington in significant numbers, it can produce a policy change disproportionate to the numbers involved. One should not assume, therefore, that the massive policy breakthroughs of the 1930s or the mid-1960s can be explained merely by the forceful leadership of the President. Equally plausible is an explanation stressing the increased willingness of an altered Congress to adopt policy changes worked out by party leaders in both branches.

The razor-thin electoral margins for Truman in 1948, Kennedy in 1960, and Nixon in 1968 suggest a long-term condition of close partisan division in the country. The fact that neither Eisenhower's personal triumphs in the 1950s, nor Nixon's landslide victory over a very unpopular Democratic nominee in 1972, broke the basic stalemate between the conservatives and liberals in Congress, reinforces this view. Since the Second World War the only period of clear and unambiguous partisan control of both the White House and Congress by either party's dominant wing has been the two years following the 1964 Democratic landslide. This was a period of historic

18

reform measures in education, health care, urban development, civil rights, and other areas. It was also a period when the public saw Congress in an unusually favorable light, giving it a 62-percent positive rating.[9] The favorable record reflected, of course, a change not in institutional structure but in Congressional membership.

The normal political deadlock has made lawmaking on controversial issues an excruciatingly difficult process. While most of the postwar Presidents have submitted proposals for some significant domestic reforms to Congress, only Lyndon Johnson signed much of it into law. In the end, for example, little remained of Truman's ambitious program but a severely watered-down housing act, whereas an act restricting labor unions was passed over his veto. While the Eisenhower and Kennedy Administrations produced some early measures aiding education, civil rights, manpower training, and other programs, these efforts were small and their social consequences marginal. Often the designs were heavily influenced by Congress. In the latter part of his Administration, Eisenhower's top domestic priority was holding down the budget.[10] President Kennedy's appeals for education aid and Medicare were futile, and he did not even venture to send serious civil rights legislation to Capitol Hill until the televised brutality of Alabama authorities toward demonstrators in Birmingham succeeded in outraging the country.[11]

When the 1964 election produced both a Presidential mandate and a working Congressional majority of non-Southern Democrats, there was a sudden outpouring of legislation touching virtually all major areas of domestic policy. This period, however, was short-lived. The GOP comeback in the 1966 Congressional elections drastically slowed the momentum of change.

President Nixon was elected without proposing any clear domestic program and submitted no significant legislation to Congress for months. Eventually he decided to continue scaled-down versions of most Great Society programs while concentrating on administrative reorganization, program consolidation, revenue sharing, and welfare reform. On most of these issues the Administration faced repeated defeats. The only real success was on revenue sharing, a proposal originally formulated by liberal economists and enjoying substantial Democratic Party support.

Over the years the general pattern has been one of inaction or ineffectual compromise. Public indecision has been intensified by institutional conflicts within Congress, and between

19

Congress and the executive branch. Congress sometimes plays the conservative and sometimes the progressive role in these conflicts, and at times the conflict has little if any ideological meaning. Critics who assail Congress for frustrating Presidential programs could just as well claim that Presidents have been frustrated because they do not speak for a national majority committed to anything. Truman, Kennedy, and Nixon all were first elected by minority votes, with Nixon receiving a mere 43 percent of the vote before his first term. Eisenhower had a mandate, but it was essentially a mandate for nothing, since he offered neither a clear set of domestic priorities nor even a definable relationship with the policies of his party. After Nixon's triumphal 1972 reelection, the President's ability to project a set of national policies was mortally injured by the Watergate scandal.

Throughout the postwar period, then, only the years immediately following the 1964 election provide a fair test of the ability of the political system to respond to a distinct electoral mandate for a reasonably clear political program. This proved to be an amazingly productive period.

The Exaggeration of Presidential Power

If this capsule history is accurate, it should be evident that the President is often neither the dominant nor the progressive partner in the shaping of domestic policy. When examined closely, in fact, many of the critics' arguments are circular. Congress is frequently described by reformers and by scholars as "unresponsive." On close examination, it often turns out that the author uncritically assumes either that the President's program actually reflects national needs, or that Congress should respond to the author's own implicit or explicit beliefs about what the primary national needs are. In fact, these goals espoused by the critics may have little or no relationship to the real desires of the local or national public constituency.

The actual distribution of power is further distorted by the fact that both reformers and scholars focus overwhelmingly on the passage of new legislation, particularly on bills the President says are very important. This not only overlooks the extremely important social consequences of alterations of taxes, appropriation levels, and regulatory structures, but also leads

observers to rate both Presidential influence and Congressional "responsiveness" on a score sheet drawn up in the White House. We let the President pick and choose the issues on which he will be evaluated. Whatever goes on the President's list is appraised as a Presidential initiative, even though all the preliminary work may have been done on Capitol Hill. The President is then credited for whatever items are enacted and Congress blamed for obstructing the rest. Often the result is a set of deceptive conclusions.

Part of the reason we let the President set the criteria of evaluation is that the political system offers little else. Usually the party organizations do little to initiate legislative programs, and the lists issued from time to time by House and Senate leaders are seldom either comprehensive or clear in terms of priorities. Probably the only real alternative to the President's agenda is an effort to actually monitor all the various issues actively under consideration within Congress at a given point in time. This is very difficult, but it would frequently reveal substantial Congressional action, or "responsiveness," on issues that have yet to reach the President's agenda.

The misleading character of the normal evaluations of Congress is particularly clear in retrospect. Congress, for example, has played the dominant role in the shaping of national urban policy and environmental protection. Although these have been major issues in recent years, much of the framework of federal policy was built during times when these issues were far less visible. The Congressional architects got little credit. Once the White House stepped in, however, the President's proposals usually became important and visible political initiatives. Whether or not they would solve the problems, they became the standard for evaluating Congress.

NOTES

[1] *Federalist Papers*, No. 48, quoted in James Burnham, *Congress and the American Tradition* (New York: Regnery, 1959), p. 95.
[2] Woodrow Wilson, *Congressional Government* (Boston: Houghton Mifflin, 1885), pp. 36, 45.
[3] *Ibid.*, pp. 61, 70, 81, 92, 100.
[4] *Ibid.*, pp. 102–03.
[5] *Ibid.*, pp. 238, 282.
[6] *Ibid.*, p. 254.
[7] Neil MacNeil, *Forge of Democracy* (New York: David McKay, 1963), pp. 53–55; Wilfred E. Binkley, *President and Congress* (New York: Vintage, 1962), pp. 241–45.

[8] David W. Brady and Naomi B. Lynn, "Switched-Seat Congressional Districts: Their Effect on Party Voting and Public Policy," *American Journal of Political Science* XVII (August 1973), pp. 528–43; Jeff Fishel, *Party and Opposition* (New York: David McKay, 1973).

[9] Roger H. Davidson, David M. Kovenock, and Michael K. O'Leary, *Congress in Crisis: Politics and Congressional Reform* (New York: Wadsworth, 1966), p. 53, citing Harris Survey data.

[10] Richard Neustadt, *Presidential Power* (New York: Wiley, 1960), pp. 75–76.

[11] Theodore C. Sorensen, *Kennedy* (New York: Harper & Row, 1965), Chapter 14.

3

WOULD a REFORMED CONGRESS BE PROGRESSIVE?

The Reform Critique

Most political scientists who have studied Congress belong to one of two major streams. The dominant group until the past generation were reformers, frequently focusing on themes similar to those first sounded in Woodrow Wilson's book. This tradition still has active and important spokesmen. More recently, however, most research on Congress has come out of the behaviorist movement. The preoccupation of this group, which is committed to a more scientific study of politics through direct observation, survey techniques, mathematical analysis of roll call votes, and other statistical methods, is to find out how Congress really works. Whereas the older tradition emphasized the legislative process, the newer one focuses on explaining the underlying relationships and behavior of members of Congress through the application of a variety of social science concepts. While the adequacy of Congress as a central institution for the making of national policy was a basic preoccupation of the earlier students, it is usually ignored by the newer group, most of whom are committed to the role of value-free scientists describing processes rather than prescribing reforms. Since the

Second World War we have been accumulating both a massive body of data on particular aspects of Congressional processes, and a series of general critiques showing little familiarity with the detailed studies. This book tries to provide more accurate and useful answers to important old questions through use of new data.

The growth of the Presidency and executive responsibilities during the Second World War, and the period of U.S. international leadership after the war, stirred deep concern about the effectiveness of Congress among political scientists still preoccupied with the traditional questions of institutional adequacy. During the war, political scientist Roland Young concluded that the President had taken "effective leadership of Congress." He alone had "the power and information necessary for formulating and co-ordinating a national policy."[1]

Congress itself was sufficiently worried to set up a joint committee on organization whose staff director, political scientist George Galloway, concluded that Congress had been in "gradual decline" for decades and was in danger of becoming a "mere ceremonial appendix to bureaucracy." During the period from the early 1900s through the war, Congress changed from a part-time assembly of a predominantly rural country isolated from world affairs and operating very few domestic social programs, to a full-time legislative body responsible for a vast array of social and economic legislation, serving an urban society with extremely heavy international responsibilities. Yet during this period Congress's major response had been simply to create more and more standing committees, with neither staff nor coordination. As they rushed from one endless subcommittee meeting to another, Congressmen, said Galloway, were "working with the tools and techniques of the snuffbox era."[2] His analysis of Congress would have sounded familiar to Wilson:

> Its internal structure is dispersive and duplicating. It is a body without a head. Leadership is scattered among the chairmen of 81 little legislatures who compete with each other for jurisdiction and power. Its supervision of executive performance is superficial. Most of its time is consumed by petty local and private matters. . . . It lacks machinery for developing coherent legislative programs. . . . Its posts of power are held on the basis of political age, regardless of ability or agreement with party policies.[3]

The situation was serious enough to bring correction of some of the most obvious weaknesses in 1946. The number of committees was cut in half and, more important, staff resources were considerably improved. Although Congress ducked the hard issues of the seniority system, the lack of party leadership, Rules Committee power, the filibuster system, and others, the reforms that did pass strengthened it.

The critics weren't satisfied. The American Political Science Association issued major reports in this period calling for more centralized party leadership and strong organized majorities in Congress.[4] In *Congress on Trial*, James MacGregor Burns saw Congressmen as lobbyists for the "dominant economic enterprise" in their districts, responding to "the small but disciplined forces of the special interests." The President, he said, spoke for the "national interest."[5]

Later, in the 1960s, Burns's *Deadlock of Democracy* portrayed each party divided into two wings, a progressive Presidential wing and a conservative Congressional wing. The Presidential wing, he said, was responsible for nationally oriented innovation while the Congressional wing was the main obstacle to needed reforms.[6] In *Uncommon Sense*, published during the Nixon years, Burns said the central need was to "generate strong and steady political power" supporting basic social and economic change. He saw Congress as the "prime *institutional* reason for the lagging social progress of the 1950s and the upheavals of the 1960s."[7]

Congressional Reformers

Reformers within Congress have echoed these arguments. Representative Estes Kefauver (D-Tenn.), later a major contender for the Democratic Presidential nomination, denounced the "blind reverence for tradition that borders on idolatry."[8] Senator Joseph Clark (D-Pa.) said that the President, the "sole spokesman of all the people," was pitted against "the gerrymandered views . . . of Senators from fifty states of vastly unequal population and the parochial viewpoints of 435 Representatives from very diverse districts which command their fierce loyalty." "In the absence of crisis," he said, "Congress cannot and will not act affirmatively except under a strong President who has a clear mandate from the people, not only because of the separation of powers and the way Congressmen and Senators came to office, but also because of the congeries of rules and customs which favor inactivity."[9]

On the other side of the Capitol, Representative Richard Bolling (D-Mo.), saw the House as a "shambles," with   25 "atrophied" leadership and "dissipated" power. Key positions went to "extreme conservatives" and "incompetents."[10] Representative Allard Lowenstein (D-N.Y.) carried criticism to a new high, during the brief period before his state legislature redistricted him out of office, by denouncing the "senility system" of committee chairmanships. Representative Donald Riegle (D-Mich.) reflected the frustration of young liberal activists within Congress in his 1972 book, O Congress:

> A continuation of business as usual in the Congress won't help us stave off approaching disasters. We're trapped by a traditional momentum that makes it impossible for us to shift into an emergency state of mind and operation and come to grips with urgent problems.
> . . . The legislative process is slow and has a million roadblocks in it. The seniority system plays a big part and there's almost no way a newer member can affect the shape of legislation. There's damn little you can get your hands on, make happen or influence.[11]

The frustration and mounting criticism of Congress finally gave birth to another serious effort to reform Congressional procedures and Congressional campaigns in the early 1970s. Major national organizations including Common Cause and the National Committee for an Effective Congress gave the reformers a kind of persistent, committed, and informed constituency they had rarely had in the past. Ralph Nader, who had gained a vast national following through his skillful exposés and campaigns on consumer issues, attempted to turn some of the same techniques against the Congressional status quo. Public reaction against the campaign scandals and the misuse of executive power generated by the Watergate investigations strengthened the reformers on Capitol Hill. In many ways, conditions were almost uniquely favorable for reform.

The first reform effort, in 1970, brought passage of a bill restricting campaign spending that was vetoed by President Nixon. However, reformers in the House succeeded in changing the rule permitting nonrecorded "teller votes"—a rule that let members vote to drastically alter or kill a bill without any record being kept of their position. Thus members could appear to support a measure on the published roll call votes and then vote to gut it without any fear that home constituents or interest groups would find out. Once it became easy to demand publication of the teller votes, participation almost doubled. Richard Conlon, staff director of the liberal Democratic Study Group, thought the change had weakened the control of committee elders over the amendment process and permitted liberals to win a number of votes they would otherwise have lost.[12] The system also had the contrary effect of making it more difficult for liberals to vote against popular conservative issues, like antibusing legislation.

A 1970 attack by liberals against more fundamental traditions met little success. In early 1970 Speaker John McCormack (D-Mass.) faced a rare challenge in the Democratic Caucus, when nineteen House liberals threatened to revolt and possibly even vote with the Republicans to organize the House the next January unless something was done. Since criticism focused on seniority, the Speaker appointed a committee to study the issue. The committee eventually recommended that any eleven members be allowed to force a vote on any committee chairman in the caucus at the beginning of a new Congress. The group proposed to distribute leadership positions more widely by forbidding any member to head more than one subcommittee, thus opening up more than thirty chairmanships. The liberals got nowhere, however, with proposals for compulsory retirement of chairmen at age seventy or for easy bypassing of the House Rules Committee.[13]

In January 1971 both Democrats and Republicans in the House adopted rules permitting caucus votes on committee chairmanships. Liberals tested the procedure by challenging the chairman of the House District Committee, Representative John McMillan (D-S.C.), a profoundly conservative rural Southerner who had blocked home rule and decent governmental services for Washington D.C., the nation's largest black city.[14] The move failed. (McMillan was ultimately defeated in a primary in his home district, whereupon the seniority system made Charles Diggs, Jr., a black Congressman from Detroit, the new chairman.) Though the new reform made it conceivable that sometime in the future a particularly outrageous committee chairman might be unseated, for the time being it was obvious that the seniority system was intact because most Democrats in the House wanted it.

January 1971 offered a good test of the mood of most House Democrats and their political complexion. The very cautious attitude on reforms was echoed by another acquiescence in the increasingly rigid reliance on seniority and predetermination in the choice of the top House leadership. In this century every man elected Speaker by the Democrats had previously served as the party's number-two leader, and the average newly elected Speaker had been in Congress for nearly twenty-six years. As

27

the pattern of almost automatic succession became increasingly inflexible, the third-ranking figure, the Whip, was developing a presumptive claim to become Majority Leader. Since the average Congressman had served only eight years, this meant that his leaders had actually been selected by a hierarchical system before he came to Congress.

The younger House Democrats had futilely attempted to depose Majority Leader Carl Albert (D-Okla.) in 1962. Now they acquiesced in his claim to the Speakership, but a liberal Arizonan, Morris K. Udall (D-Ariz.), contested the elevation of Whip Hale Boggs (D-La.) to the Majority Leader's job. Boggs won and a conservative Texan, Olin Teague, was elected chairman of the Democratic Caucus. Later, when it came to electing a new member to the extremely powerful Ways and Means Committee, liberal leader Don Fraser (D-Minn.) was defeated by the highly conservative Joe Waggonner, Jr. (D-La.).[15] There was very little support for any fundamental challenge to the status quo. The only significant change in House leadership came about in spite of, rather than because of, House Democrats. Speaker Albert and Majority Leader Boggs, concerned lest the caucus elect a conservative Whip, balanced the leadership by appointing a liberal, Representative Thomas ("Tip") O'Neil (D-Mass.), to that post. Later, when Boggs died in an Alaska plane crash, O'Neil moved up routinely to the second position.

Campaign reform proved almost equally impossible, but at least a halting step forward was accomplished by passage of the 1972 Federal Election Campaign Act. This measure lessened the prospect of rich candidates' buying nominations or elections with saturation television campaigns financed by personal funds—a trend quite evident in some 1970 primaries. The bill also set upper limits on the soaring amounts of advertising money spent per voter.[16] The measure greatly strengthened requirements for public reporting of fund raising.

The finance bill, however, made few significant changes within Congress. Indeed, some critics said it was an "incumbent's bill" which would make it even harder to challenge those in office, who were usually much better known in their districts and less dependent on advertising than their challengers. More serious campaign-spending reform, and real consideration of the possible values of public financing of Congressional campaigns, would not come until the height of the Watergate scandal in 1974.

28   The lack of enthusiasm for institutional reform within the

House was evident in the failure of a major 1974 effort to rationalize the committee structure of the House and strengthen committee resources for the first time since 1946. A House committee under the leadership of a powerful reformer, Representative Richard Bolling (D-Mo.), devised a plan to eliminate overlapping jurisdictions, increase committee staff resources, upgrade the leadership role of the Speaker, and eliminate multiple committee memberships. After many months of work in devising a plan to strengthen the committee system without infringing on too many existing prerogatives, the reformers were stunned by an abrupt and unceremonious rejection by the Democratic Caucus. A coalition of conservatives and liberals who would lose existing power bases defeated the changes. Interest groups of various stripes saw little to gain, and valued relationships to lose, through a reshuffling that brought no clear ideological benefits.

Decades of reform efforts had produced very little. Since the plaints of Woodrow Wilson in the 1880s, power in Congress had actually become more dispersed and less responsible. The seniority system had been accepted as an absolute rule, while party leadership in the House had weakened. The Rules Committee had collected great power, and Senate filibusters still regularly frustrated Senate majorities. Even the elected leadership in the House was now gained by inheritance. In spite of the tireless efforts of the reform groups, the institutional arrangements of Congress appeared to be extremely stable.

Change without Reform

Ironically, while reformers were losing battle after battle, as the years passed Congress was somehow becoming less conservative. Although the structure was the same, political and social changes altered the membership of each house, thus changing the policy impact of various rules and customs. When political scientists of the behaviorist school began to gather detailed information about the internal operation of Congress, it soon became evident that the reformers had oversimplified both their description of Congressional processes and the political meaning of various procedures.

Examined closely, for example, the description of the seniority system's inevitable magnification of the power of Southern reactionaries looked more like a comment about a particular set of political circumstances than an unchangeable rule. Recent critics of Southern power in the seniority system seldom noted the fact that liberal Democrats had long been the minority faction in a majority party traditionally dominated by Southern members. During 1947–56, for example, more than half the Democrats in each house were Southerners. During this same era the accumulation of Northern Democratic seniority was severely damaged by reverses in the 1946, 1950, and 1952 elections, each of which saw the loss of fifty or more House seats, almost all from the North. The political circumstances of the period were to be reflected in committee chairmanships in the 1960s, even as Southern strength in the Democratic Caucus was rapidly diminishing.[17]

Contrary to the argument of liberal critics that the seniority system is inherently conservative, the system is in reality inherently biased in favor of any faction that had the most seats some years earlier and that wins reelection with little turnover. Until the mid-1960s, these circumstances worked clearly in favor of the South, but they no longer do.

From the mid-1950s to the early 1970s, political conditions became far more favorable to the accumulation of seniority power by moderates and liberals. Between the 1954 election and 1974, the Democratic majority in the House was never defeated. The two dramatic political tides of the period, in 1958 and 1964, swept liberals into Congress. The only substantial GOP gains, in 1966, were more a recovery from the Goldwater disaster than any significant threat to the steady growth of Northern seniority.

Even as Northerners were strengthening their position, Southerners were losing the easy comfort of certain reelection that they had once enjoyed. The Goldwater campaign and the GOP's aggressive "Southern strategy" of the following years brought real two-party competition into substantial portions of the South. In 1964 five of the eight Alabama Democratic Congressmen lost their seats and the first Republican Representatives since Reconstruction went to Washington from Georgia and Mississippi. South Carolina's Senator Strom Thurmond switched to the GOP. While growing numbers of historically "competitive" Eastern and Midwestern states were now consistently sending Democrats to Capitol Hill, things were changing in the South. By the end of 1972, for instance, GOP Senators had been elected from Texas, Florida, Tennessee, South Carolina, North Carolina, and Virginia. The Virginia House delegation had a Republican majority.

30   Intense ideological divisions among Democrats in some

Southern states had effects similar to those produced by two-party competition. The political change in Virginia in 1966 provided a particularly drastic example of this. In 1965 Virginia conservative Democrats exercised vast power in Congress, holding the chairmanships of the Senate Finance Committee, the House Rules Committee, and the Senate Banking and Currency Committee. After the 1966 election all were gone as the Old Dominion lost a century of seniority. Senate Finance Chairman Harry Byrd resigned and his son barely fought off a tough primary challenge. Rules Committee Chairman "Judge" Howard Smith, longtime leader of Southern conservatives on the House floor, was defeated in a primary. Banking Committee Chairman Willis Robertson lost to a moderate contender, William Spong, who refused to join the Southern caucus after he was elected. In 1972 the conservative faction returned the favor by supporting Spong's extremely conservative GOP challenger, William Scott. Scott's victory again broke the cycle of seniority accumulation.

While much of the South has remained solidly Democratic in House elections, the Solid South is clearly shrinking and even the Southern Democratic Party is developing major ideological factions. The firm base of safe seats on which the South built its domination of Democratic Congresses is crumbling. An increasing number of Southerners are accumulating their seniority on the Republican side of the aisle, where it rarely counts for much.

The changes were particularly striking in the Senate, which had been described as a "Southern club" in William White's *Citadel*. Just prior to the 1958 election, there were only twenty-eight Democratic Senators from outside the states of the Old Confederacy. Most of them came from relatively conservative Border or Western states. In 1958 the Democrats gained seats in California, Connecticut, New Jersey, Maine, and such Midwestern states as Michigan, Ohio, and Minnesota. Fifteen new Democrats from the North and West tipped the numbers decisively against the Southern wing of the party. This was the precondition for future changes in the character of the Senate. Since it normally takes about a decade for a Senator to become a committee chairman, the key question was whether the Democratic seats won in the 1958 recession landslide could be held in 1964. The massive defeat of the Goldwater Presidential campaign helped consolidate the shift toward the left within the Senate Democratic delegation.

After a period of political circumstances favorable to liberals, 31 the mere passage of time meant that the political consequences of the seniority system would become less conservative. The system did not become more democratic, but it did elevate growing numbers of progressives. Contrary to popular myth, there is significant turnover in committee chairmanships, and most chairmen do not see President after President come and go. The average chairman assumes his post at an advanced age and serves for less than seven years. This average, of course, masks wide variation, and the hardy senior citizens who dominate major committees for years are far better known than those who finally succeed to power after many years of apprenticeship, only to be cheated by political tides or the Grim Reaper.

Not only is the quantity of Southern seniority power diminishing, but the quality of Southern representation is undergoing some change as reapportionment reflects both the rapid urbanization of the South and the substantial migration of Northerners into the region. The changes have been particularly dramatic in Atlanta and Houston, where voters have elected the first Southern black Congressmen since Reconstruction. In Atlanta a very conservative GOP member, Fletcher Thompson, best known for his slashing assaults on federal civil rights programs, was replaced by Andrew Young, a leading figure in Martin Luther King's Southern Christian Leadership Conference. Although most young Southern Congressmen were still voting conservative in early 1972, those from the more urbanized districts have been more likely to support domestic social programs.[18] The 1973 voting records suggested that the new Southern Congressmen elected in 1972 were substantially closer to their Northern party colleagues than any earlier group of Dixie freshman members.

More importantly, Southern members of Congress are no longer either obsessed by or rigidly unified on the race question. Historically, the most dramatic impact of Southern power in Congress had been the insulation of Southern racial practices from federal power. The Southern stranglehold, enforced through Southern power on the House Rules Committee and the Senate Judiciary Committee, through the "conservative coalition" with Republicans, and through the Senate filibuster system, was finally broken in 1964. The 1964 Civil Rights Act ended segregation in public accommodations and greatly accelerated Southern school desegregation. With the passage of the 1965 Voting Rights Act, the change in Southern society was reinforced by a change in the politics of the Deep South, spurred by a rise in black registrations. When school desegregation was completed in much of the South, and politicians considered the reality of almost a million new black voters, some of the old equations of Southern politics changed.

V. O. Key's classic study, *Southern Politics*, showed that the heart of traditional Southern solidarity in both houses was unity on racial issues. In examining 598 roll call votes between 1933 and 1945, Key found only nine votes where at least 90 percent of the Southern Senators voted against majorities of Republicans and Northern Democrats. Seven of the votes concerned racial issues, most of them were against bills making lynching a federal offense. The others concerned school segregation and federal action against job discrimination. In the House seven out of eleven votes that isolated Southern Democrats during this period dealt with antilynching legislation and action against the poll tax, which restricted black voting.[19]

Changes in the South meant that there was less political benefit and more risk in playing racial politics. Once the issue of desegregation was decided and the law firmly settled, it became far more difficult to arouse hysterical fears of racial change or to credibly promise to stop it. Once substantial numbers of blacks were voting, there was a real incentive for candidates to find ways to appeal for black votes without losing white support. With the exception of the explosive busing issue, many Southern members now sought to avoid civil rights fights. Some Southern Senators even decided to vote for the 1970 bill extending the Voting Rights Act, and against the controversial Southern judges that Nixon futilely attempted to put on the Supreme Court.

There were, of course, crosscurrents in the South. If Democrats like Senators Ernest Hollings (S.C.) and Lawton Chiles (Fla.) were moving toward the political center, the defeat of moderates in Tennessee, Texas, Virginia, and North Carolina in the 1970 and 1972 elections showed the continuing strength of the conservative tradition. The two new Southern Republican Senators sworn in in January 1973, Scott of Virginia and Helms of North Carolina, represented the far right wing of their party. While some Southern Democrats were espousing moderate positions, Southern Republicans seemed to be moving solidly into the Goldwater tradition. From the perspective of the seniority system, these complex changes meant that by 1973 almost a third of the Southern Senators were accumulating Republican seniority—power that would probably count for little, barring a major national political shift. This group in-

33

cluded most of the intense conservatives. On the Democratic side, a number of the younger members were much closer to national party positions. Within the majority party, then, seniority was giving the South less power, and that power was less disruptive to realization of national party objectives.

The changing meaning of seniority was apparent first in the Senate, where fewer years of service are needed to attain power. Majority Leader Lyndon Johnson's rule giving new members important committee assignments intensified the impact of the liberal influx of 1958. By 1971 three of the liberals elected that year chaired committees. Others ran major subcommittees and were nationally known as sponsors of important legislation. In 1970 two Senators with only six and seven years of seniority, McGovern (D-S. Dak.) and Mondale (D-Minn.), became chairmen of widely publicized select committees on hunger and school desegregation.[20]

Less dramatic but important changes were underway in the House, where more seniority is required for chairmanships and few liberals had been named to some of the most important committees. By 1971 twelve of the twenty-one standing committees were chaired by non-Southerners, but Southerners still led the three most powerful—Ways and Means, Rules, and Appropriations.[21] By 1973 the South claimed only eight chairmanships and a liberal Northern member chaired the Rules Committee.[22] Almost two-thirds of the third, fourth, and fifth seniority rankings on the committees were held by non-Southerners, while the Southerners had their full share of the three lowest committee seniority ratings.[23] A considerable equalization of seniority power by region had taken place.

One interesting possibility was that the late 1970s might bring criticism of a different kind of overrepresentation through the seniority system. By 1974 the Rules and Judiciary Committees, two of the House's most important bodies, were chaired by senior members from Gary, Indiana, and Newark, New Jersey. Five other House committees had big-city chairmen, and big-city members were second or third on the seniority ladder on such important committees as Appropriations, Ways and Means, Rules, Banking and Currency, Foreign Affairs, and others.[24] Although central cities are rapidly losing population, Congressional districts will not be reapportioned again until 1982, twelve years after the census on which the current districts are based. Not only will the big cities be overrepresented, but many of the city districts are safe seats where there is now no serious GOP opposition and seniority can easily be accumulated.

34

The Changing Role of the House Rules Committee

Even as the political impact of seniority was changing, so too was the effect of the other major targets of Congressional reformers, the House Rules Committee and the filibuster system. Since Speaker Sam Rayburn (D-Tex.) succeeded in expanding the Rules Committee in 1961, it has usually been reasonably responsive to the House Democratic leadership. While the filibuster system is still a formidable barrier to majority rule in the Senate, it is no longer an unassailable obstacle to civil rights legislation. Cloture has been achieved on a broad range of issues. On the other hand, liberals have had some success in turning the tables on conservatives by using filibusters to force delay and reconsideration of some popular conservative measures.

Close examination has shown that critics overestimated the power of the Rules Committee at its prime, and also that the 1961 enlargement of the committee made the group highly responsive to the House leadership in the great majority of cases. A relatively recent major study of the committee concluded that it was

> by and large a body which cooperates relatively closely with the leadership and with the substantive committees which come before it requesting rules for their bills. Occasionally, perhaps two to five times a session, the Rules Committee acts in a fashion which others consider to be grossly unfair or arbitrary.[25]

One sign that the committee was not totally out of touch with the House majority was the rarity of efforts to force out legislation through discharge petitions. Even though the petitions are seen as threats to the established order of committee power, a legislative body with a truly disaffected majority should have produced more than one petition signed by most members in an average year. Between 1936 and 1960 the House passed only fourteen bills discharged from the Rules Committee, and only one major bill, the law setting minimum wages and maximum hours of work, finally became law.[26]

Sometimes when the Rules Committee takes the blame for killing a bill, it is actually responding to private urgings from the House leadership or House members who wish to avoid pressure to vote for a popular bill they privately think is bad. The Rules Committee can be a convenient scapegoat.

During the 1950s the Rules Committee became a particularly serious obstacle to civil rights and education bills, issues near

35

the top of the Democratic Party agenda. When President Kennedy came to office he succeeded in convincing Speaker Rayburn to exert his great influence in a hard but successful battle to expand the committee and break its conservative majority.

When the 1964 election produced a solid liberal majority impatient to enact legislation, a much more drastic limitation on the Rules Committee was rapidly adopted. The twenty-one-day rule gave any committee chairman the automatic right to bring a bill from his committee to the House floor after twenty-one days of Rules Committee delay, if the House majority approved. This rule forced six bills to the floor in 1965, including aid-to-education, job desegregation, and union organization measures.[27]

Although the twenty-one-day rule worked and did not interfere with orderly operation of the House, it was quickly repealed after the 1966 election destroyed the House's liberal majority. An effort to reinstate the rule in 1971 also failed. Apparently most House members favored more Rules Committee power.

The committee probably retained its power of taking arbitrary action on an occasional bill, because of its general skill in avoiding confrontations on issues where there was a strong majority for action. Even though the committee chairman passionately opposed the 1964 Civil Rights Act and the poverty program, for example, the committee allowed the House to act. On some rare occasions the committee supported a leadership strategy that resulted in action more progressive than most House members favored. When the committee sent the 1968 fair-housing bill to the floor, for example, the measure went with a rule to prevent weakening amendments that might well have been adopted on the House floor.

Contrary to the popular reform images of the Rules Committee as an omnipotent villain dictating to the House, the Rules Committee has great but limited power that is most effectively exercised on legislation of the second magnitude, or through tactical delay or procedural manipulation. Delay can be a very powerful tool. If a bill likely to provoke a subsequent Senate filibuster, for example, is held up for a good part of a year in the Rules panel, the chances of a successful filibuster increase. In the final days of a session, when there is a vast amount of work to do, timing becomes immensely important and the power to delay a measure is often the power to kill it.

The Rules Committee became more representative of the

Democratic Party's majority faction when a Northern liberal finally became chairman in 1973. Neither of the two Southern members still on the committee was an old-school reactionary, and there were several liberal members. Southern spokesman Joe Waggonner (D-La.) was openly critical of the leadership's failure to consider any conservative Southerner for one of the three 1973 vacancies on the panel.[28]

The new membership of the committee dramatically changed its political function. After years of serving as a restraining influence on the House, the committee now sometimes found itself sending measures to the House floor that the House was too conservative to enact. *Washington Post* writer Richard Lyons wrote in late 1973 that the committee "has now become such a liberal sieve it is regularly being overruled by a more conservative House."[29] During 1973 the committee was defeated on the House floor thirteen times, more than 1100 percent the average rate of defeats over the past four and a half decades. Among the issues on which the committee met defeat were an effort to roll back price levels, a major program of public service jobs for unemployed workers, an effort to require Congressional confirmation of the President's nominee for director of the powerful Office of Management and Budget, and several other initiatives.

The defeats and widespread criticism in the House helped produce a partial turnabout in early 1974, when the committee suddenly denied rules to major bills on land-use policy and urban mass transit. The actions were bitterly criticized. The *New York Times* attacked the committee as "subservient" and anti-city for holding up legislation badly needed by the New York City subway system. Representative Morris Udall (D-Ariz.), a leading supporter of the land-use measure, said that committee action on that bill reflected "immoral White House double-dealing."[30] Ironically, when the Rules Committee finally reversed itself and sent the land-use bill to the floor, House conservatives killed it, too.

In part, the actions resulted from the humiliations of the 1973 session. Repeated defeats were sapping the prestige of the committee and its ability to control the flow of House business. "Members made jokes about us," said Representative Spark Matsunaga (D-Hawaii). "The chairman got tired of hearing all those jokes. If there are going to be attempts to kill a bill by killing the rule, then we had better be more careful." Chairman Ray Madden (D-Ind.) said that now "when bills come along that look like they're going to be upset on the floor, we hold

37

Table 3-1

Rules Defeated on House Floor

1961–62	0
1963–64	3
1965–66	1
1967–68	3
1969–70	1
1971–72	5
1973	13

SOURCE   Congressional Quarterly, *March 30, 1974, p. 808.*

them up until some more work can be done on them."[31] Like the conservatives before them, the liberals on the Rules Committee were learning that successful exercise of the committee's power depended upon a skillful assessment of the temper of the House.

The Rules Committee did have somewhat greater success in its effort to initiate its own legislation. A 1973 Rules Committee resolution set in motion the most searching examination of the committee structure of the House since 1946, and the committee played a major role in the development of legislation to give Congress greater control over the budget and to limit the President's ability to impound money appropriated by Congress.[32] The much-maligned committee was actually showing reformist tendencies.

The Changing Impact of the Filibuster System

Even if the seniority system and the Rules Committee no longer cast such a dismal conservative pall over the legislative process, reformers could still point to that classic antidemocratic device, the filibuster system. The Senate's self-congratulatory description of itself as the "world's greatest deliberative body" did little to obscure a record of decades of almost total paralysis in the face of open and brutal denial of basic rights to Southern blacks.

Until 1964 all twentieth-century attempts to enact significant civil rights legislation had been killed by filibusters. Decades of struggle to forbid even so intensely condemned an outrage as Southern lynchings proved futile, when Southerners repeatedly showed their willingness to bring the legislative process to a

standstill.[33] Eleven times the Senate had voted on ending filibusters against measures to curb lynching, poll taxes, job discrimination, and unfair literacy tests for voter registration.
Eleven times the two-thirds rule for ending debate had given
the South a veto. Almost half of all filibusters had concerned
racial issues, and Southerners were the leading defenders of the
unlimited debate rule.[34]

It took an epic seventy-four-day battle for civil rights supporters to finally defeat Southern resistance, vote cloture, and
enact the 1964 Civil Rights Act. Once the iron wall was broken
and the basic framework of federal law had been established,
filibusters were no longer so overpowering a barrier to legislation promoting racial change. The next year a sweeping federal
Voting Rights Act passed the Senate after little more than a
month of debate.[35] The change was even more evident in 1968,
when the Senate surprised virtually all informed observers by
breaking a filibuster against fair housing. In 1970 Southerners
permitted extension of the controversial Voting Rights Act for
another five years after only two weeks of debate, even though
the President had called for weakening the law. Only when
Senate Republicans joined the Southerners, as many did in the
1972 job discrimination filibuster, did the method of resistance
still work.

During the Nixon years some surprising things began hap-
pening with regard to the filibuster system. Filibustering became a much more common tactic, even for issues of secondary
importance, and liberals began to use the tool more frequently
for their own ends. At the same time filibuster opponents
succeeded far more frequently than in the past in cutting off
debate, and fewer and fewer members had records of consistently supporting or opposing filibusters on philosophic
grounds.

Faced with what they saw as a tidal wave of reactionary and
ill-advised Presidential proposals during the Nixon Administration, liberals used both "extended debate" and full-fledged filibusters on several occasions. Lengthy floor debate was very useful, for example, in building up national opposition to Mr.
Nixon's controversial Supreme Court nominees, thus making
possible their eventual defeat.[36]

In 1970 a brief filibuster led by Senator Proxmire (D-Wis.)
played the key role in the environmentalists' battle to kill the
supersonic transport. Proxmire's success in stopping a measure
that would certainly have otherwise passed benefited from the
fact that there were still a number of Senate conservatives

39

opposed on principle to any limitation of debate. He picked up the votes of eleven Southern and Western members on this ground, even though they had earlier voted for the SST.[37] Increasing liberal use of the system soon eroded the number of its consistent supporters.

The filibuster is merely the ultimate extreme of a system of Senate procedure that gives great weight to strongly held views of any individual Senator. Since the Senate operates under an incredibly complex and inefficient set of formal rules, Senate leaders find it necessary to keep business moving by constantly negotiating unanimous consent agreements about the scheduling of proceedings and the limitation of debate. Any individual Senator who is prepared to incur the displeasure of his colleagues can make it extremely difficult for the Senate to operate effectively. When small groups of Senators feel strongly enough about anything to threaten a filibuster—particularly when the Senate is under intense pressure for rapid handling of a wide variety of issues near the end of the session—their power is usually immense.

As the end of the 1970 session approached, Majority Leader Mike Mansfield (D-Mont.) noted that filibusters had been threatened on five major issues. "Senate rules," he said, "magnify the views strongly held by any single Member" and "project any one Senator into a position of particular predominance late in any Congressional session."[38] The leader could only appeal for restraint as tough-minded partisans, both liberals and conservatives, attempted to magnify their power over legislation through obstruction sufficient to kill a bill at this point in the session.

The 1970 logjam centered around the extremely important question of the President's power to wage war in Vietnam. One serious casualty of the stalemate was any chance for possible action on the President's welfare reform proposal, his most important domestic policy initiative. The measure had passed the House in April, but died without a vote on the Senate floor. Daniel Moynihan, a principal author of the welfare plan, describes its demise:

> . . . a filibuster immediately broke out over a foreign aid supplemental authorization which was deemed by opponents of the Cambodian incursion to lend congressional sanction to it. Another filibuster was threatened by opponents of import quotas. Labor let it be known that . . . it would rather have no bill at all. In a terse statement . . . Mansfield told his colleagues they had made a spectacle of themselves. There was nothing to do save wait until January and start again.[39]

When the new Congress came to Washington the next year, however, support for the reform was dissipated and the drive for enactment failed.

Although the filibuster system was reducing the Senate to helpless inaction on various occasions, there wasn't much interest in ending it. Shortly before he left office, Vice President Hubert Humphrey had tried to assist the chances for reform in early 1969 with a parliamentary ruling making it easier to change Senate rules. The Senate, however, reversed him. Two years later, in 1971, after a particularly bad year of filibustering, reformers waged a month-and-a-half fight over the rule but failed in four attempts to end the filibuster against closing debate on the change in the filibuster rule.[40]

An epic liberal filibuster against the draft law tied up the Senate for seven weeks in mid-1971 as antiwar Senators tried to force a rapid end to the Vietnam war. Debate was finally ended by a narrow margin of only three votes. This fight brought a major turning point in the filibuster system, as the philosophic positions of both its supporters and defenders were undermined by strong feelings about the issue. Nine Southern Senators who had consistently supported filibusters on the grounds of freedom of debate and protection of the rights of minorities in the Senate, now voted to "gag" the Senate. Suddenly the leaders of the anti–civil rights filibusters arrived at a new understanding of the system. On the other side, some traditional opponents of filibusters like Philip Hart (D-Mich.) now opposed cloture.[41] Yet another antiwar filibuster erupted after the conference committee deleted the Senate's end-the-war provision from the draft bill; as a result, the country was temporarily without a draft law as the war went on. After two months of debate the filibuster was broken by a single vote as the Southern Democrats voted two-to-one for cloture.[42]

One development lessening the political impact of the filibuster system in recent years has been the increasing success in obtaining the votes necessary to end debate. Since the cloture rule was first adopted in 1917, the Senate has shut off debate only seventeen times. Thirteen of these votes have come since 1960, and nine in the first four and a half years of the 1970s. During the 1970s, in other words, cloture votes have been coming thirteen times more frequently than during the previous decades.

The dam burst with the breaking of major civil rights filibusters in 1964, 1965, 1968, and 1972. These successes permitted the enactment of the basic structure of civil rights law

41

needed to dismantle the principal instruments of Southern discrimination, and to begin action against school and job discrimination in the North.

Liberals and moderates in the Senate have succeeded in cutting off debate on several less prominent issues. Cloture was voted for legislation providing public financing of Congressional campaigns and post-card voter registration across the country—measures intended to decrease the influence of wealthy contributors and increase the registration level of low-income voters. Debate was shut off on extending the controversial program of legal services lawyers to represent people otherwise unable to protect their rights through litigation. Conservative foreign policy filibusters against ratifying the 1972 arms limitation agreement with the Soviet Union, and against supporting the United Nations sanctions on trade with Rhodesia, were ended.

The changing perception of the system was strikingly evident in a Senate discussion of the filibuster system in late 1971. Senator Cranston (D-Calif.), a strong liberal, announced he had changed his position and would no longer vote for repeal of the filibuster rule.

> I do not consider the filibuster horrendous; I think the draft and Vietnam are far worse. I look upon the filibuster as a means, not an end. When it can be used to good purpose, I support it and I shall use it as long as the rules of the Senate permit it.

Cranston now claimed that since 1969 "the procedure has since been used almost exclusively either in support of progressive measures or against legislation which was not in the best interests of the American people."[43]

Another liberal Vietnam War critic, Senator Frank Church (D-Idaho), agreed with Cranston's analysis. "Occasionally," he said, "if the public interest is being too badly mauled, a determined minority in the Senate . . . can engage in a delaying action that often will force concessions and sometimes will even result in the rejection of the measure contested." Church thought that the success in killing the SST "boondoggle" and in substantially narrowing the Administration's proposed loan fund for bankrupt corporations, and the near success in ending the draft, made a "strong case" for keeping the rule.[44]

On several recent occasions liberal filibusters have also been defeated. In the 1960s a small band of liberals lost a battle for public ownership of the communications satellite business. Twice in the early 1970s they lost antidraft filibusters.[45] While the impact of the filibuster system has changed, it has hardly become a great liberal tool. Most filibusters still succeed, and the filibuster system is still usually more useful to conservatives who want to prevent action than to liberals who want to force it. Between 1960 and early 1974, liberals and moderates failed to win cloture thirty times. Eight times the conservative filibusters defeated efforts supported by a majority of the Senate to end the filibuster rule. Filibusters weakened the civil rights legislation eventually enacted in 1960 and 1972, delayed action for several years against discriminatory literacy tests and housing, and prevented U.S. ratification of the United Nations genocide treaty. The tactic also frustrated the labor movement's intense drive against "right-to-work" laws, defeated a constitutional amendment for direct election of the President, delayed the drive for federal financing of Congressional campaigns, and stalled the creation of a federal consumer protection agency.[46] Finally, in June 1974 it helped defeat a Senate drive for tax reform. Yet most of the time filibusters delayed rather than permanently defeated legislation enjoying broad liberal and moderate support.

Significant successful liberal filibusters were far less common. Filibusters did, however, help defend the Supreme Court's one-man, one-vote decision from a conservative attack, and helped kill the expensive SST project so hotly criticized by environmentalists. In 1972, civil rights supporters successfully employed a filibuster against a popular antibusing bill intended to drastically restrict the right of the courts to order urban school desegregation.[47] This filibuster frustrated a strong Presidential appeal for legislation that enjoyed majority support in the Senate, at the height of a national election campaign which had deeply stirred emotions on the issue.

Evaluating the full impact of the filibuster system involves, of course, much more than merely examining cloture votes. The fact that any measure may be filibustered is a constant constraint on policy-makers. It increases the disposition to compromise and greatly diminishes the likelihood of a hard battle to enact a measure that closely divides the Senate or deeply offends any significant group of Senators. In a number of cases informal filibusters or threats of filbusters succeed without any formal vote, and the matter is withdrawn. Extended debate, particularly when it is supported by the leadership who control legislative scheduling, can provide a great deal of time for developing an issue or changing national opinion. The tendency of the system toward compromise and deferral of tough divisive issues usually has a conservative impact on policy-making, while the ability to develop new issues and delay a vote until opinion changes has sometimes had a liberal or moderate impact in recent years.

Although the ideological impact of the filibuster system has become somewhat ambiguous in the early 1970s, the rule usually biases the legislative process against controversial liberal proposals requiring governmental action. Because President Nixon confronted liberals and moderates in the Senate with a variety of policy initiatives that they found worse than the status quo, this negative tool became a useful defensive measure. The system seems likely to reemerge as the leading target for critics of Congressional procedures, when a new liberal Administration next arrives in Washington.

The filibuster system is less important today chiefly because it no longer serves as the final invulnerable defense of Southern racism. Most of the old issues are gone, and most of the necessary legislation against legal segregation in the South is on the lawbooks. The filibuster rule stands, however, as a powerful barrier to the achievement of the next wave of basic social and economic reforms.

After encountering strong conservative filibusters against tax reform, public campaign financing, and consumer protection legislation, Senator Edward Kennedy (D-Mass.) concluded that this obstruction is already occurring. The Senate, he said, "is turning into rule by two-thirds." He claimed that "unless you have two-thirds, on an issue that really reaches at the important power bases of this country, you can't get a vote."[48]

Illusions about Reform

Although critics of Congressional obstructionism continue to pour forth editorials, speeches, and columns that blame Congress's failure to solve the nation's problems on its arcane machinery and undemocratic rules, it is certainly not clear that the reforms they advocate would produce a more activist, progressive Congress. In some policy areas an end to the seniority system would replace a conservative committee chairman with a moderate, while in other cases an urban liberal might lose a position of strategic power. If the House Rules Committee was replaced by a newly constituted committee appointed by the

Speaker and the GOP Leader, or newly elected by the party caucuses, the result would probably bring little change in the current policy decisions. Even the filibuster system is less of an unambiguous evil today in the view of progressives who have used it to block conservative measures. While the traditional obstacles often make Congress a tedious and stultifying place to work, particularly for young progressives on committees with very conservative chairmen, the belief that reform would free a progressive majority is an illusion fostered by those who believe in easy institutional solutions to basic political problems.

NOTES

[1] Roland Young, *This is Congress* (New York: Knopf, 1943), pp. 38–39.

[2] George B. Galloway, *Congress at the Crossroads* (New York: Crowell, 1946), pp. v, 50–63.

[3] *Ibid.*, p. 334.

[4] American Political Science Association, *The Organization of Congress* (1945); APSA, "Toward a More Responsible Two Party System," *American Political Science Review* XLIV (1950), Supplement.

[5] James MacGregor Burns, *Congress on Trial* (New York: Harper and Brothers, 1949), pp. 18–19, 31, 114.

[6] James MacGregor Burns, *The Deadlock of Democracy* (Englewood Cliffs, N.J.: Prentice-Hall, 1963).

[7] James MacGregor Burns, *Uncommon Sense* (New York: Harper & Row, 1972), pp. 114, 124.

[8] Estes Kefauver and Jack Levin, *A Twentieth Century Congress* (New York: Duell, Sloan and Pearce, 1947), pp. 226–27.

[9] Joseph S. Clark, *Congress: The Sapless Branch* (New York: Harper & Row, 1965), p. 105.

[10] Richard Bolling, *House Out of Order* (New York: Dutton, 1966), p. 12.

[11] Donald Riegle with Trevor Armbrister, *O Congress* (New York: Doubleday, 1972), p. 65.

[12] *Congressional Quarterly*, March 4, 1972, p. 488.

[13] *Washington Post*, March 20, 1970, January 14, 1971; *New York Times*, December 19, 1970.

[14] *New York Times*, January 21, 1971.

[15] *Congressional Quarterly*, January 22, 1971, pp. 176–82; Randall B. Ripley, *Party Leaders in the House of Representatives* (Washington: Brookings Institution, 1967), pp. 14–15, 26.

[16] Robert L. Peabody, Jeffrey M. Berry, William G. Frasure, and Jerry Goldman, *To Enact A Law: Congress and Campaign Financing* (New York: Praeger, 1972), pp. 208–15.

[17] Barbara Hinckley, *The Seniority System in Congress* (Bloomington: Indiana University Press, 1971), p. 41; Congressional Quarterly, *Politics in America* (Washington: Congressional Quarterly, Inc., 1969), p. 121.

[18] *Congressional Quarterly*, February 19, 1972, pp. 387–90; David R.

45

Mayhew, *Party Loyalty among Congressmen* (Cambridge: Harvard University Press, 1966), pp. 81–87.

[19] V. O. Key, Jr., *Southern Politics* (New York: Vintage, 1949), pp. 349–52, 371–72.

[20] *Congressional Directory*, 92d Cong., 1st Sess., 1971, pp. 235–37; 252–58.

[21] *Ibid.*, pp. 268–76.

[22] *Congressional Directory*, 93d Cong., 1st Sess., 1973, pp. 286–306.

[23] *Ibid.*

[24] *Ibid.*

[25] Lewis A. Froman, Jr., *The Congressional Process* (Boston: Little, Brown, 1967), p. 53.

[26] James A. Robinson, *The House Rules Committee* (Indianapolis: Bobbs-Merrill, 1963), pp. 5–6.

[27] Froman, p. 98.

[28] *Washington Post*, February 15, 1973.

[29] *Washington Post*, October 6, 1973.

[30] *Congressional Quarterly*, March 30, 1974, pp. 804–10; *New York Times*, March 7, 1974.

[31] *Congressional Quarterly*, March 30, 1974, p. 804.

[32] *Washington Post*, October 6, 1973.

[33] Franklin L. Burdette, *Filibustering in the Senate* (Princeton: Princeton University Press, 1940), pp. 133–37, 179–81, 191–99, 210.

[34] Congressional Quarterly, *Congress and the Nation*, Vol. 1, p. 1637.

[35] *Ibid.*, Vol. 2, pp. 360–61.

[36] Richard Harris's *Decision* (New York: Dutton, 1971) treats the Carswell nomination. The best coverage of the development of these historic struggles was by John McKenzie in the *Washington Post*.

[37] *New York Times*, December 20, 1970.

[38] *Congressional Record*, December 16, 1970 (perm. ed.), p. 41791.

[39] Daniel P. Moynihan, *The Politics of a Guaranteed Income* (New York: Vintage, 1973), p. 538.

[40] *Congressional Quarterly*, January 17, 1969, p. 138; *Congressional Record*, March 9, 1971, p. S2660.

[41] *New York Times*, June 24, 1971; *Washington Post*, June 24, 1971.

[42] *Congressional Quarterly*, August 6, 1971, p. 1647; and September 25, 1971, p. 1973; *Washington Post*, July 19, 1971.

[43] *Congressional Record*, September 29, 1971, pp. S15266–67.

[44] *Ibid.*, p. S15268.

[45] *Congressional Quarterly*, February 9, 1974, p. 317; March 9, 1974, p. 637.

[46] *Ibid.*

[47] *Ibid.*

[48] *Washington Post*, July 1, 1974.

4

CONGRESSIONAL INITIATIVE

The Complexities of Congressional Responsiveness

The legislative process is changing because American society is changing. In spite of strong institutional barriers and deep public suspicion of decisive federal action on domestic social problems, Congress has acted on a number of issues. The past decade has produced the first major aid-to-education program in American history; the largest subsidized housing programs; a vast growth of Social Security benefits; a massive program of medical care for the aged; a variety of new programs aimed at poverty and urban deterioration; major environmental initiatives; and enactment of the entire agenda of civil rights issues that existed a decade ago. While the Nixon Administration has brought retrogression in some of these areas, and there has been continued stagnation on a variety of other problems, it is, even so, an impressive record of social change.

The breakthroughs came largely during the brief period in the mid-1960s when there was a clear and coherent public majority supporting the program of a Democratic President and a Democratic Congress. The pace of legislative action reached its peak after the landslide for President Johnson and a Democratic Congress in 1964.

The institutional structures didn't change significantly between the Kennedy stalemate and the Johnson-era reforms, nor did they between the Johnson period and the Nixon stalemate. The fact was that Kennedy had been the first President in more than half a century who failed to make initial gains for his party in Congress, and Nixon was the first in more than a century to fail to carry either house of Congress when he was first elected. Kennedy confronted a House often solidly in the control of a conservative coalition of Republicans and Southern Democrats, while Nixon confronted a Senate with a liberal-moderate majority. In each case their Congressional opponents believed that they had broader electoral mandates than the minority Presidents, and they probably believed it with some justice. The legislative stalemate reflected public indecision at least as much as institutional unresponsiveness.

Much of the early legislative program of the Johnson Administration involved catching up with an agenda of issues developed years earlier and enjoying considerable public support for some time. President Johnson inherited the broad Democratic Party platform of the postwar period and fleshed it out with the current ideas of some of the party's academic activists. The 1964 election presented the public with a rare choice between an activist federal domestic policy and a sharp contraction of federal responsibilities. Senator Goldwater's disastrous defeat and the dramatic GOP losses in the House temporarily resolved the contradiction between desire for programs and fear of federal control. Passage of basic civil rights laws seemed to finally settle one of the issues that had divided the Democrats and complicated the development of legislation on a variety of domestic issues.

At the height of the Johnson period, legislation often poured out of Congress without careful study of controversial issues, based on the presumption that adequate funds to make the programs work would be provided after the Vietnam War ended—presumably in the near future. The liberal House majority soon disappeared, however, the war went on, and the funds never materialized. Although the public rating of Congress briefly reached a high point for recent history, reaction soon set in and GOP conservatives made a major comeback in the midterm elections.

Contrary to the reformers' picture of a public whose desires are frustrated by a recalcitrant set of institutions, this period showed that decisive legislative action produced a distinctly ambiguous reaction: an increase both in the public regard for

48

Table 4-1

Public Reactions to Speed of Integration under
Johnson Administration

	Too Fast	Not Fast Enough	About Right	No Opinion
Feb. 1964	30%	15%	39%	16%
April 1965	34%	17%	38%	11%
Sept. 1966	52%	10%	29%	9%

SOURCE George H. Gallup, The Gallup Poll (New York: Random House, 1972), polls of February 26, 1964; April 11, 1965; and September 28, 1966.

Congress and in the defeat of incumbents. Having rather quickly disposed of the less controversial issues, on which a reasonable level of consensus had been built, Congress soon reached far more contentious questions. As it moved, in just two years' time, from the relatively easy questions of desegregating hotels and restaurants to the difficult ones of urban housing desegregation, it moved from issues supported by a large majority to ones opposed by most Americans. While the Administration was advancing rapidly from the relatively settled issue of giving some federal aid to the schools, to proposals to change cities through poverty programs, model cities planning, and rent supplements to the poor, the consensus evaporated.

The vast and sudden expansion of federal domestic programs strengthened long-standing contradictions in public attitudes. People wanted more services, but less federal activity and lower taxes. They supported individual new programs while opposing big government. They endorsed the idea of equal opportunity, but increasingly said change was coming too fast and the wrong way.

Analysis of the "responsiveness" of Congress to public opinion is very difficult, because it is scarcely possible to determine at any point in time what the public really thinks about the issues as they present themselves in the legislative setting. The majority of the voters may say that they support federal aid to education, but this by no means suggests how they would vote on a complex bill that has certain effects on the district, embodies a certain degree of federal control, provides certain assistance to religious schools, and involves at least an implicit judgment about the relative priorities of a variety of domestic

49

initiatives or tax reductions. The general questions in opinion polls often show people simultaneously holding contradictory views, and poll results usually lack data relevant to the kinds of hard choices between competing values that legislators constantly face. When, for example, Congressional critics for years assailed Congress's inability to terminate the war in Vietnam, the Congressional deadlock reflected the fact that Americans wanted the war ended, but were unwilling to accept the probable consequences of a rapid U.S. pullout.[1] These incompatible desires weren't invented by Congress. The fact that the legislative process reflected them may be less an indication of organizational flaws than of the representative character of the body.

Members of Congress operate with extremely imperfect information about the desires of their constituents on many issues. Only on a handful of very salient public issues is there likely to be anything approximating a high level of public awareness and a reasonably well-formed set of policy preferences. On very sensitive and visible social issues, particularly racial questions, there is evidence that Congressmen are highly responsive to constituency attitudes. In other areas party positions appear to have more influence than differences between constituencies, and there is some evidence that Congressmen rely on information sources that basically confirm what they want to believe about local attitudes.[2]

Probably the most serious representational problem in Congress is that most members and most committee staffs must basically rely on policy analysis materials produced by agencies or interest groups. Sometimes this is supplemented by data from academic researchers. This system usually produces reasonable information about the impact of proposed policies on major economic and governmental institutions, but seldom generates good information on the impact of policies on less affluent and less organized groups in the society. This is a severe problem, not only for Congress but also for administrative policy-makers.

While Congress is frequently disparaged not only for "unresponsiveness" and a conservative bias, but also for a generally obstructionist character toward new policy ideas, this criticism is often based on a very unrepresentative selection of issues. Controversial issues are examined by both the press and scholars because they are visible at the time. Presidential issues receive special notice because of the extremely high level of attention given to Presidential actions as a matter of course. The result is that the quiet, frequently bipartisan work of

Congressional innovation often goes virtually unnoticed. Thus Congress was roundly denounced for stalemating President Nixon's welfare reform—an extremely complex proposal widely attacked by liberal and conservative groups alike—while relatively little attention was given to the easy passage of a massive child-care bill until President Nixon decided to veto it. The welfare bill would have been of substantial immediate benefit to recipients in only a few states of the Deep South. The child-care legislation would have affected the lives of large numbers of women and children across the country who now suffer from the lack of decent day-care facilities. By skillfully building Congressional coalitions, the day-care sponsors had facilitated the legislative process, but had also obscured the importance of the policy change and the significance of the Congressional innovation.

Congress and the Urban Crisis

In America's deteriorating cities social troubles have long been festering. Growing ghettos, declining urban economies, languishing school systems, and chaotic metropolitan development have been salient facts since the Second World War. Yet the country was woefully unprepared for the shock of the racial polarization and urban violence of the late 1960s, and some critics of course blamed Congress for frustrating the President's efforts to voice the needs of the cities.

Although the political system has produced only limited answers to urban problems, Congress rather than the President deserves much of the credit for whatever has been done. Until the mid-1960s there were only a handful of bills that could be clearly labeled "urban," and most of these measures had been devised on Capitol Hill. The principal author of the recent book *Congress and Urban Problems* concludes that Congress has "provided the leadership, the continuity, the persistence in formulating new policies and programs and guiding them through the political thicket of the legislative process to final decision." Executive-branch spokesmen, on the other hand, were normally "either hesitant and divided, resulting in halting and sporadic initiative, or frankly opposed, resulting in outright obstructionism."[3]

Actually the main innovators were frequently Democratic Congressmen and Senators, working together with interested groups. Even sympathetic Democratic Presidents rarely gave much attention to the issues. In fact one leading contemporary 51 student of the Presidency, Thomas Cronin, argues that the President's inescapable involvement in all manner of crises, and his heavy and unambiguous responsibility for international and military affairs, leaves him generally ill equipped for leadership on domestic policy. Most Presidents come to office with personal policy goals that are "essentially moderate and only vaguely refined." Generally the Chief Executive's role is that of a "broker for a few party priorities and as a strategically situated and important participant among vast numbers of policy entrepreneurs and political leaders." [4] The policies that eventually emerge are usually an amalgam. When the President assumes leadership there is sometimes a contribution from White House advisory groups, and always comments from the bureaucracies and clearance with the powerful pressure groups. Normally the most open, and often the most critical, scrutiny comes in hearings and subsequent negotiations with a series of legislative and appropriations subcommittees in both houses. In urban affairs sometimes the President doesn't even assert formal leadership.

If the President often serves as a broker for party objectives, the key question is where the objectives come from. No matter who first conceived of an idea, the record clearly shows that members of Congress have frequently played vital roles in translating a new perception into a public issue and, ultimately, into an accepted party position. Active members of the Democratic opposition Congresses under the Eisenhower Administration developed virtually all the issues that went into President Kennedy's legislative program. President Johnson's War on Poverty and President Nixon's revenue sharing proposals grew directly out of issues their parties developed in Congress.

Feeble as the formal structure of American parties is, party members outside the South show a pattern of broad common agreement on urban issues that reach the floor of Congress. Research shows a "dominant pattern of party voting" where "rural and small-town Democratic members voted in much larger proportions to support these urban bills than did Republicans from urban and suburban districts." [5] A study of housing bills over a fifteen-year period found Democratic House leaders, including those from the rural South, consistently supporting the pro-city position on every controversial vote. The GOP leaders, on the other hand, were prominent opponents in all but one vote during the period. [6]

The period of intense legislative activity on urban issues in the 1960s showed much the same pattern. During the 1965–69 period most Democrats were consistent supporters of programs for mass transit, housing subsidies, the poverty program, school aid for poor children, model cities, fair housing, and general domestic program appropriations. Among Republican House members only one in twenty made a similar record. Rural Democrats were more pro-city than urban Republicans. While Southern Democrats cast a significant number of votes for urban programs, Southern Republicans cast virtually none.[7]

Although the Johnson Administration played an active role in the formulation of several important urban initiatives in the mid-1960s and belatedly endorsed the main concepts in the massive 1968 housing legislation, most urban legislation has originated in Congress. Congressional initiatives first committed the country to mass transportation aid, air pollution regulation, home ownership for the poor, and a variety of other urban reforms. In 1968, after the White House had written off the possibility of enacting a fair-housing law, Congress passed it. In 1974 Congress passed a massive housing bill running contrary to President Nixon's strong effort to cut back housing programs. President Ford signed it.

The Source and Types of Congressional Innovation

Innovation in urban legislation has been only one example of Congressional leadership in the development of domestic policies. Congress has been very active in recent years in developing new employment programs, repairing some of the most blatant inequities in the tax system, protecting women's rights, granting eighteen-year-olds the vote, reforming the budget process, providing aid to higher education, creating new machinery for economic controls, greatly expanding food assistance for poor people, and a variety of other measures.

The basic source of domestic policy innovation, within national political institutions, is the liberal segment of the Northern wing of the Democratic Party. This segment of the party is usually a minority within the Democratic Caucuses in each house, and a relatively small minority within Congress as a whole. Robert Peabody, a close student of recent House leadership fights, estimates the liberal activist group in the House as numbering about a hundred or less in a typical recent year, which accounts for less than a fourth of the total House membership.[8]

When reformers join together with the Congressmen produced by the big-city organizations and the Border state and Southern moderates, or when Senate liberals combine with Democratic moderates from some Western, Border, and Southern states, a moderately liberal working majority can sometimes be assembled following large Democratic victories. Only when this happens—and it last happened in 1965–66—can one fairly say that there is a progressive majority in Congress. Looked at in this way, the record of significant domestic innovation, in the face of a normal conservative-moderate majority, is considerably more impressive.

Change comes far more easily, of course, when a Democratic President can deal with a strongly Democratic Congress. This is less because of the structural characteristics of the institutions than because of the ability of common party goals to minimize inherent institutional friction and multiple veto points in the policy process. It is true, to be sure, that a President's executive power can help engage the technical resources of the bureaucracies, and that his unique access to the mass media can sometimes greatly accelerate the process of transforming a minority position of little visibility into a salient party issue. Notable innovations have occurred, however, even when the party is limited to its Congressional base.

Observers seldom notice the extremely important role Congress often plays after the initial enactment of legislation. Both through successive amendments and through the yearly appropriations process, Congress constantly remolds ongoing programs. Most domestic grant programs are now set up for limited numbers of years. This gives Congressional committees an opportunity to reshape such programs at the time the legislation is renewed, and gives administrators a powerful incentive for complying with Congressional directives and providing program information to the committees. While single changes may not be dramatic, the accumulation of year-by-year alterations can ultimately be more important than the initial legislative process. Sometimes it is possible, for example, to launch small new programs, embodying ideas that would have no chance as separate legislation, through virtually unnoticed amendments to the statute renewing an existing program. Using the leverage of his position on the relevant subcommittee, a member can sometimes launch a program this way and hope that the program's success, or its ability to crystallize an important potential constituency, can then help turn a neglected problem into an important issue in future Congresses.

Congress can also aid the development of policy by interaction with courts or innovative bureaucrats. Virtually all social legislation involves the transfer of broad and partially undefined authority to the responsible agencies. In some cases administrators interpret their powers broadly to expand the objectives of the program. Similarly, courts may hand down broad interpretations of the "intent of Congress," thus requiring agencies to come to terms with controversial new issues. Administrative changes can sometimes be stimulated from a Congressional base, and the momentum of either kind of change can often be protected when its supporters have enough power to veto Congressional action designed to narrow the wording of the law. In effect, Congressional pigeonholing of legislation intended to override administrative or judicial policy innovation usually functions as a confirmation of the rightness of the broad interpretation of the law. This fact offers progressives in strategic positions the opportunity to broaden a program by securing inaction. As lawmaking public-interest lawyers take more and more administrative issues into the courts, and increasing numbers of liberals come into power within the seniority system, this interaction may become more important.

The Congress-Nixon Confrontation

The flow and interplay of power within the national government is often so complex and so obscure that it is virtually impossible to analyze with any precision. However, the Nixon period, with its series of dramatic institutional confrontations heightened by partisan divisions, offers a rare opportunity to view unambiguous tests of power. Through a series of case studies, the distribution of power and the ideological role of each institution will be examined in the following chapters. To avoid the distorting impact of the Watergate scandal, the great bulk of this investigation will be limited to the period before mid-1973, when the scandal began to seriously undermine and finally destroy Mr. Nixon's Presidential leadership.

Assuming office after an indecisive election where the Presidential vote was split three ways, Mr. Nixon brought with him to Washington virtually no social program except a pledge to slow down civil rights enforcement and become tougher on crime. These objectives were compatible with his goal of creating a GOP majority by adding George Wallace's extensive 1968 support to his own by the time of the 1972 election. When 55

Congressional and journalistic pressure eventually forced the new Administration to prepare a legislative program, the package was heavily weighted with organizational and managerial changes. Most of the measures concerned reshaping federal programs through revenue sharing, or through reorganization and consolidation of existing programs and agencies. The intention was to increase efficiency and provide greater local discretion in the use of the program funds. The major exceptions came in the form of an ambitious welfare program that blended progressive and conservative elements in a controversial package, and civil rights proposals that were clearly retrogressive.

President Nixon spent little time on domestic policy, except when severe political problems were apparent. The threatened economic collapse of 1971 and the energy crisis of 1973–74 made executive action essential. Heated disputes over school integration and suburban housing desegregation provoked strong conservative Presidential pronouncements. Most issues saw only intermittent Presidential involvement.

Not only did President Nixon fare very poorly in winning Congressional approval of his modest program, but he also frequently found himself fighting hard to prevent Congressional infringement on traditional executive prerogatives. Congress imposed unprecedented limitations on a wartime President, forbidding specific military acts, cutting military aid, and even suspending the draft for several months. In the end it forced termination of U.S. activities in Cambodia by the drastic step of simply cutting off the funds. While the President still retained vast powers in international affairs, Congress had become a clearer force in the making of foreign policy than it had been since before the Second World War.

In domestic policy the President experienced great difficulty in defending some generally accepted Presidential prerogatives, and found himself frequently resorting to vetoes of Congressional initiatives. Twice he lost determined drives to put nominees on the Supreme Court, and others were withdrawn without even a formal nomination. He vetoed urban and environmental measures; bills to promote education, job creation, campaign reform, and health care; and a variety of other important legislation where a Congressional majority supported a more progressive position. In spite of strong efforts, the President was unable to thwart Congressional efforts to conserve most of the legislative corpus of the Great Society. On a number of occasions he found himself eventually accepting Congressional initiatives he had originally scorned.

Summary:

Americans often tend to believe that their political problems can be solved by institutional reform. Although Congress does have procedures and ways of distributing power that are irrational and unfair to younger members, these no longer bias the system in a clearly conservative direction. In fact, some of the long-criticized procedures may have strongly liberal consequences in years to come. Much of the stalemate that exists in some areas of domestic policy probably results from a close division between conservative and progressive in recent elections and from a lack of public consensus supporting further reforms. Congress reflects the underlying political reality of the country.

NOTES

[1] Milton J. Rosenberg, Sidney Verba, and Philip E. Converse, *Vietnam and the Silent Majority* (New York: Har/Row Books, 1970), pp. 23–24.

[2] Raymond A. Bauer, Ithiel de Sola Pool, and Lewis Anthony Dexter, *American Business and Public Policy* (New York: Atherton, 1968), especially Chapters 10–12.

[3] Frederic N. Cleveland et al., *Congress and Urban Problems* (Washington: Brookings Institution, 1969), p. 355.

[4] Thomas Cronin, "The Presidency as a Domestic Policy Executive," unpublished manuscript (1972), pp. 16, 21, 27, 34.

[5] Cleveland, pp. 370–71.

[6] Mayhew, pp. 64–80.

[7] William T. Murphy, Jr., "Congress and the Cities: A Roll Call Analysis of the 89th and 90th Congresses," unpublished manuscript (1970), pp. 4, 11, 16–17, 20.

[8] Robert L. Peabody, "The Selection of a Majority Leader, 1970–71: The Candidates and Their Campaigns," unpublished manuscript (1971), p. III-23a. Peabody identified 64 members who were definitely "change oriented," 146 who were "establishment," and 45 who were "mixed or unclassifiable" in 1971.

part two

CONGRESS
and
RACIAL CHANGE

5

CONGRESS EMBATTLED

Congress in the Fight for Civil Rights

Congress has been in the midst of the battle over the rights of black Americans since its earliest sessions. With the brief exception of the Reconstruction years, when Congress was the driving force for civil rights, its record was one of continual deadlock and failure until the mid-1950s. The normal Southern domination of the Democratic party, the strength of the conservative coalition between Southerners and the GOP, and Southern control of many decisive committees and effective use of the filibuster, made legislative action all but impossible. The structure of Congress gave the South a veto, and that veto was used with force and regularity to preserve white domination. Congressional power over executive agencies meant that there was virtually no pressure against segregation in federal programs.

Perhaps the most important development in American politics during this generation has been the breaking of the Southern veto in Congress. By 1974 Congress had passed seven major pieces of civil rights legislation since the modern Congressional struggle began in 1956. Southern filibusters had been broken on four occasions, and most of the legislative framework required

A Civil Rights Chronology

1954   The Supreme Court decision against segregation in the public schools.

1957   The Eisenhower civil rights act.

1963   Civil rights demonstrations in Birmingham; civil rights initiatives by President Kennedy and Congress.

1964   The 1964 Civil Rights Act.

1965   The 1965 Voting Rights Act.
        Watts: the first big black ghetto riot.

1966   GOP gains in the Congressional election; Congress becomes more conservative.

1968   The fair-housing act.
        Richard Nixon elected President.

1969   The Senate rejects the Haynsworth nomination.
        The Philadelphia Plan supported by Congress.

1970   Defeat of the Stennis amendment.
        The Senate rejects the Carswell nomination.
        The 1965 Voting Rights Act is extended over Presidential opposition.

1972   Job discrimination legislation.
        A Senate filibuster defeats the Nixon antibusing bill.

for racial reconstruction of Southern society was in place. A major liberal filibuster in 1972 had prevented enactment of President Nixon's antibusing legislation. Congress had played a major and positive role in these significant events.

The shift in Congress reflected, on the one hand, major changes in American society producing altered local attitudes, and on the other hand, extremely important developments within the Democratic Party and its leadership structure in Congress. The Second World War began a process of change in American racial attitudes that accelerated sharply after the 1954 Supreme Court decision against school segregation. The emergence of the civil rights movement, and the dramatic confrontations between peaceful demonstrators and racist local officials in the Deep South of the early and middle 1960s, brought public awareness and commitment to its highest level in recent history. Mobilization of major elements of society, including religious and labor groups, behind the program of the civil rights movement created a national political constituency for change. In these extraordinary circumstances, GOP moderates and some conservatives joined an almost unanimous grouping of Northern and Western Democrats to break the long stranglehold of the South over legislation requiring social change.

Congress's role was not limited to legislation, and positive contributions continued long after public demands for racial change had all but disappeared. In 1968 a President opposed to vigorous civil rights enforcement was elected. The public mood had changed, and now the power of the Presidency was thrown into the balance in favor of severe retrenchment. The issue was posed to Congress in many ways, often in the glare of White House publicity. Time after time Congress rejected efforts to move the country backwards, and occasionally even took a step forward. Congressional committees gathered evidence that became highly important in slowing the national tide of reaction, particularly on school integration. Congress prevented the appointment of judges with poor civil rights records to the Supreme Court. If the United States still has a chance of building an integrated and just society, Congress deserves a great deal of the credit.

The most striking fact about the Nixon years was the importance of Congress's negative powers to delay, debate, and defeat Presidential initiatives so as to maintain the momentum of racial change. The following chapters will concentrate on the way in which many of the tools of Congressional resistance, commonly attacked by liberals, have been employed in defense of an important social goal. They will also illustrate the paradoxical fact that negative Congressional actions can often have positive social effects when Congress is asked to impede change set in motion by administrative or judicial decisions. Inaction, or defeat of the negative proposal, becomes an affirmation of the forward movement. In such situations liberals can draw on a well-developed repertoire of devices often employed by the conservatives. When the devices are used skillfully, the veto power of a liberal Congressional minority can become a veto of executive reaction.

The Rise and Triumph of the Civil Rights Movement: 1954–1965 Congress had been a graveyard for civil rights during the eight decades between 1875 and 1957. During this period there was little national interest in racial change, and the Southern veto in Congress was so strong that it prevented action even against the most unpopular aspects of the Southern system, lynching and the poll tax. When President Warren Harding called for a federal law against lynching and pressed the issue in 1921, the bill was killed. Even after the Second

World War, Congress quickly terminated the emergency Fair Employment Practices Commission established by President Roosevelt. President Truman's civil rights program was decimated on Capitol Hill. Truman even had to veto a Congressional effort to impose segregation on existing integrated schools in the South run by the federal government. The prospect for any positive legislation seemed hopeless.

The next two decades, however, brought two dramatic changes both in national attitudes and in Congress. The first change, from total resistance to token action, was begun by the 1954 Supreme Court decision against segregation in the public schools. The second change—the crucial breakthrough from symbolic action to programs requiring basic reforms—came with the rise of the civil rights movement and the emergence of strong pro–civil rights political leadership both in the White House and on Capitol Hill during 1963–64. Before the 1960s ended, Congress had been transformed from an almost completely effective barrier against human rights legislation, into the crucible of major changes in national social policy.

The 1954 school desegregation decision made civil rights a primary national issue and gave proponents of change the great advantage of the moral and legal force of a unanimous Supreme Court decision. The political impetus for change created by the Court's action, and the widespread public support that it crystallized for desegregation, first found Congressional expression in the 1956–57 struggle over the Eisenhower Administration's rights bill.

Eisenhower asked Congress for legislation to initiate federal protection of voting rights and, most significantly, to allow the Justice Department to file lawsuits to desegregate schools. Although the bill lacked the strong backing of President Eisenhower, who never publicly supported the Supreme Court's decision, Senate Majority Leader Lyndon Johnson (D-Tex.) worked out a compromise that permitted passing a law without overcoming a Southern filibuster. The resulting bill was stripped of the crucial provision allowing the Justice Department to file civil rights lawsuits. President Eisenhower might have been able to win passage of his stronger bill, but at the critical juncture he told a press conference that he himself had doubts about the central provision.[1]

After passing the 1957 law, neither the President nor Congress took any significant action for six years. During the 1960 election year a minor voting law passed, but it was inconsequential. President Kennedy responded to his narrow election victory by subordinating civil rights issues in an effort to win Southern votes for the rest of his program. Neither the President nor the Congress began the breakthrough on this issue. Public opinion changed first, stirred by the powerful demonstrations in Birmingham led by Martin Luther King. Then political leadership at each end of Pennsylvania Avenue began to move.

The Birmingham crisis galvanized the civil rights movement and suddenly put the question of racial justice at the top of the list of public issues. As national anger grew over the violent suppression of peaceful marchers in Birmingham, dozens of members of Congress submitted civil rights bills. Across the country there were mass meetings and demands for action against abuses that to the country generally had never been so visible before. When President Kennedy responded in June 1963, it was with the most sweeping civil rights bill of the century.

When Kennedy sent his civil rights package to Congress, most observers expected that it would be weakened or defeated. Even before Kennedy was assassinated in November 1963, however, Congress had actually strengthened the bill in two very important respects. The original Kennedy bill contained a weak and ambiguous section on the cutoff of federal funds to local agencies that used them for segregated programs. Under pressure of Senate criticism, including a statement by the Senate GOP caucus, the language was altered to *require*, rather than merely authorize, federal officials to end segregation in federally financed programs. This little-noticed change provided the legal basis for the massive school desegregation program by the Department of Health, Education, and Welfare (HEW) that shattered educational segregation in the South.

Congress also deserves credit for transforming a primarily regional measure into one with important national implications, when it added to Kennedy's bill a prohibition against job discrimination. House action, not White House initiative, led to the creation of the Equal Employment Opportunities Commission (EEOC), which began to use federal authority against widespread patterns of job discrimination.[2]

The 1964 civil rights fight found the liberals and moderates better organized than ever before, and the Southerners, under weakened leadership, taking a rigid position. The civil rights coalition, under the leadership of Senator Hubert Humphrey (D-Minn.), broke the longest filibuster in decades. Even though the Republican Party's most important Presidential

65

candidate, Barry Goldwater (R-Ariz.), opposed the bill, the old conservative coalition collapsed and the filibuster was voted down. Except for the Reconstruction years, when the South was denied representation in Congress, it was the first time in American history that Congress had made itself free to legislate on race relations.

The breaking of the filibuster had significance far beyond its immediate importance in making possible the passage of an immensely important law. The victory showed that the South was no longer invincible on racial issues. Civil rights forces were strong enough, on at least a few issues, to unite almost all non-Southern Senators.

The decision of many conservatives to vote to end debate weakened the plausibility of future resurrections of the old philosophic arguments for absolutely unlimited debate. Once the Southern veto was shattered, it could never quite be put back together again. Because of powerful public support, and good organization within Congress and among the lobbying groups, significant legislation could be passed.

The next year Congress quashed another filibuster to pass the most drastic piece of civil rights legislation yet proposed: the 1965 Voting Rights Act. Experience with earlier voting laws had shown that as long as federal authorities were required to conclusively prove intentional discrimination by each locality in proceedings before Southern federal judges, very little would change. After Martin Luther King captured national attention with the Selma demonstrations, in the heart of Alabama's Black Belt, President Johnson submitted sweeping legislation. The bill wrote into federal law the presumption that discrimination was taking place in states with a low level of registration and voting, using a formula that singled out six Southern states and a portion of a seventh. In the affected area literacy tests were automatically suspended, and an extraordinary provision gave the Attorney General power to veto any new state electoral legislation that might impede black registration and voting.

The bill was launched with a classic show of Presidential leadership, as President Johnson appealed to a joint session of Congress in the most eloquent speech of his Presidency. Congress responded with equal force and decisiveness. While the 1964 Civil Rights Act had taken more than a year to win passage, the Voting Rights measure sped through Congress in little more than two months. With passage of the voting law, the backlog of issues where a clear national majority supported federal action was pretty well exhausted.

Table 5-1

Changing Percentage of the Public Identifying Civil Rights as
"the most important problem facing this country today,"
before and after the August 1965 Watts riots

March 1965*	52%
May 1965	23%
Oct.–Nov. 1965	17%
May 1966	9%

* *During the struggle for the 1965 Voting Rights Act.*
SOURCE   George H. *Gallup,* The Gallup Poll *(New York: Random House,*
1972) Vol. 3, pp. 1934, 1944, 1973, 2009.

The Decline in the Civil Rights Movement: 1965–1968
Most of the major political developments in the years following
1965 damaged the momentum of civil rights forces in Congress.
1965 saw the first of the large urban upheavals, when the Watts
ghetto in Los Angeles erupted in a riot. It witnessed the emergence of the "black power" slogan, and sudden moves toward
black nationalism on the part of some important young black
leaders. Before the year was over the civil rights movement
was fragmented. The movement's supporters were divided and
confused, and the political initiative had passed to politicians
demanding "law and order" and capitalizing on white fears of
city riots.

Congress moved to the right on civil rights during 1966, and
became far more conservative after the major GOP gain in the
1966 Congressional elections. Amendments hostile to school
desegregation passed the House, and "antiriot" legislation became a very popular topic.

Even in this unfavorable climate, though, there was a majority in each house in favor of fair-housing legislation. Most civil
rights experts had thought that Congressional action on this
very controversial topic was impossible, since the change was
still not even supported by the majority of the people. In spite
of spreading rancor, huge riots in Detroit and Newark, and
violent white reaction to Martin Luther King's Chicago fair-
housing marches, the House passed a watered-down fair-housing
bill. On the Senate side, GOP opposition killed the bill through
a filibuster, but not until most Senators had voted in favor
of it. While Senate support was still far below the two-thirds
required to end debate, the measure was receiving substantial
support.

67

Congress had long been the burying place for the most modest and urgently desired civil rights measures. Now, however, it was becoming the stage for political struggle over an idea still considered suspect by much of the public. Two years later Congressional leadership produced a dramatic breakthrough on this issue.

There was, of course, a strong crosscurrent of civil rights opposition on Capitol Hill. Antiriot measures of dubious constitutionality began to pass regularly in 1966, and the House also initiated a long series of annual votes intended to limit federal school desegregation enforcement. When, beginning in 1966, it became an annual ritual for the House to send an anti-school desegregation measure to conference with the Senate, liberal seniority became a very important influence in defeating these measures. When the House and Senate pass different versions of a bill, the differences are worked out by a conference committee usually composed of the senior members of the committees that handled the bills. Liberals from each house, working with the federal agencies and civil rights representatives, found formulas to render the original text of the House bills innocuous. Language intended to prohibit school desegregation would come out as language forbidding the government to require "racial balancing"—which no one was requiring anyway. In other cases, provisions intended to roll back desegregation standards would be qualified by the phrase "except as required by the Constitution"—a modification hard to oppose. Since all court orders and virtually all administrative requirements were based on Constitutional interpretations, the amendments then became meaningless. Year after year the House majority was frustrated through the use of liberal seniority on conference committees.

Although many House members would have liked to use the committee system to attack civil rights officials, seniority had made Emanuel Celler, a civil rights supporter from Brooklyn who had first come to Congress in 1923, chairman of the Judiciary Committee. The House rules put civil rights bills and their enforcement within the prescribed jurisdiction of Celler's committee. Celler's position was critical, since the House was frequently less sympathetic than the Senate to civil rights. The Senate committee, headed by James O. Eastland of Mississippi, was eventually rendered relatively harmless by the chairman's inaction, a variety of legislative stratagems to circumvent the committee, and the appointment of a growing number of civil rights supporters from both parties.

Table 5-2

Survey Questions Reflecting Public Fears in
Late 1967 and Early 1968*

Percent that would like to see Congress pass an open-housing law	35%
Percent reporting that their attitudes toward Negroes had worsened in past months	32%
Percent favoring shooting of people looting stores during ghetto riots	47%
Percent expecting "serious racial trouble" in their big city within six months	30%

* In January 1968 the public for the first time listed crime and lawlessness as the most important domestic problem, both at the national and at the local level.
SOURCE The Gallup Poll, Vol. 3, pp. 2057, 2076, 2107, 2128.

Although there was no discernible pressure for more civil rights legislation, and the country was deeply disturbed by continuing ghetto violence, bills continued to work their way through the legislative process. During 1967 the House quietly passed two bills, the first granting the Justice Department long-sought authority to protect civil rights workers from local harassment, and the second giving real enforcement powers to the Equal Employment Opportunities Commission.[3]

The prospects for Senate action seemed dim as the civil rights workers bill came over from the House in late 1967. President Johnson was deeply preoccupied with the war, and public confidence in his civil rights policies had fallen sharply.[4] Southerners planned to filibuster against a measure extending federal protection to the "outside agitators" whom they blamed for social unrest. At a time when Northern city officials were also frequently suggesting that outside militants were responsible for ghetto riots, prospects were discouraging. Majority Leader Mike Mansfield (D-Mont.) quietly sidetracked the House bill and held it over for the 1968 session.

Congress took the initiative on civil rights in 1968—an initiative it would hold throughout the next several years. On an early test vote Senate civil rights supporters discovered they

69

were far more powerful than expected. Against the advice of the President, the Justice Department, and virtually all knowledgeable observers, a small group of Senate civil rights leaders began a fight to enact a broad federal fair-housing law as an amendment to the House bill. With the support of the Democratic leadership and the active work of young Republican progressives, civil rights forces finally won an arduous battle that involved no less than four successive cloture votes. The President played no significant role in the process and the civil rights groups never mobilized mass support.[5] It was basically a battle within the Senate, a battle to win the crucial Republican votes for cloture.

The Senate vote showed that the filibuster system no longer prevented Senate action even on relatively controversial civil rights issues. Just as the votes of the mid-1960s had shown the overwhelming support of Northern, Western, and Border-state Democrats for civil rights, so this vote showed growing strength within the GOP for action against urban segregation.

The fair-housing fight was made possible by the decision of most GOP Senators to break with the conservative position on the issue charted by Senate GOP Leader Everett Dirksen (R-Ill.) in 1966. The new Republican Senators elected in November 1966 tipped the balance within the party's Senate caucus in favor of a more moderate civil rights posture. This fact would be extremely important as the policy battles of the Nixon Administration unfolded.[6]

While Senators took the initiative in fair housing, and the House acquiesced in the broad Senate bill after the assassination of Martin Luther King, there were also some major signs of resistance on Capitol Hill. The fair-housing bill carried a vague and sweeping antiriot provision. President Johnson's proposed rent supplement program—which was intended to help disperse black families into normal apartment buildings outside ghettos—was changed to a small experimental program and subjected to veto by local suburban governments. The effort to use the new Model Cities program as a vehicle for desegregation was also lost in Congress. Even on the fair-housing issue a substantial fight was required to obtain any appropriation at all for the enforcement staff, and the money appropriated was wholly inadequate for serious enforcement.[7]

While Congress was in no mood to impose drastic changes on the country, there was still some forward momentum. But as the 1968 Presidential campaign unfolded, the GOP candidate outlined a position to the right of Congress.

President Nixon's Opposition to Civil Rights The 1968 campaign saw Richard Nixon win the nomination with vital assistance from Strom Thurmond (R-S.C.), a leading segregationist spokesman. At the Miami convention Mr. Nixon opened up some of the major Congressional issues of the following year when he criticized enforcement of existing school desegregation and voting rights laws, and promised to drastically alter the makeup of the Supreme Court. During his campaign the future President repeatedly emphasized his opposition to urban school desegregation plans requiring busing, and hammered home the Supreme Court promise.

Nixon had pledged a drastic reversal in civil rights policy to the Southern caucus at the 1968 Republican national convention. He told the Southern delegates that he opposed the new federal fair-housing law and he denounced busing, saying it would "destroy" children. He promised the South a more acceptable Attorney General and Chief Justice, and declared he was not interested in "satisfying some professional civil rights group." [8]

Early in his fall campaign, in the crucial regional television program aimed at the South, Nixon openly competed for Wallace votes with an attack on existing federal school desegregation policies. Instead of endorsing the requirement that Southern states dismantle their dual school system, Nixon supported a plan that would have maintained separate black and white schools, and placed the entire burden of any desegregation on black children willing to risk local pressures by transferring to white schools. The GOP nominee also expressed deep skepticism about the most powerful enforcement tool in the 1964 Civil Rights Act, when he told his Southern television audience that cutting off federal funds to segregated systems was "dangerous" and "going too far." [9]

When the President took office, a whole series of pending civil rights decisions soon gave him an opportunity to clarify his Administration's policies. Southern educators and political leaders urged clarification of school desegregation policies. The President, whose campaign had concentrated very heavily on winning over white Southerners, now had to define his political objectives. At the Administration's outset, national confusion was heightened when some Nixon supporters emphasized his "Bring Us Together" inaugural theme, while others waited eagerly for the fulfillment of Senator Thurmond's promise that school desegregation would soon end. Congress awaited the President's position on pending job discrimination measures, 71 and officials of the Department of Housing and Urban Development (HUD) wanted to know where he stood on major questions about the enforcement of the recently passed fair-housing law. The Chief Justice of the Supreme Court was due to retire soon and Associate Justice Abe Fortas was already under attack.

After several months of confusion and ambiguity, President Nixon turned strongly against extension of civil rights protections on virtually all of the major pending issues. The President's early statements and appointments had straddled the controversies. The Secretaries of HUD, Labor, and HEW were reputed to be civil rights supporters, but the key civil rights job, that of Attorney General, went to John Mitchell, the architect of the President's Southern strategy. Moderates found encouragement in Nixon's inaugural address. "To go forward at all is to go forward together," the President had said. "This means black and white together, as one nation, not two."[10]

Within weeks the moderates' hopes were deflated. Nixon told a press conference that he felt there was no "significant area where additional legislation could be passed that would be helpful in opening doors that were legally closed." [11] The Congressional majority supporting stronger enforcement powers for the EEOC would receive little White House encouragement. The President was soon accused of serious administrative retreats both on school desegregation and in the job discrimination program. Early HEW compromises on pending enforcement actions undermined credibility in the school program. The Administration refused to implement scheduled denial of government contracts to three large textile firms with discriminatory employment practices.[12]

As 1969 continued, the picture became increasingly dismal. After many delays the Administration made public its opposition to extension of the 1965 Voting Rights Act for another five years. This decision provoked a long Congressional struggle in which the Senate GOP Leader played a major role in battling the White House. In the housing field, action was delayed, enforcement budget requests were sharply reduced, and urban programs cut far below projected levels. In education the President undercut HEW's enforcement staff, and fired the staff's director when he continued to press for action. For the first time the Justice Department asked a federal court to delay a desegregation plan. At the same time the President fought increased funds for compensatory education.

72   While each of these struggles was of great importance, none

was so visible as the President's determined effort to name a deeply conservative Southerner to the Supreme Court. While both the Haynsworth and Carswell nomination battles were strongly influenced by other considerations as well, the judges' poor civil rights records became major points of controversy. Since developments both in the case law and the decisions of the Nixon Administration were bringing a number of highly important civil rights issues before the Court, the outcome of the nomination controversies was certain to affect American racial history.

During his first years in office, the President used his power to substantially advance desegregation efforts in but a single narrow field. Only in the desegregation of restrictive building trades unions working on federal projects in certain cities were administrative requirements substantially tightened. And even this policy was severely undermined by the President's attacks on the "quota" system during the 1972 campaign.

Throughout the first several years of the Nixon Administration, the Presidency, the traditional defender of minority rights within the federal government, became the principal hostile force. Any initiatives had to come from Congress and the Supreme Court. By 1972 President Nixon had come to actively support legislative nullification of desegregation plans that required school busing. The President even threatened to support an anti–civil rights amendment to the Constitution, in order to prevent imposition of broad urban desegregation plans. His first significant staffing decision after his 1972 reelection was to fire Father Theodore Hesburgh, an eloquent supporter of civil rights enforcement, as chairman of the U.S. Commission on Civil Rights.

School Desegregation

The Administration's First Retreat Since 1954, school integration has been the touchstone of racial change. As President Nixon took office the country was approaching completion of desegregation of rural Southern schools and nearing a decision on Southern urban school segregation. New issues were being defined in a series of Northern and Western urban school lawsuits. The President had vocally criticized Johnson Administration policies in his Southern campaign and felt the need to make some accommodation with the South. The key agencies, HEW and Justice, were in the hands of close personal as-   73 sociates of the President, and Mr. Nixon and top White House aides devoted a good deal of time to the problem.

The first signs of a new policy came in the form of adjustments on individual cases. Confusing policy statements spurred Southern resistance. Within weeks, HEW Secretary Robert Finch failed to implement scheduled fund cutoffs in several Southern school districts. In an interview with *U.S. News and World Report* he sharply attacked existing policies, and expressed sympathy for the Southern view that integration was interfering with "education." Confused Southern schoolmen, not knowing what the policy was now, began to stall once again.[13]

Congress was important as an influence in favor of continuing enforcement of the 1964 Civil Rights Act. Leon Panetta, the young HEW official who tried to keep the program operating in the face of mounting White House criticism, quickly looked to Capitol Hill for allies. A former Senate aide, he contacted acquaintances in the offices of Senate Republicans so as to generate pressure on the White House to enforce the law. Panetta saw Congressional aid as essential:

> We could count on certain strong rights advocates among Republican Senators. . . .
> On the Democratic side, Senator Walter Mondale of Minnesota had been our ally, but his approach was different: He consciously and publicly attacked Finch and the Administration at any sign of weakness . . . while hoping that would strengthen Finch's hand within the Administration.[14]

Secretary Finch, under constant White House pressure to respond to local Republican politicians in the South, found each backward step criticized by some of HEW's most important and reliable Congressional supporters. In the Administration's early weeks he met with and gave assurances to a group of liberal Democratic Senators, and to a number of GOP Senators led by Clifford Case (R-N.J.).[15]

Southern members of Congress were, of course, persistent and insistent in their arguments. During the Johnson Administration Congressional questions had received top priority attention and courteous answers, but enforcement policy was very rarely influenced. Under President Nixon White House pressure supported the protesting Congressmen rather than the enforcement program.

As the Nixon Administration moved toward announcement of a new school policy, worried civil rights supporters tried to counter the Southern influence. Senator Hugh Scott (R-Pa.), the GOP Leader in the Senate, took the extraordinary step of publicly warning a Republican President. "I'm simply serving notice," he said, "period." Six other GOP Senators and a number of Congressmen joined in appeals to Nixon.[16]

During the summer of 1969 the Administration committed itself to slowing down desegregation. The first step in the new policy came in July, when the Administration announced that the main enforcement tool provided by the 1964 Civil Rights Act—cutting off funds—was bad and would be avoided. Instead, basic reliance would be placed on the courts. The second part of the strategy was initiated in August, when the Justice Department went into federal court for the first time to seek a delay in desegregation.

The new approach was quickly rejected by a unanimous Supreme Court. The Court insisted that Southern rural desegregation must be completed immediately.[17] The decision made extensive backsliding in the South highly unlikely, even though HEW enforcement powers were no longer used.

The Whitten and the Stennis Amendments As the judicial confrontation developed, two important Congressional battles were beginning to take shape. In both, Congress would ultimately defeat proposals that received at least some Administration support.

The first proposal was the Whitten amendment. Jamie Whitten (D-Miss.), a powerful House figure, wanted to restore "freedom of choice" desegregation plans, which both HEW and the courts had concluded would mean perpetuation of segregated school systems. Attorney General John Mitchell told the House GOP leaders that passing this amendment would do no harm. After a series of close votes, with no statement from the White House, the amendment won House passage. Weeks passed before Secretary Finch was finally permitted to oppose the measure. The Senate defeated it and the conference committee rendered it meaningless.

The next struggle began in the Senate. John Stennis (D-Miss.), a leading Southern spokesman, had long been disturbed by what he saw as an unfair system requiring thorough desegregation in the South while permitting massive segregation in the North. Both the courts and HEW continued to impose special requirements on school systems that had once been segregated officially by state law. In such systems the existing Constitutional law required that local officials responsible for

75

creating and maintaining segregation bear the responsibility for eliminating it and overcoming its persisting effects. Accordingly, to redress the alleged inequity, Senator Stennis in 1970 introduced an amendment requiring an end to the legal distinction between *de facto* and *de jure* segregation, and the creation of a common policy for Northern and Southern systems. The idea of treating everyone the same seemed reasonable to many, but since the courts had not yet developed remedies for *de facto* segregation, a uniform approach would in fact prevent action in the South. Since the President had repeatedly said that the government had no authority to order desegregation of Northern cities, a common policy can only mean that urban segregation would remain everywhere.

Senator Stennis had vividly and effectively used HEW statistics to show the high level of Northern segregation, and his attack on the double standard of Northern civil rights supporters won him a few liberal allies. Senator Abraham Ribicoff (D-Conn.) made a dramatic speech accusing his fellow liberals of "monumental hyprocrisy" in pushing desegregation in the South while doing nothing in the North. Northern communities, he charged, "have been as systematic and as consistent as southern communities in denying the black man and his children the opportunities that exist for white people."[18] Other civil rights supporters argued that Ribicoff had naively fallen into Stennis's trap.

As the struggle developed and passage of the Stennis amendment became a serious possibility, the President wavered. The White House rejected a statement of opposition drafted by Commissioner of Education James Allen, Jr. The President's press secretary ambiguously commented: "To the extent that the uniform application amendment offered by Stennis would advance equal application of the law, the Administration would be in full support of the concept." Later an Administration spokesman claimed that the White House had no position at all on the amendment. Two days before the Senate vote, Mr. Nixon issued a statement supporting neighborhood schools and declaring "school desegregation problems should be dealt with uniformly throughout the land."

The day of the final vote produced an almost comic illustration of White House indecision. Senate GOP Leader Hugh Scott had devised a plan to add language to the Stennis amendment designed to render it meaningless, and he thought he had the President's support. On the Senate floor he faced the humiliation of having his statement of the Administration's position openly contradicted by another GOP Senator, who had information from a ranking Presidential aide that the White House really favored the Stennis proposal. With the President seeming to be in a tacit alliance with the Southerners, Scott's tactic failed by a single vote and the Senate passed the Stennis proposal.[19]

While the House had a long tradition of actions against school desegregation requirements, the Stennis vote was the first break in the Senate's recent record of support. The Mississippian's victory was widely viewed as a fatal blow to the faltering cause of integration in American society. Across the country, newspapers and magazines gravely announced that integration was dead.[20]

The obituary was premature. Liberals with seniority dominated the conference committee, and wrote a final version of the education bill that eliminated the Stennis plan. HEW was directed to formulate two distinct policies, one for *de facto* and another for *de jure* segregation, and to enforce each uniformly. The conference rejected the majority preference of each house for restricting desegregation requirements, and left the status quo intact.[21]

Although the conferees were sharply criticized, their report was eventually accepted. In fact, when the vote finally came up, President Nixon had changed ground again. His long-awaited policy statement on school integration finally conceded the futility of further resistance to desegregation of the rural South. Instead, he now tried to make a very strong legal distinction between the Southern situation and urban Northern segregation, vigorously opposing any extension of requirements causing modifications in the neighborhood school plan. Following this shift, the Senate decisively rejected the Stennis approach.[22]

Perhaps the most significant final product of the Stennis controversy was the creation of a special Senate committee to investigate the whole desegregation controversy. Under the chairmanship of Senator Walter Mondale (D-Minn.), the committee assembled a skilled staff and conducted two years of hearings that provided a very important forum for criticizing the Administration's policy positions, for working out constructive alternatives, and for trying to keep national attention focused on successful integration experiences. The hearings included close grilling of Administration spokesmen and continual monitoring of agency performance. The committee's efforts led to drastic revision of the President's desegregation assistance program.

The Emergency School Aid Act of 1970 The deep split between the White House and the civil rights supporters on Capitol Hill again became evident during the long fight initiated by President Nixon's Emergency School Aid Act of 1970. The bill had its beginning as a constructive afterthought to the President's largely negative statement on school desegregation. The chief political intention was to cushion the burden of change for the Deep South's school system, which the Supreme Court had ordered to desegregate immediately. Even at this early stage, however, two serious issues arose. First, the President's program was basically aimed at the South, whereas Northerners wanted it made clear that money would be available for urban desegregation programs as well. Secondly, while the President wanted to protect himself on the volatile busing issue by prohibiting the use of the funds for pupil transportation, the leading GOP education spokesman in the House, Representative Al Quie (R-Minn.), refused to introduce a bill with the antibusing strictures included. The critics succeeded in modifying the initial legislation.[23]

After the initial millions were spent, Congress proved a highly effective critic of abuses in the program, with hearings and reports showing that much of the money had been committed in a frenzied rush. Some funds went to districts energetically working to maintain segregation, while very little was spent on new ways to make integration work.[24]

Pressures brought to bear by civil rights organizations and their Congressional allies were sufficient to provoke a major reorganization of HEW's procedure in making the grants. The Mondale committee hearings provided the basis for a thorough redrafting of the Administration bill in the Senate. The new version, clearly designed to provide incentives for integration, reserved money for specific purposes recommended by desegregation experts and civil rights organizations. Before the Senate could act, however, the House in late 1970 passed the Nixon bill, including the President's antibusing language. Mondale refused to capitulate and the bill was held over until the next session.

The following spring the Administration compromised with Senator Mondale and Senator Ribicoff, and agreed to support a new measure. As eventually passed by the Senate, the bill incorporated strict standards of eligibility and reserved substantial amounts of money for metropolitan area desegregation programs. The Senate strongly rejected antibusing language.[26]

A less noticed but potentially more important feature of the

Senate debate was the vote on Senator Ribicoff's amendment requiring every metropolitan area to prepare a ten-year school desegregation plan. Although the issue was new, and there was no evidence of public support for the idea of busing children across suburban-city lines, the amendment received a substantial favorable vote. The large majority of Northern Democrats voted for the plan, including all the party's prominently mentioned Presidential candidates, and the amendment received a total of thirty-five votes.[27] Senator Ribicoff had begun the process of creating a new public issue.

The continuing Congressional battle over what became the Emergency Education Act of 1972 will be analyzed more extensively in a later chapter on educational policy. At this stage it is sufficient to note that the initiative for school desegregation had passed decisively from the White House to Congress. The Administration's major interest during its first years was in finding some way to moderate the political consequences of Southern objections to desegregation. At the same time the main task of Congressional civil rights supporters was to defeat destructive proposals that enjoyed at least tacit support from the Administration—a job that Congress handled with great success during the first three years of the Nixon Presidency.

A Mounting Controversy: The Turmoil over Busing A new and more violent phase of the school desegregation struggle began in late 1971. A series of Southern urban desegregation plans, prepared in compliance with the Supreme Court's new ruling requiring desegregation through busing in Southern cities, was causing turmoil in major portions of the South. The issue really became explosive, however, after federal judges in Detroit, Michigan, and Richmond, Virginia, ordered school authorities to adopt desegregation plans covering entire large metropolitan areas. This attack at the heart of suburban prerogatives generated a very strong national reaction—a reaction rapidly reflected both in the House and in the President's office.

The House adopted a series of sweeping anti-integration proposals in November 1971. After heated debate, the Senate voted down the House provisos in favor of a relatively meaningless compromise designed by the Majority and Minority Leaders of the upper chamber. Both Leaders also joined in attacking the proposal for a Constitutional amendment forbidding school busing that was then under active White House consideration. In an historic turnabout, the Senate leadership

79

was protecting the enforcement of Supreme Court civil rights decisions from Presidential opposition.

The President responded to Congressional inaction and public concern by proposing two bills. The first would deny federal courts the right to require busing during a moratorium imposed by law—a proposal raising very serious Constitutional difficulties because of its infringement on the autonomy of the courts. The second bill was announced as a fulfillment of the President's pledge to equalize school quality in existing segregated schools, but actually provided only for increased concentration in the use of existing educational funds. This second bill also permitted school systems desegregating under existing court orders to reopen the court cases and fight the whole issue out again. Finally, the President said that if Congress should fail to take sufficiently strong action, he would be willing to support a movement for a Constitutional amendment. This statement was strongly criticized on both sides of the aisle in the Senate.

The school issue showed the change between Presidential and Congressional leadership in civil rights in a strikingly clear form. The Eisenhower and Kennedy Administrations had gone to Congress for additional authority to make the 1954 decision truly the law of the land, and President Johnson had used that authority vigorously. President Nixon, however, came asking for a retreat. Though the Senate had long been the bastion of Southern power, it was now the main arena for defense of school desegregation initiatives. The House seniority system had long been accurately denounced as a major barrier to racial justice, but it now served to protect civil rights programs from a hostile House majority. In spite of the Administration's heated battles both in Congress and in the courts, the job of desegregating the rural South was largely completed by the fall of 1972. The proportion of Southern black children in formerly white schools had doubled during the Nixon Administration. Congressional vetoes of Presidential antibusing policies shielded the courts' efforts to enforce the Constitution. Defensive power had liberal consequences.

Job Discrimination

Congressional initiative had been responsible for the creation of a federal law against job discrimination, and during the Nixon Administration Congress waged a hard-fought battle to give the enforcement agency real powers. President Nixon opposed the effort.

EEOC: An Agency without Real Power The title in the 1964 Civil Rights Act prohibiting unfair employment practices was the one section of the landmark act for which Congress was wholly responsible. President Kennedy's 1963 bill had skipped over the controversial issue, which had produced futile fights in Congress after Congress during the postwar period. The title had been added in the House Judiciary Committee by Democratic liberals, urged on by the AFL-CIO. Its final form was determined in Senate negotiations designed to win the vital support of GOP Leader Everett Dirksen.

The 1964 compromise produced an agency charged with fighting discrimination but in reality possessing few powers. The Equal Employment Opportunities Commission (EEOC) could investigate complaints and make a tentative ruling on the facts, but there its powers ran out. It had no authority to order the discriminating company to change its practices. By late 1971 the agency had received more than 81,000 complaints, with new ones flowing in at a rate of 32,000 a year, but it could only attempt to negotiate changes with the companies involved, then send the cases over to the Justice Department for possible litigation by its tiny Civil Rights Division staff. The system imposed years of delay for victims of discrimination, while the lack of enforcement powers severely undermined the authority of EEOC negotiators.[28]

President Johnson had asked that the EEOC be given cease-and-desist powers to order companies to correct biased practices, and the issue was nearing decision when Mr. Nixon took office. But even within their existing narrow range, EEOC enforcement activities came under Republican attack very early in the new Administration. Senate GOP Leader Everett Dirksen warned EEOC Chairman Clifford Alexander that "either this punitive harassment of business is going to stop . . . or I'm going to the highest authority in this Government to get somebody fired." The next day the White House announced that Alexander would indeed be removed. While the President had every right to name a new chairman, the timing seemed threatening. In his resignation letter Alexander charged a "crippling lack of Administration support."[29]

After resigning as chairman, Alexander still held a seat on the commission. The Assistant Attorney General for Civil Rights, Jerris Leonard, broke bureaucratic protocol to attack

81

his statements and suggest he leave government completely:

> The EEOC was a commission born in optimism but I hazard to say that it has been a commission operated in cynicism on the theory that an occasional newspaper headline could supplant effective investigations and effective hearings.
> . . . one wonders whether, considering current accusations, it would not be morally sound and wise, although financially detrimental, for those critics to resign their $36,000-a-year jobs right now.[30]

A New Alliance: Congress and the Bureaucrats The Alexander controversy deepened questions about the Administration's commitment to fair-employment practices that had been raised earlier by its handling of a case involving three large Southern textile companies. All companies receiving federal contracts were required by executive order to submit plans for ending job discrimination. During the final year of the Johnson Administration there had been investigations and negotiations of serious job problems in three textile giants with large Defense Department contracts. The facts of the cases were dramatic. In Dan River Mills, for example, the company had assembled a clerical staff of 475 women without hiring a single black. All but twenty of the firm's 1,424 black employees were paid less than the company's average wage.[31]

As President Nixon took office, sanctions were about to be imposed for the first time, denying contracts to companies that were concentrated in South Carolina, home state of the President's leading Southern ally, Senator Strom Thurmond. The issue was seen as extremely important both by Southern politicians and by civil rights groups wishing to set a precedent through action against a particularly notorious industry. Weeks after taking office, the Nixon Administration reversed the earlier Defense Department decision and awarded the contracts. Regarding the civil rights issue, they relied on verbal assurances from company officials—assurances that did not meet established standards.

The Administration decision prompted a rapid Congressional investigation, illustrating once again the importance of growing liberal seniority on committees and subcommittees. It happened that Senator Edward Kennedy was chairman of an obscure Judiciary subcommittee, Administrative Practice and Procedure. By liberally defining his subcommittee's jurisdiction, Kennedy put the Administration on the spot. During the hearings Alexander outlined the weaknesses of the agreement, and a Labor Department official from the office responsible for supervising compliance throughout the government, said the Administration had violated Labor Department and Defense Department rules. Senator Mondale attacked:

> The law cannot be what the personal judgment of one official may determine it to be at a particular time. An effective compliance program involving hundreds of companies and billions of dollars cannot be conducted on the basis of personal oral assurances between a defense official and private industry officials.[32]

The hearings revealed serious harassment of a Presidential appointee, and illustrated a tacit alliance between a Congressional committee and responsible civil rights bureaucrats. Similar alliances between committee conservatives and bureaucratic standpatters had often bedeviled liberal reformers in the past. As civil rights officials within the executive branch leaked a whole series of important documents, the difficulties of defending the altered policy were magnified. The alliance now focused liberal pressure on a conservative President.

In the end, Congressional criticism did not succeed in reversing the textile decision. It did, however, multiply the costs of the compromise and dramatically warn other officials of the risk of further steps backward. Mondale's committee put school officials and Justice staff members under similar pressure. Civil rights supporters, including liberal Republicans, also watched other agencies. When the Transportation Department, for instance, apparently weakened requirements for employment practices of highway builders, there was sharp criticism. The net result was to give bureaucrats who want to operate stable, noncontroversial programs the impression that obviously poor performance regarding civil rights could cause political trouble.

Policy-making on issues not receiving wide national publicity is often accomplished through interaction of Congressional and bureaucratic specialists and the representatives of the concerned constituencies. Job discrimination policy within the Transportation Department was an example of an issue where enforcement supporters within the department could use the fact of Congressional inquiries and hearings to bring the issue to the top of the department and obtain some forward movement. In effect, a relatively low-level Congressional-bureaucratic alliance could move policy somewhat against the general drift of the Administration.

The Philadelphia Plan More important than these early battles was the shaping of the Administration's policy on the issues of granting enforcement powers to the EEOC, and the development of a program to force desegregation of the labor force employed by companies with federal contracts. The case against the existing system had been fully outlined by Richard Nathan, a scholar active in GOP politics whom Nixon named assistant director of the Budget Bureau.

> The Equal Employment Opportunities Commission . . . was not given enforcement powers and lacks jurisdiction. . . .
>
> . . . its critics contend that it has never been given the financial resources and political support necessary to do its job properly. As for the contract compliance program, its requirements have not been put into statutory form and Congress has on several occasions succeeded in undermining this program by withholding funds and authority for it to operate. Finally, political restraint in dealing with entrenched institutions, such as the apprenticeship training system, the public employment network, and large corporations with government contracts, often have a serious limiting effect on programs and activities of the Federal Government in the field of equal employment opportunities.[33]

Nathan concluded that clear White House support, stronger policies, more money, and a better organization structure were essential to significantly change employment practices. Only in the latter part of the Johnson Administration, he said, had there been clear Presidential commitment to the program, as shown by appointment of a strong EEOC chairman and a request for a doubling of appropriations. Regulation of federal contractors had been weakened by ambiguous requirements and by failure to demonstrate the seriousness of the policy by actually cutting off some contracts. Although the Labor Department had begun to impose specific desegregation goals on construction contractors in Cleveland and Philadelphia, Nathan believed that the department's close ties with the AFL-CIO had prevented any serious action against segregationist union policies.[34]

President Nixon inherited from Johnson both a record of White House support for EEOC enforcement powers, and the first stage of a program to tighten requirements for affirmative action. The Administration's first major positive decision was to impose the specific numerical goals for craft union desegregation on federal contractors in the Philadelphia area. Amid nationwide black demonstrations against segregation in the building trades, the Administration's Philadelphia Plan shifted the burden of proof in discrimination cases from the victims of segregation to employers who could not meet their targets for employing a fair share of minority workers.

The construction industry was an excellent target, with 2.9 million workers and a record of almost total segregation in some of the higher-paying trades. During the summer of 1969, black demonstrations organized around the issue succeeded in stopping work on hundreds of millions of dollars of scheduled construction in several cities, while demanding promises that specific numbers of black workers be hired. The government was deeply involved, since as much as two-thirds of new construction activity in some cities involved government funds.[35]

The Nixon Administration at first had fewer inhibitions than the Democrats in facing this issue. The question split two vital elements of the Democratic Party, blacks and labor, neither of which then had any significant influence in the GOP.

After the Labor Department's June 1969 announcement of the Philadelphia desegregation goals, the policy was assailed both by labor leaders and by conservatives. An AFL-CIO official described the plan as "unworkable," and ailing Senate GOP Leader Dirksen unloosed one of his last salvos against a program that made "preference as to race" a condition for getting a job.[36] John McClellan (D-Ark.), the powerful chairman of the Senate Government Operations Committee, asked the Comptroller General, the Congressional official who must countersign all government checks, to reject the policy. In response the Comptroller General ruled that the plan was illegal.[37] The Administration stood behind the plan, claiming the Comptroller General had no authority to interpret civil rights laws and insisting there was an urgent need for action. Senator Dirksen then announced that he would try to write riders into appropriations forbidding payment of contracts containing racial quotas.[38]

Dirksen's threat was very serious because the most powerful lobby on Capitol Hill, the AFL-CIO, had broken with civil rights organizations on this issue. George Meany, AFL-CIO President and a member of the highly segregated plumbers union, claimed that there was no serious problem and that blacks should try to get into apprenticeship programs. Such programs, however, had only about one black for every twenty-four whites. The national convention of the building trades unions

85

resolved that they were "100 percent opposed to a quota system."[39]

Congressional pressure was exerted on both sides. A leading civil rights opponent, Senator Sam Ervin (D-N.C.), used his subcommittee to launch a hostile investigation. On the other side, the two Massachusetts Senators and Speaker McCormack, who represented a Boston district, openly asked the Labor Department to develop a similar plan for Boston. Nine Senators supporting the plan issued a statement as Ervin's hearings opened. Since labor had always been an extremely important force in enacting civil rights legislation, however, the program was in real trouble.

The issue came to a head in the closing days of the 1969 session. The decision was reached during action on an appropriations bill that not only sharply cut the EEOC budget, but also contained a rider prohibiting the use of any federal funds to finance contracts that the Comptroller General believed to violate federal laws. The Labor Department attacked the rider as a blow that would "destroy one of the most effective civil rights tools available to this Government and would set back the course of civil rights." "The Senate," the department continued, "could not possibly be contemplating any more disastrous piece of legislation at this time in our nation's history."[40] Nonetheless, the Senate upheld the committee by a 52-37 margin. Joining the conservatives were a group of men with good civil rights records who were very close to the labor movement, including Majority Leader Mansfield.[41]

After defeat in the more liberal chamber, the fight went to the House. Before the House vote, the White House intervened with a statement of support from the President and a Labor Department attack on the AFL-CIO. The Administration commitment created strange alliances in the House, with Gerald Ford (R-Mich.), the House GOP Leader, in the vanguard of a civil rights fight for the first time in memory. Before the final vote the President again escalated pressure with a strong statement criticizing the tactics of the program's opponents and even threatening to veto the entire bill unless the rider was removed. Members eager to adjourn for Christmas were thus put under strong pressure.

As the final vote approached, labor pressure on the House intensified and civil rights leaders found themselves wondering about the motivations of the Administration. AFL-CIO President Meany dispatched telegrams saying labor was "firmly opposed to quota systems which are illegal, un-American and in and of themselves discriminatory." Representative Gus Hawkins (D-Calif.), a black Congressman from Los Angeles who had been unable to obtain Administration support for his bill to give the EEOC enforcement powers, hoped the new attitude was a "first sign of repentance." NAACP lobbyist Clarence Mitchell thought the Administration was pressing so hard because the issue divided blacks and labor:

> It is amazing that the same administration which has sought to destroy the voting rights bill, which is against strengthening existing equal employment opportunity legislation, which has been guilty of outrageous footdragging in school desegregation, now suddenly is on a great crusade to save the Philadelphia Plan. It is very odd that at the beginning of the year the administration was perfectly willing to let the textile industry continue employment discrimination . . . [and] now is enthusiastically cracking down on discrimination that involves labor unions.[42]

The House supported the Administration 208-156. Senate Majority Leader Mansfield then threatened to keep the Senate in continual session throughout the Christmas period, unless the Senators accepted the changes necessary to prevent a veto of the essential appropriations measure. The Senate complied 39-29.[43] The President had won his first and only victory for civil rights, and Congress had provided at least an indirect legislative mandate for the new program.

The consequences of the victory, however, turned out to be disappointing. In most major cities the Administration decided to rely on voluntary "home-town" plans rather than federal requirements. Contractors soon fell behind their goals even in Philadelphia. Although contractors shifted black employees from other assignments to the federal projects, it took a hundred threats of contract cancellations before the second-year goals were reached. Even in Washington, D.C., contracts fell far behind goals in half the trades covered. A year after Congress supported the program, black employment in the affected unions had risen from 1.01 to 1.54 percent.[44] A program that was weakly administered, and that focused on a handful of unions in a few cities in a single sector of the local labor market, could have only limited impact. In 1972, after Presidential nominee George McGovern was assailed within the Democratic party for support of a "quota system," the President reversed himself. Seeking labor support, he denounced all forms of quota systems, thus undermining his one civil rights accomplishment.

87

More Power for EEOC? While President Nixon had provided temporary leadership in establishing the principle of the Philadelphia Plan, most civil rights supporters gave a higher priority to the battle to grant the EEOC enforcement powers. Early in the Administration the Justice Department had actively considered support for cease-and-desist power, and EEOC Chairman Robert Brown reported that the President had pledged complete support for the agency. Cease-and-desist powers, the chairman stressed, were "absolutely imperative."[45] This power would allow EEOC to order companies to end discrimination.

Civil rights forces then took the initiative: thirty-four Senators, including the leaders of the moderate wing of the GOP, co-sponsored an Equal Employment Opportunities Enforcement Act proposal in June 1969.[46] Almost two months later, after a hard battle within the Administration, the President submitted a much narrower proposal. In place of cease-and-desist power, the agency would merely get its own right to sue rather than rely on the Justice Department staff. The Senate bill provisions, which extended coverage to employees of state and local governments and to those of small companies, were left out. A spokesman for the Leadership Conference on Civil Rights described the bill as "a joke."[47] At the hearings Senator Eagleton (D-Mo.) saw it as "another of a sequence of events where pious pronouncements were made but ended in a surrender." One participant said it was "a Munich on the Potomac."[48]

The Senate bill came to the floor in 1970 and a powerful bipartisan coalition rapidly rejected the President's limited approach. The key vote on cease-and-desist brought a 41-26 victory for civil rights forces. Since the House had twice passed similar bills, the twenty-two-year effort to get a workable job discrimination act now seemed near final success. The Southerners, exhausted from a filibuster against electoral college reform, put up only slight resistance. On final passage the bill sailed through the Senate 47-24. Passage came without any significant White House involvement on either side, and without any serious lobbying from the civil rights coalition, racked as it then was by internal division over the proper approach to the job issue.[49]

Senate action had come on October 1. But for one last time the House Rules Committee, which had long been a major burying ground for human rights measures, delayed House action. Although a bill had been reported out by the House Education and Labor Committee in August, Rules Committee Chairman Colmer (D-Miss.) had failed to even schedule hearings by early December. At this point Representative Hawkins (D-Calif.) filed a discharge petition to try to force committee action. Seventy-five members signed it the first day.

Chairman Colmer, however, refused to change his position, even after renewed open appeals from the House Democratic leadership. The Mississippian, who had generally been cooperative, now threatened to delay nine other important measures if the job bill was pushed. Colmer said the bill was "vicious" and he had no intention of complying with the Speaker's request. A majority of the members of the committee could have forced action, but they made no move to do so. (In fact one key member, Representative Richard Bolling (D-Mo.), was on vacation in the Caribbean, and had refused to return even to cast the decisive vote to save a major consumer protection bill.[50] Bolling was a liberal critic of the House and author of an angry book strongly critical of its procedures.)

The bill was now in trouble. There was not enough time to gather signatures for the discharge petition. A Senate effort to get the bill to the House floor by tacking it onto some other measure passed by the House was frustrated by Senator Sam Ervin's threat of a filibuster. Everyone was eager to get home after a long session, and few believed the little-noticed enforcement bill to be of sovereign importance. The conditions were ideal for maximizing the Rules Committee chairman's power of delay, and so the bill died.

Nothing more was seen of the bill until mid-1971. When the House Education and Labor Committee took up the issue again, the old bipartisan spirit was replaced by strong GOP opposition, crystallized by the President's alternative measure. The committee vote was almost a straight party division. The Rules Committee now reported out the bill without a great fight in mid-July. Opponents apparently believed that the conservative coalition would successfully amend the committee bill on the floor to conform with the President's limited proposal.[51]

When the House vote came in September 1971, the conservative coalition was successful by a narrow margin, and the Administration's bill was substituted for the cease-and-desist measure. Shortly after the House action, the Senate again opened hearings and again reported out a cease-and-desist bill with unanimous committee support. The bill was reported out at the end of October but delays, including the threat of a filibuster and a number of amendments dealing with school busing, brought postponement to the beginning of the next session. Another year was lost.

The first several weeks of the 1972 session were largely consumed by a Southern filibuster, with implicit Administration support, against strong enforcement powers. In a closely divided Senate, civil rights forces were plagued by the absence of several active Presidential candidates, all of whom supported cease-and-desist. After weeks of battle and apparent success in winning a narrow victory, civil rights supporters failed to obtain the necessary two-thirds margin they needed for breaking the Southern Democratic–Republican filibuster. Republican conservatives, led by Senator Peter Dominick (R.-Colo.), refused to provide the needed votes so long as the key enforcement powers remained. With time and patience running out after a long debate and a whole series of cloture motions, the conservatives won.

The resulting bill was some improvement on the existing procedures, but it still had many of the old weaknesses. The important advance was the extension of coverage of federal job discrimination law to state and local public agencies accounting for far more jobs than the federal civil service. The new law might, for example, provide some outside leverage in the heated local conflicts over alleged discrimination in police forces and in the hiring and promotion of teachers. The EEOC was given the right to go to court directly itself, rather than rely on the Justice Department. This was seen as a gain, since the Justice Department's overburdened Civil Rights Division had seldom given high priority to the complex employment cases. Fundamentally, however, the commission was still forced to rely on the tedious, expensive, and time-consuming process of case-by-case litigation. This procedure has been hopelessly inadequate in the past. The President had won the basic issue in his battle against more vigorous enforcement.

The job discrimination fight underlined the limits of Congressional power in civil rights areas where positive action, rather than a mere veto of a White House initiative, was required. Given the President's ability to mobilize Congressional Republicans, and the continuing power of the conservative coalition in blocking legislation through Senate filibusters or committee delays, even moderately controversial measures actively opposed by the President could rarely pass.

90

Summary: Civil Rights Momentum Slowed

The struggles over school desegregation and job discrimination policy during the first term of the Nixon Administration illustrated the dramatic change in the President's relationship with American blacks and both the successes and shortcomings of Congressional efforts to preserve the momentum of racial change. The President was hostile to school desegregation from the beginning and his position encouraged bitter Congressional battles. By narrow margins, the Senate prevented a drastic reversal of national policy. On the job discrimination question, the record was far more confusing, given the President's opposition to enforcement power for the Equal Employment Opportunity Commission, and his changing positions on desegregating the construction unions working on federal building projects. In the legislative arena White House resistance overcame the earlier support in both houses for a greatly strengthened EEOC. With the President supporting a filibuster, Congress could take only a very small step forward.

NOTES

[1] Richard Neustadt, *Presidential Power*, (New York: Wiley, 1960), pp. 75–76; and J. W. Anderson, *Eisenhower, Brownell, and the Congress*, (University, Ala.: University of Alabama Press, 1964), pp. 40–43, 88–89, 121–22, illustrate Eisenhower's changing positions during 1956, and his switch against the bill in 1957.

[2] These provisions became Titles 6 and 7 of the 1964 Civil Rights Act, 78 Stat. 241.

[3] Congressional Quarterly, *Revolution in Civil Rights* (Washington: Congressional Quarterly, Inc., 1968), pp. 81–83.

[4] Gallup Poll in *Washington Post*, November 12, 1967; Roper Survey in *Congressional Record*, November 28, 1967, p. S17782.

[5] Author's interview with Harry McPherson, former aide to President Johnson, January 29, 1971.

[6] The split was evident in 1967, when Senator Robert Griffin (R-Mich.) led successful opposition to Dirksen's effort to outlaw the use of federal funds for desegregation plans designed to overcome racial imbalance in the schools (*Congressional Record*, November 28, 1967, p. S17838). In early 1968 it was the unexpected level of GOP support for fair housing that set in motion the successful battle to win passage of the law against housing discrimination.

[7] The House Appropriations Committee initially voted to deny the HUD civil rights officials any money at all to enforce the new law. It required a major effort to obtain even a small fraction of the appropriation request.

[8] Garry Wills, *Nixon Agonistes* (Boston: Houghton Mifflin, 1970), p. 261.

[9] Gary Orfield, "Civil Rights: Nixon's First Test," *Nation*, January 20, 1969, pp. 79–82.

[10] Congressional Quarterly, *Civil Rights: Progress Report 1970*, (Washington: Congressional Quarterly, Inc., 1971), p. 18.

[11] *Ibid.*

[12] Senate Judiciary Committee, Subcommittee on Administrative Practice and Procedure, *Hearings, Equal Employment Opportunity Procedures*, 91st Cong., 1st Sess., 1969, pp. 25–158.

[13] *U.S. News and World Report*, March 10, 1969; Gary Orfield, "The Politics of Resegregation," *Saturday Review*, September 20, 1969, pp. 58–60, 77–79.

[14] Leon E. Panetta and Peter Gall, *Bring Us Together* (Philadelphia: Lippincott, 1971), pp. 74–75, 131–32.

[15] *Ibid.*, pp. 132–34.

[16] *Ibid.*, pp. 202, 211.

[17] *Alexander v. Holmes*, 369 U.S. 19; statement of July 3, 1969, in *New York Times* of July 4, 1969.

[18] Congressional Quarterly, *Civil Rights: Progress Report 1970*, p. 40.

[19] *Ibid.*, interview with Kenneth Davis, May 26, 1972.

[20] See for example *Time*, March 9, 1970.

[21] Congressional Quarterly, *Civil Rights: Progress Report 1970*, p. 40.

[22] *Ibid.*, pp. 40–41.

[23] Earl Browning, Jr., "Emergency School Assistance: Financing the Desegregation Retreat," unpublished manuscript (1971).

[24] Report of General Accounting Office reprinted in *Congressional Record*, March 16, 1971, S3293.

[25] *Washington Post*, December 23, 1970; December 30, 1970.

[26] *Congressional Quarterly*, April 30, 1971, pp. 964–66.

[27] *Ibid.*, April 23, 1971, p. 932.

[28] Senate Committee on Labor and Public Welfare, Subcommittee on Labor, *Hearings, Equal Employment Opportunities Act of 1971*, 92d Cong., 1st Sess., 1971, pp. 53, 71.

[29] "Notes in the News," *The Progressive*, May 1969, p. 5.

[30] *Washington Post*, April 23, 1969.

[31] Senate Judiciary Committee, Administrative Practice Subcommittee, *Equal Employment Opportunity Procedures*, 91st Cong., 1st Sess., 1969, pp. 111–12.

[32] *Ibid.*, p. 104.

[33] Richard P. Nathan, *Jobs and Civil Rights* (Washington: U.S. Commission on Civil Rights, 1969), p. 10.

[34] *Ibid.*, pp. 109–10, 252.

[35] Alex Poinsett, "Crusade Against the Craft Unions," *Ebony*, December 1969, pp. 33–42.

[36] *Congressional Quarterly*, July 11, 1969, p. 1237.

[37] *Congressional Record*, August 11, 1969, pp. S9602–07; *Congressional Quarterly*, July 11, 1969, p. 1237.

[38] *New York Times*, August 7, 1969; *Washington Post*, August 8, 1969.

[39] *Columbia State*, September 1, 1969; *Washington Post*, September 22 and September 23, 1969.

[40] *Congressional Record*, December 18, 1969, p. S17132.

[41] *Ibid.*, p. S17151.

[42] *Washington Post*, December 24, 1969; letter from Mitchell to Speaker McCormack, December 22, 1969, in *Congressional Record*, December 23, 1969, p. H13085.

[43] *Washington Post*, December 24, 1969; *Newsweek*, January 5, 1970, p. 50.

[44] *New York Times*, May 3, 1970; *Washington Post*, December 13, 1970; U.S. Civil Rights Commission, *Federal Civil Rights Enforcement Effort*, 1970, p. 20.

[45] *Richmond Times-Dispatch*, April 26, 1969; *Congressional Record*, June 2, 1969, p. E4505, quoting *Christian Science Monitor*, May 22, 1969.

[46] *Congressional Record*, June 19, 1969, p. S6740.

[47] *Washington Post*, August 9, 1969.

[48] *Ibid.*, August 12, 1969.

[49] *New York Times*, October 1 and October 2, 1970; *Congressional Record*, October 1, 1970, p. S16914.

[50] *Washington Post*, December 7 and December 11, 1970; *New York Times*, December 3 and December 10, 1970.

[51] *Washington Post*, May 5 and May 15, 1971; *New York Times*, May 5, 1971.

6

CONGRESSIONAL VICTORIES: VOTING RIGHTS and the SUPREME COURT

Voting Rights

The Voting Rights Act: A Record of Success and Resentment Coming after a period of the most dramatic racial change in the twentieth century, the Nixon Administration and its Congress faced a wide array of portentous civil rights choices. Few were so important as· the 1970 Voting Rights struggle and the Congressional battle to prevent the elevation of civil rights opponents to the Supreme Court. The Voting Rights Act had been widely hailed as the cornerstone of black political participation in the Deep South, but it was due to expire in 1970 unless Congress renewed it. The President opposed renewal. The Supreme Court had, of course, been of decisive importance, both in beginning the modern civil rights drive in 1954 and in sustaining the process of change in the succeeding years. Blacks consistently identified the Court as the government institution most responsive to their needs. The prospect of a drastic reversal in direction by the Court, following closely the change in the executive branch, was deeply disconcerting. On each of these issues Congress took a stand. In each case the struggle ended with decisive Congressional victories.

In the mid-1960s it seemed clear that if there was any civil rights issue on which there was deep and broad accord among Americans, it was that the right to vote must be secured for Southern blacks. The 1957 and 1960 civil rights laws had been predominantly concerned with this issue, which became the major concern of the Kennedy Administration as well. In 1964 the country had ratified a Constitutional amendment against the poll tax, and in the following year both the President and Congress had given massive support to the new Voting Rights Act. This act contained the most far-reaching provisions of any of the civil rights legislation, and had been rapidly upheld by the Supreme Court.

Voting rights raised no sensitive social question and were a real issue only in a small fraction of the country. The law affected but six states and a section of a seventh, and most of these had abandoned the two major parties to vote for George Wallace in 1968, thus lessening their leverage over national policy.

Most important, from the perspective of civil rights groups, the law was working. It was one of few civil rights measures that had made a rapid, unambiguous, and dramatic impact. More than 800,000 new black voters registered in the affected states. In states where there had been no black officials, there were now hundreds. Black voting strength began to help turn the balance of power within the Democratic Party of the South

Table 6-1

Increase in Percentage of Blacks Registered to Vote in
First Two Years of Enforcement of the 1965 Voting
Rights Act in the Six States Covered by the Law

	Registration Level before Enactment	Registration Level Two Years After
Alabama	19.3%	51.6%
Georgia	27.4%	52.6%
Louisiana	31.6%	58.9%
Mississippi	6.7%	59.8%
South Carolina	37.3%	51.2%
Virginia	38.3%	55.6%

SOURCE   *U.S. Commission on Civil Rights*, Political Participation (*Washington: GPO, 1968*), *pp. 12–13.*

from the old segregationist wing to a moderate wing more preoccupied with improving governmental services than with exploiting racial polarization. In states such as Mississippi and Louisiana, where virtually no blacks had been allowed to vote, blacks suddenly became visible in state politics, whereupon whites began calculating strategies to exploit this new source of votes. The problems of the South did not disappear, of course, but the situation showed obvious improvement and significant further potential.

Most resistance to the law was based not on the voting issue but on the drastic changes in state and local powers imposed by the law. In order to get at very deep-seated problems, Congress had been forced to strike at the roots of local power. Not only were states and localities covered by the act forbidden to employ literacy tests, but they could not alter their existing electoral laws in any way without approval of the Attorney General. This grant of veto power over state legislation to an appointed federal official was unprecedented and strongly resented. Resentment was deepened by the triggering mechanism. The states covered were those where less than half the population of eligible voters registered and voted in 1964. Even after registration rose substantially above this point, the same states remained subject to special restrictions. The clear assumption of the law was that the politicians of these states, if given half a chance, would speedily find new ways to restrict black political strength. In point of fact, the Civil Rights Commission documented a variety of ways whereby this was already being done in the late 1960s, even within the existing restrictions.

Voting Rights Extension: The Battle in the House President Nixon responded to the anger of the Deep South with criticism of "regional legislation," and an implied commitment to do something about the objectionable features of the Voting Rights Act. After the President was elected, however, his Administration delayed presenting its position on the issue. Since the law automatically expired in 1970 and a Senate filibuster against renewal was expected, the bill's supporters thought it vital that House action take place in 1969. The pressure on the Administration grew.

Even so, Attorney General Mitchell postponed his appearance before the House Judiciary Committee to unveil the Administration's proposal five successive times. The Justice Department was reported to be working on fourteen proposed changes in the law. By 1969 reports were circulating widely that the Administration would call for replacing the law with a nationwide prohibition on literacy tests. The Attorney General was known to favor ending his power to veto state electoral laws.[1] Consequently, even before the Administration made its position public, GOP civil rights supporters were on the attack. The leading GOP spokesman on civil rights in the House, Representative William McCulloch (R-Ohio), insisted that the law must simply be extended. Senator Robert Taft, Jr. (R-Ohio), declared, "The need for extension of the act is clear." [2]

When Attorney General Mitchell finally testified, he insisted that he could not "support what amounts to regional legislation." In place of the existing law he called for a bill temporarily suspending literacy tests across the country, and for an end to state residency requirements for voting in Presidential elections. On the crucial issue the Attorney General proposed to end the automatic Justice Department review of state legislation, and to go back to a case-by-case procedure where the Justice Department would have to go into court and win a decision against each evasive measure.

The Administration's bill eliminated the one section that caused the most resentment in the South. In March the Supreme Court had upheld the Justice Department's right to review three changes in Mississippi's laws, and only a month before the Attorney General's testimony the department had vetoed the state laws in question. The Mississippi state attorney general had described this provision for federal vetoing of state legislation as the one section "we cannot live with." Clarence Mitchell, the leading black spokesman in Washington, immediately characterized the Administration bill as "a sophisticated but nonetheless deadly way of thwarting the progress we have made." [3]

The intensity of the attack on the Administration's bill was so great that it seemed the proposal was doomed. Five days after the Attorney General testified, the *New York Times* reported that the bill was "regarded as all but dead." President Nixon's appointee as head of the Civil Rights Commission had denounced it as "a distinct retreat" that would "turn back the clock to 1957," and GOP members of the Judiciary Committee had come out against it. After a meeting with the President, House Republican Leader Gerald Ford (R-Mich.) announced that the whole battle was "just a matter of tactics." "You know there will be an extension," he said. "It's just a question of whether it will be done in a package or in a two-step proce- 97 dure." The Administration was ready to permit a "compromise" that would first extend the voting rights measure and then consider the broader issues in the Nixon proposal.[4]

Momentum in favor of extension grew as the Judiciary Committee acted quickly and overwhelmingly in support of a simple bill prolonging the program for five more years. Amid threats of delays in the Rules Committee and of a Southern filibuster when the bill reached the Senate, civil rights forces pressed for rapid action.[5]

A Rules Committee delay, however, provided time for the Administration to build new support for its proposal. Under pressure, Republican members who had initially shown little enthusiasm for the Attorney General's bill, now united behind the President's proposal. On November 18 the Rules Committee reported the bill out with a special rule that worked to the advantage of the Administration program. During a long session of the committee, three non-Southern Democrats supported a conservative move to bring the Judiciary Committee bill to the floor under a rule permitting opponents to move to substitute the President's measure. If the Rules Committee had not taken this course, civil rights supporters might well have succeeded in obtaining a parliamentary ruling that the Administration program was out of order as an amendment, since its scope was so different from the extension bill.[6]

When the bill came to the House floor in early December, the Administration intensified pressure on House Republicans. The measure was an essential piece of the White House Southern strategy. Staff members from both the White House and the Justice Department were actively lobbying, and the President appealed for "every effort" on behalf of the weaker bill. As the final vote approached, Speaker McCormack announced the outcome would be determined by the willingness of about sixty Republicans to stand with the civil rights forces against the Administration.[7] Gerald Ford, the House GOP Leader, led a strong effort to ensure those votes for the substitute bill.

After debate, the House sustained the Administration position and substituted the weaker bill by a vote of 208-203. Only forty-nine Republicans voted for the extension bill and ten Northern Democrats supported the President.[8] Civil rights supporters were stunned. NAACP spokesman Clarence Mitchell asserted the defeat was "engineered by the President of the United States," who "has sold us out in order to get the segregation vote in the South."[9]

The Voting Rights Fight in the Senate Attention now shifted to the Senate, where resistance was expected to be more intense. Through a parliamentary maneuver the bill was sent to the hostile Senate Judiciary Committee with directions from the Senate to report the bill to the floor by March 1, 1970. As the fight shaped up, Senator Sam Ervin once again threatened a filibuster, and Senate Republican Leader Hugh Scott repeated his commitment to extension of the existing law. Scott said he hoped a "compromise" could be worked out that would preserve the key section of the 1965 law and also incorporate some of the nationwide protections proposed in the Administration bill.[10]

Senator Ervin was bitter about the Senate limitations on the Judiciary Committee. The procedure, he claimed, was only used on "so-called civil rights bills." (The limited referral procedure had, in fact, been an essential liberal tactic to circumvent the power of Juiciary Committee Chairman Eastland, a staunch segregationist.) Said Ervin:

> I hope that my friends who advocate equal rights for all men will have a moment of repentence, and agree to allow Senators from the United States, even those who come from these seven conquered provinces, an equality of rights under the Senate rules, and let the bill go to the committee, and thus permit the committee to hold hearings on the bill.[11]

The Senate was less favorable ground than the House for the Administration's effort to hold Republican votes. The Republicans in the Senate had voted almost unanimously for the Voting Rights Act in 1965, the only dissenter being Strom Thurmond. Five of the seven GOP members of the crucial Judiciary Committee, including each of the party's two top leaders, favored extending the existing powers. Nonetheless, the issue would probably be decided by the seriousness with which the President pressed for GOP support of the Southern filibuster.[12]

During early 1970, as public attention and Senate action focused on the controversial nomination of Judge G. Harrold Carswell to the Supreme Court, Republican and Democratic civil rights supporters in the Senate worked out a compromise bill. Senator Scott was repeatedly expressing his hope that the Administration would permit preservation of the key powers. The civil rights organizations lined up behind the Scott proposal.[13] Hearings on the bill, however, were delayed because of the lengthy Judiciary Committee consideration of Judge Carswell. After the Judiciary Committee voted in favor of Carswell, Majority Leader Mansfield took advantage of the Southerners' desire for this confirmation by announcing he would not schedule action on the nomination until after a vote on voting rights.[14]

When the House bill came to the Senate floor, ten members of the Judiciary Committee, led by Senators Scott and Philip Hart (D-Mich.), presented their substitute bill. On the other side, the manager of the Administration bill, Senator Roman Hruska (R-Neb.), underlined the President's unqualified support for the weaker measure. A long and difficult battle seemed to lie ahead, if there was to be a workable law in force when the old one expired in August.

Most of the debate was taken up by Southern Senators detailing the changes in the South that had made the law unnecessary, arguing the Constitutional issues, and talking at length about the "subjugation" of the South. Senator Thurmond saw the 1965 law as an aberration that must be ended.

The first tests came after only a few days of debate, and the civil rights forces showed surprising strength. A motion to table the strong bill failed 47-32. The next day two weakening amendments were defeated by a far more massive margin, and Southern leaders were disheartened. Confronting the fact of probable defeat and eager to get to the Supreme Court vote before growing opposition jeopardized Carswell, the Southerners lost their disposition to fight a serious battle for delay. Here was a clear instance where one of the key strategies of Southern civil rights opponents—filibuster—was nullified by the Majority Leader's use of his very important power to schedule legislative action.

Now, ironically, the major problem came from the other side. Senate Majority Leader Mansfield and Senator Edward Kennedy (D-Mass.) decided the bill was a good vehicle for granting the vote to all American eighteen-year-olds. This would change existing procedures in all but two states, and introduced a highly controversial issue into a bill that already had severe problems. There was serious legal doubt about whether Congress possessed the authority to change state election laws without a Constitutional amendment. Even the liberal chairman of the House Judiciary Committee, Emanuel Celler (D-N.Y.), was known to have grave doubts about the Mansfield-Kennedy approach.[15] Some civil rights supporters felt it was reckless to pyramid controversial measures and thus increase the risk of defeat.

100   The vote for eighteen-year-olds was sprung by surprise on

the Senate by liberals skeptical about the possibility of dealing with the question through the Constitutional amendment procedure. There was no great support among the public for the change, and referendums had usually been voted down in states where the issue was on the ballot. The Administration maintained that it was unconstitutional. The issue, however, posed an uncomfortable dilemma for Senators. Few wished to be identified as enemies of political participation by a group that was bearing the brunt of an unpopular war and that would probably be given the vote anyway. When the final vote came, the novelty and the Constitutional difficulties of the amendment were lost sight of in a rush to support a winning cause. The amendment passed 64-17.[16]

Once the voter-age issue was decided, the Senate moved rapidly toward a final vote on the entire bill. The opposition seemed to collapse as only a handful of intense civil rights opponents attempted to keep the Senate tied up. In the end the Southerners abandoned their filibuster after only two weeks of debate.

The main consequence of the debate had not been to weaken the bill but to make it more powerful. As the bill neared final Senate action, it contained not only the section vital to civil rights groups, but also nationwide bans on literacy tests and excessive residency requirements for participation in Presidential elections. In addition, the measure incorporated a major political reform that had only recently been given no chance for speedy action: the eighteen-year-old vote. A measure that had gone into the Senate weakened severely by House reverses emerged dramatically as a more powerful bill than anyone had expected. The tactical need of the conservatives to gain an early vote on Carswell blunted their major opposition weapon.

The final vote was almost anticlimactic. The Scott-Hart bill was substituted for the Administration bill by a 51-22 majority, and then the whole bill was promptly passed by a lopsided 64-12 majority. The one remarkable thing about the last vote was the weakness of the Southern opposition. Only eleven Southern Senators were on the floor to cast hostile votes. Four Southern members actually voted in favor of the bill, including Senator William Spong (D-Va.), whose margin of victory had been provided by Southern blacks.

The weakness of Southern support for the President's position was partially explained by the changing complexion of Southern politics. Blacks were gaining political power, and white politicians were increasingly reluctant to be openly identified with hostile legislative proposals. A national Gallup poll showed two-thirds of white Americans and about half of Southern whites favoring strong federal intervention to protect the voting rights of black citizens.

Two Southern Senators, overheard in the Senate cloakroom, expressed the new situation. "Don't ask me to go out there and filibuster," said Senator Ernest Hollings of South Carolina, who had been elected by black votes. "I'm not going back to my state and explain a filibuster against the black voters." "Look fellows," announced Georgia's conservative Senator Herman Talmadge, "I was the principal speaker at the NAACP conference in my state last year." [17]

The President found himself taking a position not only substantially to the right of the national majority, but even to the right of a growing number of Southern politicians and much of the Southern white public. The Senate, which has often been attacked as the burial place of civil rights measures proposed by the more progressive Presidency, now held the line on a central issue. Senate Republicans, under strong White House pressure on both voting rights and the Carswell nomination, broke decisively with the President to support a voting bill coauthored by the GOP Senate Leader.

Senate action was encouraging to civil rights supporters, but the problem still remained of working out an agreement between the Senate and the House on the voting-age provision. Judiciary Chairman Celler had repeatedly stated his serious Constitutional objections to the eighteen-year-old vote provision, and he could force the writing of a new bill in a conference committee where he would lead the House conferees. There also was the problem of obtaining a favorable rule from the House Rules Committee, which had sided with civil rights opponents on the last test.

Shortly after the Senate action, Chairman Celler announced that he had changed his mind. In spite of his "personal reservations about the power of Congress to affect residency requirements for voting and to ban literacy tests generally," he now conceded that these questions could be safely left to the courts. The Voting Rights Act was "of such paramount national importance that it must be effectuated as promptly as possible and at a minimum of risk." [18]

The President, on the other hand, escalated the pressure on Congress with a long letter to Minority Leader Gerald Ford opposing the Senate action on the voting question. He called it "an unconstitutional assertion of Congressional authority in an area specifically reserved to the States." The President called on the House to remove the teen-age voting section from the bill and to consider it separately as a Constitutional amendment.[19] This would, of course, have unleashed a new House-Senate conflict shortly before the Voting Rights Act was due to expire, and would have permitted the Senate to begin a new filibuster on the conference report.

Attention now focused on the Rules Committee. Unless the Committee sent the bill to the floor with a rule forcing the House to accept or reject the whole Senate package, there was a high probability that the bill would be amended on the floor. As the Rules Committee vote approached, the House GOP Policy Committee supported the President's approach.[20] When the decisive vote came, however, the Rules Committee voted 8-6 against sending the issue to conference, and then voted to send it to the floor under a rule forbidding amendments.[21] The Rules decision greatly aided the civil rights forces. A committee which had often been a central obstacle to civil rights bills now provided vital assistance.

After a leadership delay to permit the favorable lobbies to organize support, the bill came up for final action on June 17. During the closing debate Minority Leader Ford implied that the President might veto the bill in its present form. On the key test vote, however, the House voted 224-183 to proceed to an immediate vote on the Senate bill, which it then passed by a two-to-one margin.[22] The Voting Rights Act had been preserved and the eighteen-year-old vote would soon be a reality.

The President's voting rights initiative had failed because the President was unable to rally his own party against a civil rights law expressing the broad public consensus for voting rights. While there was some possible political logic to the move as an attempt to enlarge the GOP Presidential vote in the South, it was both morally offensive and politically senseless from the perspective of the moderate GOP Senate leadership.

Race and the Supreme Court

The Fight over the Haynsworth Nomination Perhaps the most dramatic of the many struggles between Congress and President Nixon over the nation's racial policy came in the long and bitterly fought controversies over the nomination of two very conservative Southern judges to the Supreme Court.   103

For month after month, from August 1969 through April 1970, the attention of the country was focused on the sharpest conflict between Presidential and Congressional powers in the appointment of Justices since the Administration of President Ulysses S. Grant. In a nation where the Supreme Court had become the symbol of the government's movement toward racial justice, the struggle had elemental political importance.

Presidents had come to expect confirmation of Supreme Court nominees almost as a matter of course. While there had been a good deal of criticism of several nominees, the only twentieth-century defeat was suffered by President Hoover in 1930. On that occasion the President, weakened by the Depression disaster, had been unable to win confirmation for Judge John Parker, who was severely attacked for hostile attitudes by the labor movement and the NAACP. Since that time no Presidential choice was voted down, although a 1968 filibuster forced President Johnson to end his effort to elevate Justice Abe Fortas to Chief Justice.

President Nixon had experienced no difficulty in naming a new Chief Justice, and expected none in filling the seat vacated by the resignation of Justice Fortas. He had promised to name conservatives to the Court and confidently set about doing it. The new Chief Justice, Warren Burger, had been confirmed with virtually no opposition, in spite of his very conservative record on the Court of Appeals and his relatively undistinguished legal background. The Senate Judiciary Committee held a perfunctory hour-and-a-half hearing, largely devoted to favorable statements by Senators. The committee didn't even bother to issue a formal report before the Senate vote. After a three-hour discussion on the Senate floor, Burger was confirmed by a 74-3 vote.[23] With this easy victory in selecting the nation's fifteenth Chief Justice, the President seemed in a very powerful position.

In filling his second vacancy, the President turned to an unknown federal appeals court judge from South Carolina, Clement F. Haynsworth, Jr. Although Judge Haynsworth was criticized by civil rights groups as a conservative member of a Southern court that had handled a great deal of civil rights litigation, no significant Senate fight was expected. Many liberals had strongly argued during the 1950s and 1960s against Southern opposition to nominees based on civil rights grounds, and ideological attacks were widely seen as illegitimate. The

104 Senate's role in the confirmation process had atrophied, so

much so that no one seriously thought a nomination of a President could be defeated.

The early assessments on Haynsworth were optimistic. Senate Minority Leader Dirksen saw "no difficulty" in winning speedy confirmation for the South Carolina jurist. Dirksen granted that liberals would object to the judge's "somewhat moderate" civil rights record, but he maintained that the country was moving "slowly but surely in the conservative drift." "Look how generously the country accepted the nomination of Burger," he remarked.[24] Southerners and conservatives greeted the new appointment enthusiastically and no Senator expressed opposition. In spite of vigorous criticism from the NAACP and the Leadership Conference on Civil Rights, the chances of the opponents seemed exceedingly slim.[25] Even after several weeks of discussion, Senator Philip Hart (D-Mich.), a leading civil rights advocate, declared the Senate should confirm a nominee if he were "competent in the law and honest." [26]

The scheduled hearings were postponed by the death of Senator Dirksen, a leading member of the Judiciary Committee. Even this delay, and charges that Haynsworth had decided cases involving a financial conflict of interest, did not shake the confidence of the judge's supporters. As the hearings were about to open there was still no opponent of the nomination on record in the Senate, and certainly no one seemed eager to lead what would surely be a losing battle.

The hearings created Senate opposition and made the nomination a focus for a national political struggle between Senate liberals and moderates on one side, and on the other a President who committed his political resources strongly to the effort. The Haynsworth nomination fight was a classic illustration of a seldom noticed variation of the filibuster approach to the legislative process. By greatly prolonging the highly publicized hearings, critics succeeded in focusing attention on the judge's record and creating a major new national issue. While the President clearly enjoys unequaled access to the news media at any given point in time, the sustained impact on public opinion of a long and well-orchestrated hearing can be vast.

As the hearings and subsequent debate continued, the Administration was hit by a whole series of statements by opponents, and by new revelations of conflict-of-interest charges. Black organizations increased the intensity of their attacks, and attention was forcefully called to the judge's record on labor issues by strong opposition from the AFL-CIO, backed up by the organization's powerful lobbying staff.

105

Judge Haynsworth's civil rights record was strongly criticized by the Leadership Conference on Civil Rights and other major black organizations. A number of Senators said that his insensitivity toward racial problems, his narrow construction of civil rights precedents, and his reversal by the Supreme Court on several issues, were major reasons for their votes against confirmation.

On the ethics question, many were not satisfied with the judge's explanations of how he came to cast important votes in a case decided in favor of a textile firm that had a big contract with a vending machine company of which he was part owner. In another case, where Haynsworth had purchased stock in a company whose case was still active before his court, he had clearly, although unintentionally, violated the American Bar Association's canon of ethics.

Senate Republicans were beginning to feel actively uncomfortable, both about the civil rights charges and about the ethical problems. However, they still expected to go along with the President. The first sign of open resistance came when Senator Brooke (R-Mass.) released a letter to President Nixon recommending withdrawal of the nomination. Brooke wrote that Haynsworth's "treatment of civil rights issues is not in keeping with the historic movement toward equal justice," and that his confirmation would deeply concern those who "look to the Court as the indispensable instrument of equal justice under law." Brooke warned Nixon of growing opposition:

> If this nomination is put to the Senate, it will be extremely embarrassing to those of us who face a great conflict between our principles and our sense of obligation to you. It may well be that there will be sufficient votes to deny Judge Haynsworth's confirmation.[27]

The next day Senator Mondale (D-Minn.) made a similar appeal to the President: "If the Supreme Court—the one institution to which black Americans have been able to look with confidence—is turned around, there will be no reason for those in the South committed to resist change to act in any way other than according to their convictions."[28] Senator Harrison Williams (D-N.J.) announced he would vote against Haynsworth because of his "regressive judicial thinking in at least two areas vital to the majority of America—the areas of labor and race relations."[29]

The President tried to head off opposition with a strong show of support. Both in a letter to Minority Leader Hugh Scott and in a meeting with GOP leadership, he underlined his support of Haynsworth and his belief that there was no substance to opposition charges. The President, however, could not win the support of either of the top two Senate Republican leaders. Although the Republicans at the White House meeting warned him that there were at least ten GOP members likely to vote against Haynsworth, the President decided to go all out for the nominee after an Administration count showed him likely to win confirmation by a six-vote margin.[30]

Within days of the President's decision, his position was seriously eroded by the announcement of Senator Robert Griffin (R-Mich.), the assistant GOP leader, that he would vote no. Griffin had led the fight against Justice Fortas. On the same day a pillar of the Republican establishment, Senator Margaret Chase Smith (R-Maine), announced her opposition on ethical grounds. Even Haynsworth's chief Senate sponsor, Senator Hollings of South Carolina, conceded that the nomination was seriously threatened.[31]

With some vote counts already showing a hostile majority, pressure on the President to withdraw Haynsworth's name grew. Haynsworth himself was reported to have doubts about the wisdom of continuing the battle. Even conservative spokesman Senator Barry Goldwater (R-Ariz.) asked the President to withdraw the nomination. Very active opposition by labor and civil rights groups was generating a good deal of critical mail to Senate offices, and opposition grew during the long succession of widely publicized attacks made possible by the dragging out of the confirmation proceedings.[32]

The President responded by deciding to exert his power in a direct test with the Senate. In a rare news conference in his office, he went into the case in detail, claiming that hostile Senators had resorted to "vicious character assassination" of a qualified judge. The President said he wouldn't withdraw the nomination even if Haynsworth asked him to. He belittled the ethical problems, and on the civil rights issue insisted that "a judge's philosophy is not a proper basis for rejecting him from the Supreme Court."

> If Judge Haynsworth's philosophy leans to the conservative side, in my view that recommends him to me. I think the court needs balance, and I think that the court needs a man who is conservative . . . in respect of his attitude towards the Constitution.[33]

The President's limited view of the Senate's responsibility was hotly disputed. Senator after Senator rose on the floor to disagree with the President's assessment of the ethical question. In many cases they asserted that the Senate had a special responsibility to consider the public record of men to be given vast lifetime responsibility to help determine the meaning of the Constitution.

As the vote neared, the White House drive for confirmation became intense. Ralph Smith of Illinois, an obscure Republican appointed to fill the seat vacated by Senator Dirksen's death, was invited to the White House four times and pressured by his Governor until he reversed his early opposition to Haynsworth. The White House orchestrated a campaign against Senators who privately told the President of their opposition to the nominee. Another Republican freshman, William Saxbe (R-Ohio), reported all kinds of urging: "Businessmen and defense contractors I'd never heard of began calling me. . . . And some would add a reminder that they'd contributed to my campaign."[34] Similarly, Senator Len Jordan (R-Idaho) reportedly told other Senators that he had been under extraordinary pressure to change his vote:

> This crowd knows how to kill a senator. They play rough. They go to all your political leaders and put the pressure on you. I'm up for re-election and I presume they want to get my votes on some issues in the Senate until then, but they're pretty short-sighted if they think this is the way to do it.[35]

The pressure even extended to a threat by House GOP Leader Gerald Ford to initiate impeachment proceedings against Justice Douglas on conflict-of-interest grounds. He said that the standards applied to Haynsworth should also be applied to men already on the bench. Senate Majority Leader Mansfield called the threat "counterproductive." An even more unusual development came when Chief Justice Burger violated tradition by urging confirmation on Senators he met at social functions.[36]

During the days of final debate the civil rights issue figured prominently in public statements. Senator Symington (D-Mo.) noted that through Supreme Court decisions "in recent years many Americans have won important rights of citizenship." [37] Senator Metcalf (D-Mont.) attributed the nomination to the Administration's Southern strategy, and said the President was "unwilling to chance the appointment of a Justice who will decide vital issues of the day on the merits." [38] Senator Jacob

Javits (R-N.Y.) based his opposition on the conclusion that Haynsworth "persists in error—persists, after years and years, in the view that the old was right and the new is wrong, particularly on this critical civil rights question."[39]

In spite of the gnawing opposition in the Senate, the country's liberal establishment was by no means united against Haynsworth. The law professors who went before the Judiciary Committee all appeared in support of the judge. Neither of the nation's most influential newspapers, the *Washington Post* and the *New York Times*, called for the Senate to vote the nomination down, although both proposed that the President withdraw Haynsworth's name. Congress was not responding to a great national wave of indignation, then, but to an issue that Congress itself had created.

The final vote came on November 21, after three months of intense political warfare. In eleven minutes the roll was called and the future course of the Supreme Court was altered. On the vote the President was opposed by seventeen members of his own party, including three top Senate GOP leaders, as the nomination failed 45-55. The ten-vote margin of defeat was the largest ever achieved in a Senate-Supreme Court fight. The President had taken a stand on an issue where Presidents are rarely defeated, and in spite of very unusual and intense personal and administrative efforts, he was smashingly beaten. The result was to revive an almost forgotten but very important Senate power.

The Fight Renewed: The Carswell Nomination President Nixon responded angrily to what he described as an affront both to the Presidency and to the South. Attorney General John Mitchell analyzed the defeat as "a reflection of the failure of some in the Senate to recognize the President's constitutional prerogatives." Insisting that his election gave him a mandate to change the Court, the President declared that he would send the Senate another nominee with the same "legal philosophy." Senator Hruska (R-Neb.), who had led the fight for Haynsworth, announced that labor and civil rights organizations had won a "hollow victory." GOP Leader Hugh Scott said he expected another conservative nominee.[40] Though the President had been seriously defeated, it was not yet clear why. Many thought that the defeat might have no lasting ideological impact on the Supreme Court. The President had suffered his first major setback in Congress, but he was determined to win the next round.

109

After the ordeal of the Haynsworth struggle, no one expected a serious fight on the President's next choice. So long as the President submitted a candidate without obvious personal deficiencies, he was expected to be confirmed routinely. Senator Mike Mansfield, for example, said it would be "fine" if the President wanted to select a conservative Southerner, "if he's cleared thoroughly in advance." The other major Senate Leader, Hugh Scott, said that a "strict constructionist" from the South would be the ideal candidate. Vice President Agnew, campaigning in the South, promised that "this administration will appoint, and will see confirmed, a Southern strict constructionist on the Supreme Court." [41]

On January 19, 1970, the President announced his nomination of Judge G. Harrold Carswell to the Supreme Court. The fifty-year-old Florida judge had been thoroughly checked for conflict-of-interest questions and had no significant record of labor cases. The President had cleared the appointment in advance with Senator Scott, who promptly pledged his support "without qualification." Within the past year Carswell had been confirmed unanimously by the Senate to a seat on the Fifth Circuit Court of Appeals.[42]

Civil rights groups had strongly protested Carswell's appointment to the Fifth Circuit and now immediately attacked the Supreme Court nominee, claiming that he had been more hostile to black litigants than any other federal judge in Florida. The criticisms had made no impact on the earlier appointment, but now they were suddenly given new credibility by the discovery of a white supremacy speech Carswell had once made when running for the Georgia state legislature in 1948. The speech blasted civil rights proposals of the Truman Administration and concluded with a sweeping statement of Carswell's position:

> I am a Southerner by ancestry, birth, training, inclination, belief, and practice. I believe that segregation of the races is proper and the only practical and correct way of life in our states. I have always so believed, and I shall always so act....
> I yield to no man as a fellow candidate, or as a fellow citizen, in the firm, vigorous belief in the principles of white supremacy, and I shall always be so governed.[43]

After a Florida reporter unearthed the speech, Carswell promptly declared the ideas were "obnoxious and abhorrent to my personal philosophy." Attorney General Mitchell dismissed the speech as remarks made "in the heat of a political contest more than 20 years ago." [44] Confirmation still seemed certain. The GOP Senate leaders and even Senator Edward Kennedy (D-Mass.) argued that a man should have the right to change his mind. Several days after the nomination, only two hostile witnesses had asked to testify before the Senate Judiciary Committee, and the commitee expected to finish hearings in a day or two.[45]

Carswell's 1948 speech had alerted potential opponents, however, and stimulated rapid research into the nominee's record. Gradually information emerged suggesting that the judge's attitudes had not changed. A Rutgers University law professor, John Lowenthal, wrote a letter to the *New York Times* reporting on his experience in defending civil rights groups before Carswell. Carswell, he alleged, "was well known to both local and out-of-town lawyers as a vigorous opponent of civil rights." In his letter and in later testimony before the committee, Lowenthal detailed cases in which Carswell had shown open hostility to civil rights lawyers. The office of Senator Proxmire (D-Wis.) found a Yale Ph.D. dissertation analyzing the records of Southern federal judges and placing Carswell firmly in the "segregationist" category. The Senator cited it in his speech announcing opposition. Duke University Law Professor William Van Alstyne, when contacted by a newspaper reporter, said he found Carswell far inferior to Haynsworth, whose nomination he had supported. In his later Senate testimony Van Alstyne would develop the "mediocrity" issue that severely weakened Carswell. From Tallahassee came the story that Carswell had helped incorporate a private club in 1956 that had taken over the city's public golf course to prevent desegregation—an issue that would bring extensive questioning during the hearings.[46]

Still, when the hearings opened, confirmation seemed certain. Judge Carswell, confident and effective in contrast to the timorous Haynsworth, was praised by early witnesses and won the effusive support of Senator Scott. When the liberals' early efforts to question Carswell produced no significant breakthroughs, few Senators even attended the hearings.

After three days of testimony, the hearings seemed to be almost over. When the opposition finally got a chance to testify, the conservative committee chairman, James Eastland (D-Miss.), held off the serious civil rights testimony until late afternoon, when there was little news coverage. The committee decided to hold a final day of hearings the following Monday. Senator Eastland, who had permitted delays the last time, was 111 now hurrying everything through. Senator Scott predicted speedy Senate confirmation with from eighty to eighty-five favorable votes.[47] The President reaffirmed his strong support for his choice, arguing that Carswell's record was "impeccable and without a taint of any racism." He predicted overwhelming Senate Support.[48]

The testimony during the final days of hearings was damaging, but seemed to make little political difference. A Justice Department lawyer testified that Carswell had openly expressed his hostility to civil rights workers in his courtroom. A civil rights lawyer stated he had heard the judge advising a prosecutor how to circumvent a civil rights decision by an appellate court. A New York University law professor who had practiced before him testified that Carswell was "insulting and hostile" to black lawyers. Louis Pollak, Dean of the Yale Law School, asserted, "The nominee presents the most slender credentials of any man put forward in this century" for the Court.[49]

Increasingly worried about Carswell but hopelessly outnumbered, the liberals began to stall, relying on a variety of devices often employed by conservatives. Senator Birch Bayh (D-Ind.), who was emerging as leader of the opposition, confronted the Judiciary Committee with a motion tying electoral college reform to the Carswell issue. Southern conservatives had long opposed direct election reforms, which would mean national regulation of suffrage, and Strom Thurmond filibustered against the Bayh motion. The committee recessed, thus delaying a move to report the nomination to the Senate floor.[50]

Carswell's opponents next resorted to the right of any committee member to hold a matter over a week before a final vote, so that it was February 16 before the Judiciary Committee voted. On that date the nomination was supported by an overwhelming 13-4 vote and sent to the Senate floor. More time was consumed, however, when the liberals got ten days for preparation of their minority report on the nomination.[51] Carswell nevertheless came out of the committee stage in a far stronger position than Haynsworth, holding the unanimous support of all committee Republicans.

The next important delay came with a decision by Majority Leader Mansfield to call up the controversial voting rights bill before scheduling the nomination for a vote. Mansfield thus put conservatives in a procedural vise: they must either shorten the voting rights filibuster and thus permit extension of a law much criticized by them, or permit momentum to build against a very conservative Supreme Court nomination.[52] Frustrated Carswell supporters, certain they then had a majority, would see weeks pass and opposition gradually mount.

One by one, Senators announced their opposition. In the law schools and in the press there was a growing tide of criticism that had an impact on the lawyers in the Senate, and began to create broad public interest in the conflict.

On March 13 Senator Mansfield called up the nomination. Liberals were still so far from a majority that there was some thought of trying a filibuster like the one that killed the Fortas nomination in 1968. Senator Scott led off the discussion with a strong defense of the Florida judge.[53]

The growing criticism within the legal profession was fed by a famous statement by Senator Hruska during the first full day of Senate debate. The Senator met disaster in trying to play down the widespread allegations that Carswell was too mediocre for the Supreme Court.

> Even if he were mediocre, there are a lot of mediocre judges and people and lawyers. They are entitled to a little representation, aren't they, and a little chance. We can't have all Brandeises and Frankfurters and Cardozos and stuff like that there.[54]

Hruska charged that the whole issue was merely a ploy by those who really opposed Carswell's failure "to promote the civil rights revolution of the past decade." [55]

Both the Hruska statement and the unusual action of two of Carswell's prominent colleagues on the Fifth Circuit Court, who criticized his nomination, fed the growing belief in the legal profession that the nomination was an affront to the Court. From law schools across the country, and from members of the local bars, came letters and petitions asking Senators to defeat the nomination.[56] The growing criticism of Carswell's technical incompetence provided a politically useful basis for an opposing vote by members who would have been highly uncomfortable opposing confirmation merely on ideological grounds.

As the debate dragged on with lagging interest in the Senate, Carswell suffered a slow erosion of support. Opponents who believed they had thirty votes against confirmation began to think that sufficient delay would bring the total to forty or more. Four Republican Senators who had earlier favored the nomination now said they were undecided.[57]

The final two weeks of delay—necessary to build up support   113 against Carswell—were gained through an implicit threat of a filibuster. With the debate consuming day after day and criticism growing on all sides, the nominee's supporters agreed to postpone the final vote to a specific date, rather than risk a concerted and indefinite filibuster. As this agreement was reached, Carswell's prospects for the first time seemed uncertain.[58]

As the showdown approached, the President claimed that opposition Senators were seriously infringing on the proper authority of the Presidency. After restating his "total support" for Carswell and dismissing opposition charges as "specious," his letter defined the central issue as

> the Constitutional responsibility of the President to appoint members of the Court—and whether this responsibility can be frustrated by those who wish to substitute their own philosophy or their own subjective judgment for that of the one person entrusted by the Constitution with the power of appointment.[59]

The Senate, he said, should not deny him "the same right of choice . . . which has been freely accorded to my predecessors of both parties." [60]

The President's letter was resented and hotly disputed by several Senators, who argued that the Senate had coequal responsibility in selecting members of the Supreme Court. The assertion that the Senate had no real role in the process lacked appeal for most Senators and actively irritated some. The Haynsworth fight had settled this question.

When the final votes came, Carswell supporters first took heart when they repulsed an effort to send the nomination back for more committee hearings on the new issues raised during the debate. Then, two days later, the Senate surprised the country by voting to defeat the Carswell appointment 51-45.[61]

The critical votes against confirmation were provided by Senator Marlow Cook (R-Ky.) and Senator Margaret Chase Smith (R-Maine), both conservative members of the President's own party. Senator Cook was concerned both about Carswell's lack of personal capacity and about his poor record on civil rights. Senator Smith's vote may have been lost, in part, through a false report, circulated by the White House staff, that she had said she would support Carswell. This ploy got back to Senator Smith before the vote and infuriated her.[62]

The White House had employed intense political pressure on behalf of Carswell, sustaining its efforts right up to the day of the vote. Senator Richard Schweiker (R-Pa.) was told by a White House staffer, just as the vote began, that his vote was crucial, and that "there isn't *anything* you couldn't get for your state from the White House as a result." Senator Howard Cannon (D-Nev.) likewise came under heavy pressure; some reports claimed that he was offered the assurance of a weak GOP opponent in the fall if he voted right. Senators Smith and Cook had both received strong personal appeals from the President at the White House. All voted against Carswell.[63]

The President chose to use his defeat for political purposes in the South, claiming that the Senate decision was based on a bias against that region:

> I have reluctantly concluded—with the Senate presently constituted—I cannot successfully nominate to the Supreme Court any Federal Appellate Judge from the South who believes as I do in the strict construction of the Constitution. Judges Carswell and Haynsworth have endured with admirable dignity vicious assaults on their intelligence, their honesty, and their character. They have been falsely charged with being racist. But when all the hypocrisy is stripped away, the real issue was their philosophy of strict construction . . . and the fact that they had the misfortune of being born in the South. . . .
>
> I understand the bitter feelings of millions of Americans who live in the South about the act of regional discrimination that took place in the Senate today.[64]

The President's charge was hard to sustain in the face of the fact that four Southerners had cast votes against Carswell. Moreover, few knowledgeable observers would take seriously an argument that such GOP stalwarts as Smith of Maine and Prouty of Vermont were opposed to strict construction. Even more dramatic rebuttal of the President's charge would come from the voters of Florida. Less than two weeks after his Senate defeat, Carswell resigned his position as a federal judge to enter the race for a Florida Senate seat being vacated by the incumbent. Even though he entered the race with the support of Florida's other Senator and the Governor, and made a major issue of the Supreme Court fight, the Florida voters rejected him in the primary. In the general election they turned from the Republican Party altogether to send an almost unknown moderate Democrat to Washington.[65]

Carswell's campaign demonstrated that his critics had been right. He harshly attacked school desegregation decisions and the Court's effort to protect the rights of accused criminals. The voters in the Florida Republican primary, however, de-

115

feated him by an almost two-to-one margin. After the election Senate GOP Leader Hugh Scott, who had kept his pledge to the White House to vote for Carswell's confirmation, said that Carswell was a "racist" who "got what he deserved." Describing his vote on the Senate floor, Scott now confessed, "I have a considerable sense of guilt that I did a damn foolish thing."[66]

The Supreme Court fights saw the Senate withstand immense political pressure and the full force of Presidential leadership to defeat two successive Supreme Court nominees and to severely question the power of President Nixon. Although there were important additional issues in both cases, the weak civil rights record of each nominee very plainly played a role in making Senators decide to wage a serious battle, and in determining the votes of many members. It was the Senate, the old bastion of reaction, that now defended the tradition of Supreme Court leadership in civil rights that had developed since 1954. The Presidency, on the other hand, employed Court appointments as a form of regional political patronage, and even in the face of powerful Senate opposition, used the full weight of its authority to press for confirmation of highly conservative Southern judges who were insensitive to problems of segregation.

Summary: The Presidency and Congress Reverse Their Roles

American politics offer few examples of so massive and rapid a shift in political perspectives as that affecting civil rights policies in early 1969. The White House, recently occupied by the most determined civil rights supporter in the history of the Presidency, had now passed to a President committed to stemming the tide of change in race relations. No longer the leading advocate for black Americans, the President now in fact often seemed to be the principal enemy.

Like a movie running backwards, the first years of the Nixon Presidency brought a succession of retreats to positions held much earlier in the racial struggle. Voting rights for black Americans were fine, Congress was told, but not if the cost for a workable law was a provision singling out the states where the President wished to make political headway. Why not, the
Attorney General asked, "strengthen" the law by making it

apply across the country, and then quietly remove enforcement powers? Congress rejected this plan.

School desegregation had been a dominant theme of civil rights discussion since 1954. Nothing provided so clear a test of the role of political leadership on a difficult and controversial racial issue as did school policy. The Nixon Administration began dismally and moved steadily toward a position of obstinate resistance to the settled law of school desegregation. Whereas under President Johnson HEW and the Justice Department had actively accelerated desegregation, under the Nixon Presidency HEW stopped enforcing the 1964 Civil Rights Act, while the Justice Department repeatedly went into court against civil rights litigants.

The issue came up repeatedly in Congress. Time after time the White House and the Justice Department gave active or tacit encouragement to those attempting to legislate a rollback of desegregation requirements. Time after time liberals holding seniority in the House, and moderates and liberals in the Senate, defeated these efforts. Finally, in 1972, the President went dramatically on television to press Congress to enact sweeping antibusing legislation restricting the power of the federal courts in desegregation cases.

Clearly, there was nothing in the institution of the Presidency to assure any responsiveness to civil rights claims of black Americans. The circumstances of the last two decades had produced an unreal optimism about necessary support from the Presidency.

Only in the field of job discrimination did the President achieve even a temporary and ambiguous record. While using his power briefly to prevent restrictive legislation and thus protect the experimental effort against union discrimination in Philadelphia, the President simultaneously made it impossible to enact a fair-employment law with a serious enforcement mechanism. This battle the Administration won.

The whole sweep of the change was most evident in the Supreme Court fights. In the 1950s President Eisenhower had nominated moderates to the Court over the bitter objection of Southern segregationists. Presidents Kennedy and Johnson had followed with further nominations of moderates and liberals, despite similar objections. President Nixon, however, named only conservative justices, and his first two Southern nominees both had records showing a distinct distaste for the legal developments that had begun in 1954. Leading Southern critics of the Supreme Court in the 1950s and 1960s now became almost 117 the only enthusiastic defenders of the new nominees. The President employed his power very drastically to accomplish his purpose, but the Senate defeated both efforts.

America entered the 1970s under grim warnings from a succession of Presidential commissions and from many sensitive political leaders that the nation faced imminent danger of fragmentation into two separate, unequal, and hostile societies. It also entered the decade in a time when long-established political loyalties were breaking loose, particularly in the South. The President chose to exploit the second change to try to create a new Presidential majority in the American electorate— a fundamentally conservative majority. The strategy accelerated and exploited racial division. If we still have a chance of building a single society, much of the credit belongs to Congress.

NOTES

[1] *Washington Post*, June 19, 1969.
[2] *Ibid.*, June 20, 1969.
[3] *Ibid.*, June 20 and June 27, 1969.
[4] *New York Times*, July 2, 1969; *Washington Star*, July 2, 1969.
[5] *New York Times*, July 11 and July 18, 1969.
[6] *Ibid.*, November 19, 1969; *Washington Post*, November 26, 1969.
[7] *New York Times*, December 11, 1969; *Washington Post*, December 11, 1969.
[8] *Congressional Record*, December 11, 1969, p. H12184; *Congressional Quarterly*, December 19, 1969, p. 2664, roll call no. 150.
[9] *Washington Post*, December 12, 1969; *Washington Post*, December 13 and December 16, 1969; *Atlanta Constitution*, December 13, 1969.
[10] *Congressional Record*, December 15, 1969, p. S16707.
[11] *New York Times*, December 19, 1969.
[12] *Washington Post*, February 11, 1970.
[13] *Ibid.*, February 19, 1970.
[14] *New York Times*, February 19, 1970; *Washington Post*, February 11, February 19, and February 26, 1970.
[15] *Congressional Record*, March 12, 1970, p. S3585.
[16] *Ibid.*, March 13, 1970, p. S3714.
[17] *Chicago Daily News*, March 14–15, 1970; Gallup Poll in "America's Mood," *Look*, November 18, 1969, pp. 23–32.
[18] *Congressional Record*, April 8, 1970, p. H2737.
[19] *Ibid.*, April 28, 1970, pp. H3610–11.
[20] *Washington Post*, June 3, 1970.
[21] *Ibid.*, June 5, 1970.
[22] *Congressional Quarterly*, June 19, 1970, p. 1570.
[23] *Ibid.*, June 13, 1969, p. 1010.
[24] *Atlanta Constitution*, August 19, 1969.
[25] *New York Times*, August 19, 1969.
[26] *Congressional Quarterly*, September 12, 1969, p. 1685.

[27] *Congressional Record*, October 1, 1969, pp. S11660–01.
[28] *Ibid.*, October 2, 1969, p. S11740.
[29] *Ibid.*, October 3, 1969, p. S11838.
[30] *New York Times*, October 3, 1969.
[31] *Ibid.*, October 9, 1969; *Columbia State*, October 8, 1969.
[32] *Newsweek*, October 20, 1969.
[33] *Washington Post*, October 21, 1969.
[34] *Newsweek*, December 1, 1969, pp. 21–23.
[35] *Washington Post*, November 15, 1969.
[36] *Ibid.*, November 10, 1969; *New York Times*, November 8, 1969.
[37] *Congressional Record*, November 13, 1969, p. S14273.
[38] *Ibid.*, November 17, 1969, p. S14468.
[39] *Ibid.*, November 20, 1969, p. S14771.
[40] *Washington Post*, October 9 and November 21, 1969; *New York Times*, September 27 and November 22, 1969; *Atlanta Constitution*, November 22, 1969.
[41] *Trenton Times-Advertiser*, November 23, 1969; *Washington Post*, October 27, 1969.
[42] *Atlanta Constitution*, January 20, 1970; *Washington Post*, January 20, 1970.
[43] *New York Times*, January 23, 1970.
[44] *Ibid.*
[45] *Washington Post*, January 23, 1970.
[46] *New York Times*, January 25, 1970; *Congressional Record*, January 27, 1970, pp. S632–33; *Washington Post*, January 25, 1970.
[47] *Chicago Daily News*, January 30, 1970.
[48] *New York Times*, January 31, 1970.
[49] *Ibid.*, February 3, 1970.
[50] *Washington Post*, February 4, 1970.
[51] *Ibid.*, February 17, 1970; *New York Times*, February 17, 1970.
[52] *Washington Post*, February 18, 1970.
[53] *Congressional Record*, March 13, 1970, p. S2729; *New York Times*, March 10, 1970.
[54] *Washington Post*, March 17, 1970.
[55] *Ibid.*
[56] *Washington Post*, March 18 and March 19, 1970.
[57] *Newark Star-Ledger*, March 21, 1970; *Washington Post*, March 20, 1970.
[58] *Washington Post*, March 26, 1970.
[59] *New York Times*, April 2, 1970.
[60] *Ibid.*
[61] *Washington Post*, April 7 and April 9, 1970.
[62] *Wall Street Journal*, April 9, 1970; *New York Times*, April 9, 1970.
[63] *Newsweek*, April 29, 1970, pp. 37–38.
[64] *Congressional Record*, April 10, 1970, p. S5571.
[65] *New York Times*, April 21, 1970; *Congressional Quarterly*, September 11, 1970, p. 2229.
[66] Reg Murphy and Hal Gulliver, *The Southern Strategy* (New York: Scribners, 1971), pp. 146–50.

119

part three

CONGRESS and the SCHOOLS: MONEY, RACE and CHANGE

7

FEDERAL AID:
ITS PRIORITY
and DIRECTION

Education: A History of Controversy

Although Americans have constructed a remarkable system of
public education, the relationship between the schools and the
national government has always posed a set of particularly difficult political problems. The American political tradition pic-
tures the schools not only as the key institution underlying the
promise of equal opportunity, and as the major solution to a
variety of social problems, but also as a peculiarly local function
where any hint of federal control must be avoided. The clash
between those who assert that federal resources are essential to
ensure real equality, and those bitterly opposed to any erosion
of local and state control, has been going on for over a century.
This continuing clash has often been intensified or even over-
shadowed by struggles concerning the impact of federal school
policy on racial segregation, or on the future of the huge parochial school system of the largest religion in America. Perhaps
no other issue can so effectively illustrate the strengths and
weaknesses of the Congressional policy-making process.

After the Second World War Congress was widely blamed
for frustrating the efforts of Presidents Truman, Eisenhower,

An Education Chronology

1961 Kennedy education bill fails.

1964 Lyndon Johnson elected President in a landslide; the liberal Democrats gain control of Congress.

1965 The Elementary and Secondary Education Act (ESEA). Enforcement of school desegregation guidelines begins.

1966 GOP gains in the Congressional election; ESEA henceforth under heavy attack.

1967 ESEA is extended in weakened form for two more years.

1968 Richard Nixon elected President in a close election.

1969 ESEA is extended for another two years.

1970 Nixon vetoes a school appropriations bill as inflationary; the veto is sustained.

ESEA is extended in expanded form.

Nixon vetoes a second school appropriations bill; the veto is overridden.

1971 Nixon signs the next school appropriations bill without a fight.

1972 Senate filibuster kills Nixon antibusing bill.

The Emergency Education Act of 1972.

Nixon vetoes successfully two more school appropriations bills.

Nixon reelected President.

1973 Nixon obtains lower school appropriations, but is forced by the courts to release impounded education funds.

1974 Congress rejects Nixon antibusing proposal.

Congress rejects the Nixon revenue-sharing bill and extends ESEA.

President Ford signs bill.

and Kennedy to win passage of some kind of federal aid. President Kennedy gave top priority to a school bill, but it died in the House Rules Committee.[1] Critics often saw the Presidency as the champion of education, unable to prevail over a conservative, fragmented Congress that allowed disgruntled pressure groups to veto any significant action.

The dam broke on Capitol Hill in 1965. By the end of that year, with the passage of the Elementary and Secondary Education Act, the federal government was transformed from a relatively insignificant force in American education into a source of massive new funding, of major demands for changed educational concerns, and unprecedented pressure for racial change in Southern schools. Both federal funds and federal leverage grew suddenly and vastly.

124

President Nixon took office as a conservative opponent of the new federal role, assuming power at a time when national educational policy was at a pivotal point. Major changes had been set in motion, but the changes had stirred deep tensions. For several years Congressional Republicans and Southern Democrats had been fighting for a return to the tradition of unbridled local control. The 1965 education act was due to expire only months after Nixon took office, offering the new President an immediate opportunity to influence the basic structure of federal school aid.

Major decisions had to be made on three central issues in education policy:

(1) Whether the federal government should insist on local action to meet the special needs of poor children, or simply hand funds to state and local education authorities through revenue sharing.

(2) Whether the scale of federal aid should level off, be cut back, or expand to play an increasingly important role in school finance.

(3) Whether federal officials should continue to vigorously enforce the school desegregation requirements of the 1964 Civil Rights Act, or those requirements should be weakened by legislation or administrative reversals.

After a period of hesitation and indecision during which Congress took the initiative, the President came down strongly on the conservative side on each of these three policy dimensions. In a remarkable reversal of the pre-1965 period, the Nixon era found Congress generally fighting to preserve the momentum of educational change against a President committed to reaction. The President not only drew on the full range of his positive powers and influence, but also made lavish use of his veto. He also fought for his policies by asserting a broad power to refuse to spend Congressionally appropriated funds (impoundment), and a right to ignore his duty to enforce the 1964 Civil Rights Act. These later decisions eventually drew the courts into the policy confrontation.

The President pressed hard for a change of direction. In most cases, however, Congress resisted and Congress prevailed. While basic innovation or broad expansion of the programs was all but impossible under these circumstances of confrontation, Congressional supporters did at least preserve the legal and administrative framework for future educational change. The President was most successful in holding down the school budg- 125 et. Through an extraordinary series of vetoes and impoundments, he substantially slowed, but did not reverse, the momentum for expanding federal aid. In the face of intense executive resistance, Congress maintained much of the most basic change to date in the federal role in American education.

As the energy of the Presidency was thrown into the battle to reverse educational policy, the role of some major instruments of Congressional power was transposed. The House Appropriations Committee, for example, which was famous for its inclination to cut back the social program requests of liberal Presidents, now found itself in the unfamiliar role of rejecting the conservative White House budget requests in favor of considerably more liberal funding of school aid. Liberal supporters of civil rights enforcement in the Senate even had recourse to that classic Southern tool, the filibuster, in order to defeat legislation the President was sponsoring to prevent urban school desegregation. It was a drastic reversal of the recent tradition.

The Education Background

A Tradition of Inaction   Until 1965, Congressional fragmentation over a number of the bitterly divisive issues involved in school aid helped forestall enactment of any significant school aid measure. Congress seemed clearly behind the current of public opinion reflected in responses to Gallup Poll questions about federal aid.

Congress was blamed for obstruction, but much of the trouble actually arose from serious divisions among those who supported federal aid—divisions reaching into the heart of the Democratic Party. While most Americans wanted federal aid

Table 7-1

Surveys of Public Opinion about Federal Aid to Schools

Year	Percent in favor	Percent opposed	No opinion
1949	43%	33%	24%
1957	76%	19%	5%
1960	65%	25%	10%

SOURCE *Gallup Polls of January 10, 1949; February 10, 1957; and February 19, 1960, in George H. Gallup,* The Gallup Poll (*New York: Random House, 1972*), Vols. 2, 3.

in the early 1960s, in a 1961 Gallup Poll most also opposed giving aid or even loans to Catholic schools. Catholics, on the other hand, favored such grants by more than a two-to-one majority, and favored loans by more than a four-to-one majority. Catholics made up a very important segment of the Democratic Party, and constituted a majority of the population in a number of Congressional districts. On another explosive issue, about a fourth of the public believed that federal aid should be withheld from Southern school systems refusing to desegregate. This percentage was much higher in the Eastern part of the country.[2] Such a condition, of course, was then totally unacceptable to Southern Congressmen.

Congress didn't create these divisions, but it did provide a setting where they could be forcefully expressed. It had procedures and fragmented committee power that their advocates could often use to veto proposed legislation. The education question showed with special clarity the serious differences within the Democratic coalition. Particularly in the House, where the electoral districts are relatively small and homogeneous, the battles showed real divisions of interest and goals among Democratic Congressmen representing big-city Polish communities, rural Southern Protestant whites, California suburbanites, and black ghettos. During the 1940s and early 1960s the religious issue shattered the Democratic coalition, while during the 1950s the race issue likewise seemed ruinously divisive.

Congressional obstructionism was widely blamed when Congress killed the Eisenhower Administration's modest school construction bills, intended to help overcome a very severe classroom shortage. After the 1954 Supreme Court decision, the NAACP and Harlem's black Congressman, Adam Clayton Powell (D-N.Y.), insisted that any school aid program deny funds to states defying the constitutional requirement for desegregation. The Powell amendment produced monolithic Southern opposition that helped defeat bills in both 1957 and 1959.[3]

Interestingly enough, although the Powell amendment was widely condemned by nationally prominent liberals in the 1950s because of the obstacle it created to enactment of a school bill, the fight in the House set the stage for inclusion in the 1964 Civil Rights Act of a provision forbidding federal aid for any program in which discrimination was practiced. Just as the NAACP had suspected, this provision proved to be crucial to the federal drive against Southern school segregation during the Johnson Administration. What contemporary critics in the

1950s saw as obstructionism actually was a very important element in the development of a progressive policy.

President Kennedy tried to achieve a breakthrough on federal aid by subordinating the racial issue, only to divide his party on the religious question. Kennedy obtained Representative Powell's promise not to introduce his amendment, and the Kennedy Administration sent no civil rights legislation to Congress for two and one half years. The first Catholic President felt, however, that he couldn't support aid to parochial schools, and it was impossible for Congress to find a compromise over this divisive issue. Nothing happened.

A Landmark: The Elementary and Secondary Education Act of 1965   In 1965 a century of failure was swept aside and the Elementary and Secondary Education Act (ESEA) was rapidly enacted. Virtually all observers concede that the most basic political reason for this victory was not something that happened within Congress, but the immense Democratic victory in the 1964 elections. The election gave non-Southern Democrats and their allies clear control of both House and Senate. It also put the President in an extremely powerful position. Given these political changes and the strong commitment to federal aid of both the President and the chairmen of the key House and Senate committees, it became very probable that a bill would be passed. This likelihood increased the power of the Administration in bargaining with concerned groups, and multiplied their incentive to reach agreement so as to be included in a program that seemed increasingly inevitable. The momentum was increased by President Johnson's record of intense interest in education and by his skill in legislative politics. The Rules Committee, the forum often used by the conservative coalition to kill school bills, was neutralized in one of the first actions of the new Congress—adoption of the twenty-one-day rule that permitted easy bypassing of the Rules panel.[4]

The race issue caused no trouble in 1965. There would be no Powell amendment because the 1964 Civil Rights Act had made a requirement of nondiscrimination in all federal programs the general law of the land. The South had been beaten, but nothing much had changed. The Office of Education, in fact, did not even issue its desegregation policies until several days after President Johnson signed the federal aid bill into law.

Meanwhile the religious conflict was circumvented by changing the focus of aid from schools to needy students. Senator Wayne Morse (D-Ore.), chairman of the Education subcommittee, and his staff director, Charles Lee, had introduced a modest version of such a bill in 1964, only to have it opposed by the Administration. The next year President Johnson's education task force arrived at a similar idea on a much larger scale. In early 1965 the Administration proposed its audacious bill, which included a billion dollars for educating poor children, a large program to encourage educational innovation, and other major elements including library services and funds to strengthen state departments of education.

The bill was received with grateful enthusiasm, and with a common determination by Congressional education supporters to exploit existing momentum and push it through intact before any of the old disputes reemerged. The measure was passed by the House just two and a half months after the President proposed it. Although most Republicans and Southern Democrats voted against the bill, it passed by a large margin. In a highly uncharacteristic move, Senate supporters deferred to the House and followed a rigid strategy of passing the bill without any amendments, so as to avoid a conference committee and further votes in both houses. Within two weeks of House action, the Senate passed the bill 73-18.[5]

This victory came about because the 1964 election gave progressives control of the House for two years. The most important precondition for success was the gain of thirty-eight House Democratic seats, many of which had passed from very conservative Republicans to unusually liberal Democrats. For years Democrats had been showing strong and increasing support for federal aid, while GOP support had fallen. On critical tests the support of House Democrats had risen steadily from 53 percent in 1956 to 80 percent in 1965. While two-fifths of the GOP members had voted for the 1957 bill, 96 percent had opposed the 1961 bill and little more than a fourth supported the 1965 act. In the House in 1965, the Elementary and Secondary Education Act was supported by every freshman Democrat who had displaced a GOP member, and by an incredible 98 percent of all Northern and Western Democrats.[6] More than anything else, the passage of this act was a victory for the progressive wing of the Democratic party—a victory reflecting both the 1964 electoral landslide and the success of the party's leaders in devising a formula to overcome the longstanding religious division.

Renewed Conflict over ESEA   The 1965 law settled the fact that the federal government would be involved significantly in   129 education, but many of the old disputes soon surfaced again. Contrary to assertions in many civics books, passage of a law is usually only the first step in a continuing political struggle over the nature and size of the new program. Once the common goal of the various groups to get some program into operation had been attained, their conflicting interests revived. Within two years the program would be racked by battles over race, federal power, and even allocation formulas. When the time came to extend the program in 1967, opposition was so strong that survival of the ESEA structure was seriously in doubt.

The most explosive conflict was over school desegregation. Southern conservatives had always maintained that a big federal aid program would bring federal interference with race relations. Their experience during 1965 and 1966 seemed to confirm this fear with a vengeance. When ESEA became law, most school districts in the South remained totally segregated. But the new HEW standards for enforcement of the 1964 Civil Rights Act meant that Southern districts would receive the badly needed federal money only if they began desegregation in 1965, and made genuine progress toward a wholly nonracial school system by September 1966. These were serious and traumatic changes for many Southern communities where people had become convinced that segregation could be maintained indefinitely, or that token integration was the worst that could ever happen. It was the first time a federal agency had ever seriously used the fund cutoff power to force change on sensitive local social issues. When a federal bureaucracy required far more change in two years than the courts had in twelve, the political attacks on the agency were bound to be severe.

While the South was concerned about new federal power over desegregation, school leaders in other regions opposed the growing impact of the Office of Education on educational change. Although the 1965 law contained the traditional guarantee of local control of the schools, the fact was that the whole design of the program was intended to foster change in the local status quo. The act in effect declared that state and local officials had failed to provide adequate schooling for poor children, and that new educational methods were needed. The financial leverage, particularly in the section financing educational innovations, was intended to foster experiments favored by Office of Education officials and the experts who advised them, rather than the changes that local officials might endorse. There was an implicit assumption that the education establishment needed incentives to respond to critical education problems that it had hitherto ignored. As these assumptions began to become evident in the administrative process, criticism mounted.

The legislative process gave members of Congress a succession of opportunities to remold the program. The annual appropriations battles provided a chance for attack by the conservatives of the Appropriations committees, and a forum for the continuing tug-of-war over the distribution formula. Big-city Congressmen, for example, favored special recognition of welfare children, while Southerners would be greatly assisted by a national minimum standard of payment.

There were also annual disputes over the level of appropriations. Liberals in Congress, for instance, complained in 1966 that President Johnson had cut almost a quarter of a billion dollars from the Office of Education's request for the new program, leaving the latter without adequate funding. There was already a substantial Congressional constituency for putting more money into the schools than the President, faced with rising Vietnam expenditures, felt he could afford.

Like most new domestic programs, ESEA expired automatically in two years unless Congress extended it—a procedure that guaranteed continuing Congressional involvement and close monitoring of agency performance. Unfortunately for advocates of ESEA, the 1966 midterm elections wiped out the liberal gains of 1964 in the House, and restored the power of

Table 7-2

Composition of the House of Representatives before and after the 1964 and 1966 Elections*

	Republicans	Southern Democrats	Northern Democrats
88th Congress (1963–64)	177	105	153
89th Congress (1965–66)	140	101	194
90th Congress (1967–68)	187	91	157
91st Congress (1969–70)	192	88	155

* 218 votes are necessary for a majority when all members vote.

SOURCE Congressional Quarterly Almanac, 1963, p. 741; 1964, p. 1015; 1966, p. 1399; 1968, p. 960.

the conservative coalition. Republicans defeated a number of young liberals, taking fifty-two formerly Democratic seats and losing only five, for a net gain of forty-seven seats.[7]

With the race issue fraying the loose bond between Northern Democrats and Southern moderates, opponents had an excellent opportunity to attack ESEA before the massive effort was really off the ground. The conditions were very favorable: the President was losing his popularity; conservatives were gaining political strength; the Office of Education still had serious administrative problems; and white resentment against black riots and the black power movement was growing, even as HEW came under bitter attack in the South for its desegregation requirements.

The mortal threat to the program suddenly became clear in early 1967. House Democratic leaders were shocked to learn that a Republican plan might well pass that would turn ESEA into a kind of education revenue sharing, where the federal money would be turned over to state officials to use as they chose with very few federal strings attached. In a long and dramatic fight the House leaders stalled the bill while education groups, the White House, and committee members worked to put the coalition back together again.

Liberals found themselves fighting for the status quo. Their main argument was that tampering with the existing, painstakingly constructed compromise would reopen all the old deep wounds. A promising program, aimed at those most in need, would give way to endless and perhaps fatal bickering. ESEA supporters worked hard to mobilize those most suspicious of state control: the big-city superintendents who never got their share of state funds, and the Catholics whose aid would be jeopardized where state constitutions contained absolute prohibitions against aid to religious schools. At the same time, Democrats were working for Southern support by urging certain civil rights changes and a distribution formula that would send more money to the poor Southern states.

Although ESEA survived, the federal role was weakened. Control over the program of educational innovations was turned over to state departments of education. The House passed an amendment limiting HEW's civil rights enforcement powers. When the House bill reached the Senate, there was further trouble over the race issue. After the Southern caucus threatened to filibuster, and GOP Leader Dirksen nearly succeeded in prohibiting the use of federal funds for school busing, HEW accepted a compromise weakening its cutoff power through elaborate procedural guarantees to Southern school systems.[8]

Nor was this the end of Republican and Southern Congressmen's hostility. The following year the House Appropriations Committee sent an education appropriations bill to the floor with a proviso cutting the heart out of HEW's desegregation program. The House sustained the Southern position on two successive votes, and only a favorable conference committee prevented real danger to civil rights enforcement.[9]

Not only was the program politically vulnerable at the time of the 1968 election, but it was also already in trouble in terms of its projected growth. In fiscal year 1968 Congress only appropriated 43 percent of the amount authorized for that year by the original legislation.[10] The budgetary pressure of Vietnam had lowered President Johnson's request for funds and had produced growing concern on Capitol Hill about inflation induced by spending programs. The original plan for a rapidly expanding program accounting for a growing proportion of the nation's school needs was abandoned in favor of operation at a stationary level, with small increments of funds.

The Nixon Attack on the Budget

Congress Acts First The 1968 election brought Richard Nixon to the White House. In his April 1969 message to Congress on domestic legislation, the new President didn't even mention ESEA.[11] Mr. Nixon in fact had no developed program. He saw his job much more as one of conducting foreign policy and of bringing coherence to the great collection of programs he had inherited, than as one of fighting for new laws.[12] In an early message to Congress the President responded to mounting criticism of his lack of initiatives in domestic policy with a defense of postponement.

> Merely making proposals takes only a typewriter; making workable proposals takes time. . . .
> . . . where more time is needed, we will take more time. I urge the Congress to join with the Administration in this careful approach to the most fundamental issues confronting our country. Hasty action or a seeking after partisan advantage either by the Congress or Executive Branch can only be self-defeating and aggravate the very ills we seek to remedy.[13]

While the President was gradually formulating his program, however, House Democrats rapidly set out to protect the Ele-   133 mentary and Secondary Education Act. Just ten days after the President took office, House Education and Labor Committee Chairman Carl Perkins (D-Ky.) took to the floor to set in motion the effort to extend ESEA before the new Administration could formulate an alternative position. Perkins had surveyed some four thousand school superintendents across the country, and now reported that they wanted the federal aid bill extended with larger appropriations.[14]

While Congressmen are often pictured in textbooks as the passive recipients of the urgings of pressure groups, here their role was clearly different: the committee leaders actively mobilized the constituents of the programs they wished to continue, then used hearings and floor debate to provide a platform for the pressure groups they helped generate. In contrast to the textbook image, both executive agencies and groups within Congress do in fact frequently try to stimulate the organization of pressure groups to function as local constituencies for the programs they support. In this case the ESEA supporters organized so fast and so well that the Administration didn't get a program off the ground that year.

Hearings began quickly and the Committee Democrats voted out a bill providing a five-year extension and authorizing up to $5 billion a year. The committee sent the bill to the floor, calling it the "No. 1 priority education need."[15] The fact that Congressional leaders were ready to act before the executive branch had even formulated a policy, was an interesting rebuttal of another stereotype: that of a Congress unable to function without the White House calling the signals.

Democrats were trying to force the issue and deny the new President any significant influence on the basic school program throughout his first term. The strategy was particularly audacious, since the House GOP had fought bitterly for a very different type of school aid only a year before Mr. Nixon's election. As the Democrats rushed the bill to the House floor, the GOP committee minority reported its "intense frustration."[16]

In the end, a split in Democratic ranks forced the party leaders to make some compromises. Representative Edith Green (D-Ore.), a maverick with considerable influence on school legislation and close ties with Southern conservatives, urged a shorter extension.[17] Even Speaker McCormack's unusual personal appeal on the House floor failed to stop the GOP-Southern coalition's drive for a shorter extension. For the Republicans the stakes were very high. "Make no mistake about it," said one member, "this bill is a test round on whether the Democrats can deep-freeze the Great Society until it's ready to be exhumed by a Democratic President in four years."[18]

The critical vote produced a strong 235-184 margin for Mrs. Green's compromise. The House voted to extend ESEA only two more years, and to take the first small step toward cutting down federal controls over the way the money could be spent. The President praised the conservative accomplishment.[19]

However, the dramatic defeat of the five-year bill obscured some basic facts. The central educational program of the Johnson Administration had been extended at least well into the third year of a GOP Presidency. A program with numerous critics, which had almost been killed in 1967 in spite of very strong Presidential support, was now preserved in the face of Presidential opposition. Given the normal gestation period for major new legislation, it was unlikely that the President could change education policy before he had to face a reelection campaign. Not only would the program continue, but the House had supported a very large authorization level. While authorization figures only set the ceiling, not the floor, on future yearly appropriations, a high figure generates expectations and raises the aspirations of lobbyists.

A central liberal program had survived the Presidential transition. The President had not used the good will and strong influence of the "honeymoon" period of the new Administration to reverse school policy. Given the mounting strength of local constituencies that grow up around major grant programs after several years of operation, the President had lost his last real opportunity to fundamentally reshape the basic structure of federal aid.

The President's Drive for Cutbacks Although the Nixon Administration had only vague ideas about many educational issues, it had a strong and consistent position on budgetary matters. Perhaps the most basic motivation behind the whole long struggle culminating in the enactment of ESEA had been the need for more federal resources for overburdened local school systems. The basic idea was that the federal government would relieve the great pressure on local tax systems by assuming a growing share of national school costs. This was, of course, a very expensive proposition. Educational costs were climbing so rapidly that even maintenance of a constant fraction of the nation's school budget required a substantial yearly increase in federal money.

135

The fiscal impact of the growing federal responsibility for education was frightening to Nixon Administration officials working within the tight budgetary framework set by the new President's pledge to cut taxes. If educational costs grew rapidly, it would substantially narrow the already small range of fiscal options available to the President. From the first year of the Eisenhower Administration to the last year of the Johnson Administration, federal aid to education had increased from less than $0.3 to $4.1 billion. During the 1965 fiscal year, federal school costs had been only about a third of the level reached four years later.[20] There was strong pressure from the affected constituencies for rapid continued growth of the programs—pressure reflected in the high authorization figures written into the bill extending ESEA.

The Administration responded to the dilemma with some recommendations for sharp cuts in the education budget proposals that President Johnson had sent to Congress only weeks before leaving office. President Nixon wanted to actually cut spending $450 million below the previous year. In the midst of a school year where the average cost of educating a student had gone up more than 12 percent since the previous year, the President was calling for a major cutback in federal dollars.[21] His own school officials were directly opposed.[22]

Racing a common threat, the education groups rapidly formed a coalition against the President's program. The Emergency Committee for Full Funding of Education Programs organized around the lowest common denominator of winning full authorized levels of annual appropriations for all the major school programs. The various education lobbies, totaling some fifty national organizations, collected funds and hired a very influential former Congressional staffer, Charles Lee, to coordinate the operation. Lee had run the staff of the Senate Education subcommittee during the period when all the major school bills of the mid-1960s had been hammered out, and he had extensive contacts with a wide variety of groups and members of Congress.

With survival of their programs at stake and severe and rapid budget cuts threatened, the groups found common ground. While some might fully agree, for instance, that the impacted areas program* was a waste of money, they were glad to ally themselves with forces that had real influence in almost every

---

* This was a popular old program that gave unrestricted federal aid to school districts "impacted" by students from military bases or from families of other concentrations of federal employees.

136

Congressional district in the country, and that had a remarkable record of defeating attempts by successive Presidents to cut back the program. With a small budget and an office in a hotel near the Capitol, Lee could draw on the extraordinary web of Capitol Hill contacts developed by all the various groups, and the leaders of the Emergency Committee could pool their capabilities to mobilize diverse and important constituencies at home. The programs involved were simultaneously able to rally local mayors and school boards, the huge teachers organizations, the book publishing and education materials industries, state school officials, the Catholic Church leadership, and many other interests ranging from supporters of vocational education to defenders of children needing rehabilitation. Obviously, such constituencies had to be taken seriously in Congress.

Instead of exploiting the many potential divisions within the education groups and within Congress, the Administration's budget posture created an unprecedented sentiment for unity. A simple common program was developed, calling for a united fight to raise the education budget by a billion dollars.

The coalition reflected a broad consensus about the need for more money, which even had some supporters within the Administration. In early June 1969, for example, the Cabinet Subcommittee on Education called for federal help in meeting normal school costs in every district, and for rewards for states making special efforts. The report contained HEW data documenting the very difficult job local officials confronted in even maintaining existing school services.[23]

The impact of mounting concern about the Nixon budget cuts was apparent in early June, when HEW Secretary Robert Finch appeared before the Senate Labor and Public Welfare Committee. He heard the ranking Republican member, Jacob Javits, attack the cuts as "severe" and label them a threat to the priority of education. The proposals, Javits concluded, "have the effect of repealing some . . . programs by eliminating their funds entirely. Other programs face emasculation because they stand to be funded at less than half the authorizations." Chairman Ralph Yarborough (D-Tex.) expressed his angry conclusion that school programs had "taken one of the heaviest blows of all" in the Administration's domestic program retrenchments.[24] On the floor, Senator Edmund Muskie (D-Maine) called for Congressional initiative.[25]

Rebellion on the Floor   Usually a President committed to holding down expenditures on domestic programs can count   137 on crucial support from the House Appropriations Committee, the predominantly conservative and vastly powerful group that initiates all spending bills. Normally the President's request provides the beginning point for the committee, which sets out to cut down the executive-branch recommendations. The basic premise of the committee's work is that there is waste to be eliminated. Committee members usually see themselves as the taxpayers' representatives in guarding the Treasury from visionary schemes of bureaucrats. The most detailed study of the committee yet prepared shows that more than three-fourths of the time executive proposals are cut.[26]

At the time of the budget battle, not only did the Appropriations committees in both houses reflect the conservatism of their members, but their influence had been further magnified by the rarity of successful challenges to their recommendations. Over a twelve-year period committee bills were adopted without change more than 87 percent of the time.[27] The committees had so much power over so many projects, and were so respected for their specialized knowledge and careful work, that they could seldom be reversed.

The Nixon cuts, however, were too much for the House Appropriations Committee, and a rebellious mood on the floor soon warned committee members that they might in fact suffer embarrassing defeats unless they proposed substantial increases in the President's budget. The signs of unusual pressure were apparent as the Appropriations subcommittee was finishing up its hearings. After months of examination of concerned officials, the subcommittee was flooded by members of Congress bringing with them educational leaders from all over the country to push for full funding. Education and Labor Chairman Carl Perkins, for example, came before the subcommittee with a group calculated to demonstrate the range and force of the coalition now forming around the budget fight. He brought leaders of the American Association of School Administrators and the U.S. Catholic Conference, a state education expert from Alabama, the President of a major southwestern state university, and the director of instructional materials from a Washington suburban school system that enrolled many children of Congressmen.

Perkins and others came to these meetings armed with information detailing the devastating impacts of the budget cuts in the operation of specific local programs across the country. The mounting pressure on the subcommittee was evident in an exchange between Appropriations Subcommittee Chairman

Daniel Flood (D-Pa.) and the Catholic spokesman, after the religious leader spoke of a coming "tidal wave" of protests:

> MR. FLOOD   You mean there is another one coming?
> MONSIGNOR DONOHUE   You have not heard from the Catholic schools yet.
> MR. FLOOD   Oh, yes, I have.
> MONSIGNOR DONOHUE   Not to the extent that you may well hear in time.
> MR. FLOOD   We have been using the term "avalanche" here.[28]

Even before the House showdown, there was a successful assault on the Appropriations Committee in the Senate in June. Education supporters succeeded in writing into a supplemental appropriations bill an amendment permanently exempting the Office of Education from any spending ceiling Congress might later set. The amendment carried 52-43, as GOP Leader Dirksen berated the "very effective school lobby."

The decisive fight, however, came in July, when the House Appropriations Committee brought the HEW bill to the floor. The Committee had increased Mr. Nixon's budget somewhat, but it was wholly unprepared for the impressive lobbying effort staged by the groups in the full-funding coalition. The National Education Association (NEA) brought in teachers, while the National School Boards Association arranged for influential board members from the home districts of undecided Congressmen to visit them in their offices. The special interest groups outlined the consequences of the votes for the programs that individual members cared most about. Watchers were conspicuously present in the galleries to prevent members from backtracking on nonrecord votes. One opponent apparently even underwent a last-minute conversion when he spotted his local bishop up in the gallery watching. There was even a coordinated command operation, including active sympathetic Congressmen on the floor reporting back information. The pressure was strong enough to convince even the GOP national chairman, Representative Rogers Morton (R-Md.), to oppose the President.

The vote ended in a stunning defeat for the President and the Committee on Appropriations. The floor manager for the Administration, Representative Robert Michel (R-Ill.), declared: "Our committee has been rolled for more money than I can recall in all my years as a member."[29]

After the House victory the bill was delayed for months in the Senate. In October 1969, House Appropriations Chairman

George Mahon (D-Tex.) brought a routine "continuing resolution" to the floor to permit HEW to continue spending at the previous year's level. However, even before the Senate voted on the new appropriations bill, education supporters decided to resist this resolution and try to force HEW to spend at a higher level.

Representative Mahon saw the proposal as an unprecedented attack on his committee and on the integrity of the appropriations process. The powerful Texan appealed to the House's respect for the committee system and for regular procedure.

> I do not want to see the Committee on Appropriations discredited. Like other Members of this House, I do not want to be humiliated, or have the feeling myself, or have others feel, that I have failed to do my job, or that the 51 members of the Committee . . . have failed to do their job.[30]

Even this rather plaintive appeal from one of the dominant figures of the House, however, could not deter the education backers. More than half the total membership, led by Representative Cohelan (D-Calif.), had already submitted resolutions calling for immediate opening of the federal coffers. Even Mahon conceded the weakness of his position when he offered an alternative proposal increasing the budget $600 million. Mahon told the House that he had been assured that the Senate Appropriations subcommittee would report a bill out within two weeks.

The President tried to defeat the House measure. Minority Leader Ford announced that the President supported the Appropriations Committee. In fact, the White House said it would not spend any more money even if it were appropriated. "Approval of this resolution," Ford informed the House, "is an act of total futility, if you add on the Cohelan amendment. You will not get one more penny for all of these schoolchildren." Ford even threatened a Presidential veto, which would leave the entire executive branch without funds and members of the House without their paychecks.

Representative Brademas (D-Ind.) replied for the measure's supporters, expressing their frustration and anger:

> I must say, Mr. Chairman, I am getting a little resentful of the attitude taken by some Members of this body. They in effect say to those of us who do not sit in the Appropriations Committee, "Who do you think you are?" . . .
> . . . in July of this year, by a vote of 293 to 120, the Mem-

bers of the U.S. House of Representatives went on record as saying, "Mr. President, we think education is very important." . . . Look at the press gallery here. They have been writing articles about the fact that there is something new going on this year in the Congress of the United States. For Congress is at long last becoming responsive to the concerns and priorities of the American people.

. . . I hope that having voted 2 to 1 in July for education, we are not going to hide behind a little parliamentary maneuvering that the public does not really understand and turn our backs on that commitment.[31]

When the vote came, the Appropriations Committee was routed. The House supported the increase 177-124.[32]

Conservatives blamed their defeat on the powerful new education lobby. Congresswoman Green (D-Ore.) said the school groups had made "a mockery of the legislative process" for a measure "that will last for a possible 30 or 60 days. . . . We are building up a lobby in this country that will make it impossible for us to exercise our best judgment as to what ought to be done in terms of quality education." Representative Mahon called the school group "the second most powerful lobby" in America.[33]

While the skillful organization of the school groups was certainly extremely important, the fact that the groups were successful in the House after repeated failures within the executive branch, requires an explanation. In spite of a chronic need for school funds across the country, the President's broad constituency and freedom to innovate had not led to a favorable White House response. From the White House perspective, problems of financing the Defense budget and controlling inflation had much higher priority than the needs of collapsing school systems. Congressmen—who tend to be responsive to the demands of any significant, unified, and powerful element of their constituencies—gave education a far higher priority.

The battle also, of course, illustrated some of the difficulties of Congressional policy leadership, especially in the face of a hostile committee chairman. To assemble a broad enough coalition to win, the bill's supporters had to fight for the lowest common denominator of all the groups: more money for everyone. The result was a bill that expanded programs of dubious importance along with those badly needed. In its inefficient way, however, the bill would accomplish the broad objective of pumping additional funds into the schools, with a significant fraction of the money going to systems facing fundamental problems.

The very day the House acted, thirty-five Senators introduced a measure with the same objective. "I feel confident that the Senate will uphold and even increase the amounts voted by the House," said Senator Montoya (D-N.M.). Since Congress was certain to approve higher appropriations, he observed, "the present continuing resolution represents the imposition of an unnecessary hardship on federally funded education programs."[34] Two weeks later the Senate made good Montoya's prediction by passing the resolution and sending it to the President.

President Nixon signed the resolution. With funding authority for most of the executive branch about to expire, he had little choice but to accept the bill authorizing the continuation of programs until Congress passed the regular appropriations bills. He did say, however, that he would impound the money.[35]

As the end of the session approached, the Senate finally voted on the regular HEW appropriations bill. After working out a compromise on a civil rights issue with the House, the conference committee report was finally adopted by the House on December 22.

The President was still threatening to veto the bill. The Christmas recess was coming up and the Constitution gives the President the right to an absolute veto—a "pocket veto"—when Congress is not in session. Senate leaders decided to deal with this threat by delaying final Senate action on the conference report until the new session in January 1970.[36]

The Senate strategy provided an interesting example of how the changing role of the President in education legislation was reflected in Congressional tactics. In earlier years education supporters had often held their legislation until the end of a session to deny the chief opponents, conservative Southerners, an opportunity to develop a major civil rights fight in the Senate. Now a major education bill had to be delayed until the next session to protect it from its new principal enemy, the President.

Veto and Compromise: January 1970   The first day of the new session, the Senate adopted the HEW money bill by a very strong margin of 74-17, dramatically challenging the President's program even before he had a chance to deliver his State of the Union address.

The reverse came in the face of White House resistance. The President's top advisor told the lobby representatives that a veto was certain, and tried unsuccessfully to turn the health group representatives against the education forces. The bill's supporters tended to see it as an effort, in Senator Mansfield's words, to move toward a balance "between foreign and military needs and our domestic needs." "It is strange," said the lobbyist for the American Federation of Teachers, "that President Nixon, who vigorously promoted billions and billions of dollars for an ABM missile system . . . now says it's inflationary to spend $1 billion extra for sorely needed school and education programs." Senator Kennedy called the issue "a basic matter of priorities," and pointed out that the sum of all appropriations bills was still billions below the President's budget.[37]

The President sought public support for his position with the first veto ever signed before a national television audience. He described the bill as "the wrong amount for the wrong purposes and at the wrong time." While conceding that the programs were "politically popular," he charged that the bill was inflationary and that it "is in the vital interests of all Americans in stopping the rise in the cost of living." Congress, he asserted, should not force hurried and wasteful spending in the "same old programs." He sharply attacked the inequities in the impacted areas program and its failure to direct funds where they were most needed. The televised speech stimulated heavy mail in favor of the veto and led Senator Muskie to express his concern about Presidential tactics that created "an imbalance of forces."[38]

Access to national TV time is a principal asset of Presidential leadership. It is one that must be husbanded in order to avoid overexposure and public resentment. The way a President employs his television time is perhaps one of the best indices of his judgment about which issues are most important. This dramatic initiative clearly showed the high priority the President gave to holding down spending on social programs. It also illustrated the power of direct mass media contact with the people in enabling the President to turn the issue of proper support for the schools and health care into a question of "big spending" and inflation.

The education and health groups found themselves locked in a tough battle against a mobilized executive branch to gain enough Republican votes to create a two-thirds majority against the President. School and health lobbies launched "Operation Override," which brought some five hundred volunteer lobby- 143 ists into the House and Senate office buildings, while on its side the Administration pressed very hard for party loyalty. The Administration also sought to hold its forces together by quietly assuring supporters that the President would subsequently accept a smaller bill raising funds by about $450 million.

Congressional Democrats were delighted to be leading a fight for education during a Congressional election year. Senator Vance Hartke (D-Ind.) claimed that the President was using the bill as a scapegoat for inflation and economic stagnation. The President, he said, ignored the fact that Congress had sliced $5.6 billion from the Nixon budget, and would have cut deeper had not the President fought so hard for ABM and SST funds.

> Without Presidential support, Congress has tried to improve our education and health programs. . . . It is surely unrealistic to insist that Congress restructure these programs in the midst of the appropriations process. It is ironic that, having offered no leadership or guidance, President Nixon now criticizes those who are trying to meet some of our desperate domestic needs for being less than perfect.[39]

The House Democratic Steering Commitee, seldom able to agree on any major issue, unanimously resolved that the bill "must be given top priority." Majority Leader Carl Albert (D-Okla.) urged members "to demonstrate their courage of conviction." "The appropriations process," he reminded them, "is basically the prerogative of the Congress of the United States." In changing the priorities in the President's budget, he insisted, Congress had responded to "the insistence of the American people that education be given more, not less, support."

More surprising was the conversion of Appropriations Committee Chairman Mahon. Long an opponent of increased expenditures, he now called for overriding the veto. It was, he pointed out, already more than seven months into the fiscal year, and many districts had made commitments based on the increase voted by both houses. Congress, he maintained, could not be blamed for inflation, but only for transferring $5.6 billion from Mr. Nixon's programs to education, social security, and the housing bill. Even if the veto was beaten, the final budget would be within 0.2 percent of the original request.[40]

The Republicans argued economics and echoed the President's veto message. "In the past decade," declared the House

144 GOP Policy Committee, "the free spenders . . . created deficits

of $57 billion." This had produced an "increased cost of living" and all governmental programs were seriously threatened by inflation. Representative Al Quie (R-Minn.), the party's leading school expert, remarked that it was too late in the year for school districts to spend all the money carefully anyway. At the same time he assured worried members that the President was ready to reach a reasonable compromise after his veto was sustained.[41]

Since vetoes come to a vote almost immediately, there was little time, in the day and a half between the veto and the House vote, for a national debate or for receipt of regular constituent mail. The lobbying on both sides, however, was intense. The pressure focused squarely on the eighty-six Republicans who had voted against the President earlier.

The effort to change their positions began with the television speech, which had suddenly redefined the issue. Officials all over the executive branch made contacts with GOP Congressmen's offices needing program commitments. "The veto vote," said a high HEW official, "was regarded as similar to the Senate vote on Haynsworth in its importance and we told the Members so. The President couldn't afford to lose it on a number of grounds." [42]

The White House wrote to all GOP members during the recess, and agency officials telephoned them to urge party loyalty. One Congressional aide commented, "When five, six, seven Administration people begin contacting you, that's ridiculous." Groups including the U.S. Chamber of Commerce, the American Farm Bureau Federation, and the National Association of Manufacturers worked to generate local mail supporting lower appropriations.

The net impact of the lobbying supporting the President was impressive. Representative Durward G. Hall (R-Mo.) reported that 55,000 telegrams had been sent to Congress following the veto speech. When he checked his colleagues' offices he learned that the wires were overwhelmingly in support of Mr. Nixon.

The pressures on the other side were also very strong. The education groups, which had defeated the President by great margins on six votes already, made every effort to hold their gains. A centralized operation combining the strength of the huge teachers groups, the large and very effective AFL-CIO legislative staffs, the college representatives, the National School Boards Association, and others, represented a combination of lobbying power seldom seen on Capitol Hill. Lobbyists received detailed instructions and information was pooled twice daily.

145

In the end, however, the pressure for party regularity prevailed and the President's veto was sustained. The education forces fell fifty-two votes short of the required two-thirds majority, as fifty-seven Republicans who had earlier supported higher spending levels now voted with the President. The President even succeeded in turning around GOP members from liberal districts carried by Humphrey in the 1968 Presidential election.

The composition of the House minority that sustained the President's veto indicated something about the political base the President was representing. The President was strongest with older members and those from rural and suburban areas. Almost 80 percent of Congressmen representing cities voted to override the veto.[43]

The President's success in upholding his veto of money for very popular and widely supported programs, illustrated the broad sweep of negative power the veto gives to a President able to maintain. his leadership over a substantial fraction of his party in Congress. By calling on party loyalty and using the mass media to recast the issue, the President succeeded in imposing his will.

There was still no 1970 appropriation bill, however. When yet another round of Congressional action was finished, the contest ended in a compromise with the President agreeing to accept part of the increase in school funds. The House added a third of a billion dollars to the President's latest offer, and rejected a GOP effort to give the President discretion over 2.5 percent of the money. In so doing, it ignored Minority Leader Gerald Ford's warning of a virtually certain veto.

The final compromise with the Senate resulted in a bill raising the education budget a total of about $600 million from the President's initial request, and giving him the right to withhold 2 percent of the HEW appropriations. Although the President had singled out the impacted areas program for particular criticism in his veto message, ridiculing its tendency to channel aid to rich suburban districts that did not need it, he now accepted a bill that provided the largest increase for this program and cut back proposed increases for schools serving poor children. In his fight, one commentator remarked, the President had "saved the bathwater and thrown out the baby." [44]

The struggle between the President, wishing to sharply cut back school expenditures, and the Congress, pressing for substantial expansion, resulted in a limited success for Congress.

146

The budget did grow: the Office of Education would enter subsequent budgetary tussles with an established base appropriation more than $.5 billion higher than the President wanted. More than that, the Appropriations Committees, the White House, and the GOP leadership had all experienced the high political costs of restricting school programs, while the Democrats had produced an issue for the fall elections. The conflict was a significant episode in the intensifying White House–Congressional conflict over national priorities.

Veto and Presidential Defeat: August 1970 Well before the 1970 HEW appropriation bill was signed (after two-thirds of the fiscal year had already elapsed), another chapter of the epic confrontation was unfolding as Congress worked on the bill for the 1971 fiscal year.

President Nixon did not try to cut school programs in his new budget, but rather aimed to hold the figure to a modest increase. The President proposed to spend $3.8 billion, a figure that was up $600 million from the one he had submitted in the previous January, and very close to the program he had reluctantly accepted in the end.

The bill was further increased by the House Appropriations Committee, which added $300 million to the President's request. The bulk of the new money went to the ESEA program for poor children, college student loans, and vocational education, with smaller increases for a variety of programs. The net impact of the year of political battle was to persuade the powerful committee to bring to the House floor a bill almost a billion dollars above the one it had tried unsuccessfully to defend a year earlier.

Given the increased committee budget, the education groups made no major effort to raise the figure. The House was spared the intense political pressure of the previous years. The Emergency Committee for Full Funding of Education Programs made an unsuccessful floor effort to restore an $80-million cut in impacted areas money. The school groups were not deeply concerned, however. The director of the Emergency Committee conceded that "it's not a bad bill in many respects."[45]

The Senate Appropriations Committee compounded the President's difficulties by raising the bill another $390 million. When the bill finally passed the Senate, it was about a billion dollars over the President's request.

Just seven months after vetoing one school bill, the White House was presented with another appropriation measure far exceeding the President's proposal. When the conference committee finished its work on the bill and both houses gave final approval, the net increase stood at $453 million. Education supporters hoped that the compromise would be acceptable to President Nixon. The bill went to the President with an overwhelming show of support on Capitol Hill. Final Senate passage came on an 88-0 vote, while the House approved the measure 357-30.[46]

As the President considered the bill, there were powerful political reasons for signing. Not only did the bill have very broad Congressional support, but the polls showed public opinion favoring better school financing. The President had already weakened his position in a series of losing battles with Congress. Within the last year he had been rebuffed on two Supreme Court nominees and had encountered very serious difficulties in defending his ABM and SST programs. That summer the Senate had struck at the President's authority in foreign affairs by passing the Cooper-Church amendment forbidding the use of any appropriated funds for extension of the American invasion of Cambodia.

Furthermore, the President had been badly defeated in Congress earlier that same summer after he vetoed a very popular hospital construction bill without even talking to GOP Congressional leaders. Less than a hundred members of the House and only nineteen members of the Senate had stood with the President.[47] He was clearly vulnerable.

The President had to decide not only on the Office of Education bill but also on a big appropriation for the Department of Housing and Urban Development. Observers thought he might well veto the HUD bill, which had a less organized and less powerful constituency, and quietly sign the school measure.

President Nixon, surprising his own advisors, decided that consistency on the inflation issue required a veto of both bills. Worried GOP Congressional leaders told the President that he would not only be defeated on the school bill, but would also put men up for reelection under terrible conflicting pressures.[48]

The President claimed, in his veto message, that his budget proposal and his forthcoming bill for desegregation assistance already made ample provision for education. Congress, he insisted, had merely raised "spending on old approaches that experience has proved inadequate." He described his veto as an essential step to "hold down the rising cost of living."

148

> Taken individually, there is much that can be said in favor of every spending bill. . . .
>
> But a President is not elected to see any one bill in isolation. He must see them as part of a whole, because his constituency is 200 million Americans.
>
> Acting in the best interest of the nation as a whole, and concerned with the average family struggling to make their incomes meet rising prices, I have drawn the line against increased spending.[49]

The President used his message to claim the role of representative of a truly national constituency that critics of Congress have often claimed for the Presidency. That constituency was interpreted by him as supporting the assignment of a relatively low priority to education. Rather than chance the marginal inflationary impact of an addition of far less than 1 percent to the federal budget, the President chose to risk the further weakening of overburdened public school systems, particularly in the large cities. Mr. Nixon's chosen role had very little resemblance to some of the romantic textbook descriptions of Presidential progressivism.

Congressional reaction was angry. Senator Magnuson (D-Wash.), the bill's floor manager, expressed weary surprise. Pointing out the tremendous effort to complete action on the school money bill earlier than any time in the past twelve years, and also the great consensus behind the compromise, he was appalled to be facing another fight just weeks before the new school year.

> We thought that 445 yea votes out of 475 voting Members of the House and Senate was substantial enough to impress the President on what the legislative branch considered an appropriate minimum amount of Federal money to help provide a better education.[50]

Senator Yarborough (D-Tex.) condemned the President for failing to speak to "the state of the education system or its needs" while instead blaming the general problems of the economy on school expenditures. "The bill," the Senator asserted, "was vetoed not because of its relationship to the education system, but for its relationship to the price structure. I ask Senators to consider when they can recall any administration program for a military contract limited and cut back because of its impact on the economy." [51] "I am for fighting inflation as much as anyone," declared Senator Quentin Bur-

149

dick (D-N.D.), "but I must question the President's logic in continually asking the poor, the sick, and the schoolchildren to carry the burden of this fight." [52]

After a short debate the Senate voted. The President was defeated 77-16. Not a single Democrat voted to sustain the veto, and even a large majority of Republicans turned against Mr. Nixon.[53]

The House quickly joined the Senate. The battle was settled and the President had another serious Congressional defeat. The budget was enlarged and the school programs had a bigger base for future contests. Far from being held at a fixed level that would gradually be eroded by inflation, the federal school commitment was still a growing one.

The same battle over money unfolded again in 1971, but the President had learned from his earlier defeat and accepted the decision in Congress. In April 1971 the House passed a bill $130 million over the President's request, and failed by only four votes to support the effort of the Emergency Committee for Full Funding to add another $728.6 million. The fear of another bruising and divisive battle influenced the outcome of the House vote, as did the failure of the education coalition to pull its legislative package together until just days before the decisive vote.[54]

On the Senate side the President's program was badly beaten. The Senate bill was more than $900 million over the Nixon proposal. In conference the two houses agreed on a budget halfway between the House and Senate figures, thus setting the stage for another possible veto.

The President signed the bill. He announced that there would have to be "offsetting reductions elsewhere in the budget to maintain fiscal stability." For the first time since he took office, the President approved a school funds bill as it came from Congress. "This will make Federal funds available to schools and colleges earlier than at any other time in recent years," he announced, adopting one of the arguments recently used against him, "thus permitting careful planning for the fall term by our educational institutions." [55]

Two costly battles with Congress had raised the priority of education. The programs had not changed significantly and the inflation problem remained very serious—so serious that the President would embark on a drastic new economic policy the next month. Nonetheless, the President signed. The largest education appropriation in American history—$5,146,000,000—quietly became law.[56]

NOTES

[1] Robert Bendiner, *Obstacle Course on Capitol Hill* (New York: McGraw-Hill, 1964); Hugh Douglas Price, "Race, Religion, and the Rules Committee: The Kennedy Aid-to-Education Bills," in Alan F. Westin, ed., *The Uses of Power* (New York: Harcourt, Brace, and World, 1962), pp. 1–77.

[2] George H. Gallup, *The Gallup Poll* (New York: Random House, 1972), Vol. 3, pp. 1712–13.

[3] James L. Sundquist, *Politics and Policy: The Eisenhower, Kennedy, and Johnson Years* (Washington: Brookings Institution, 1968), pp. 155, 187.

[4] Eugene Eidenberg and Roy D. Morley, *An Act of Congress* (New York: Norton, 1969), pp. 7, 241–42; Stephen K. Bailey and Edith Mosher, *ESEA: The Office of Education Administers a Law* (Syracuse: Syracuse University Press, 1968), pp. 37–38; Congressional Quarterly, *Congress and the Nation*, (Washington: Congressional Quarterly, Inc., 1969), Vol. 2, pp. 719–20.

[5] Bailey and Mosher, pp. 27–28.

[6] Philip Meranto, *The Politics of Federal Aid to Education in 1965* (Syracuse: Syracuse University Press, 1967), pp. 91–92.

[7] Congressional Quarterly, *Politics in America*, 3rd ed. (Washington: Congressional Quarterly, Inc., 1969), p. 68.

[8] Eidenberg and Morley, pp. 207–11; *Washington Post*, December 6, 1967; Gary Orfield, *The Reconstruction of Southern Education: The Schools and the 1964 Civil Rights Act* (New York: Wiley, 1969), Chapter 7.

[9] *Congressional Record*, June 26, 1968, pp. H5655–56.

[10] *Ibid.*, p. H5617.

[11] Congressional Quarterly, *Nixon: The First Year of His Presidency* (Washington: Congressional Quarterly, Inc., 1970), pp. 45-A–46-A.

[12] Rowland Evans, Jr., and Robert D. Novak, *Nixon in the White House: The Frustration of Power* (New York: Random House, 1971), pp. 10, 12.

[13] *Nixon: The First Year*, p. 45-A.

[14] *Congressional Record*, January 30, 1969, pp. H607–11.

[15] *Ibid.*, April 21, 1969, p. H2819.

[16] *Ibid.*, p. H2823; *Congressional Record*, April 22, 1969, p. H2888.

[17] *Congressional Record*, April 22, 1969, p. H2898.

[18] *Ibid.*, April 23, 1969, pp. H2888, H2972, H2997; *Newsweek*, May 5, 1969, p. 32.

[19] *Washington Post*, April 24 and May 1, 1969.

[20] Tax Foundation, *Facts and Figures on Government Finance* (New York: Tax Foundation, Inc., 1971), p. 169.

[21] Charles L. Schultze with Edward K. Hamilton and Allen Schick, *Setting National Priorities: The 1971 Budget* (Washington: Brookings Institution, 1970), p. 61.

[22] *New York Times*, June 5, 1969; House Committee on Appropriations, Subcommittee on Departments of Labor and Health, Education, and Welfare, *Hearings, Departments of Labor and Health, Education, and Welfare Appropriations for 1970*, Part 5, 91st Cong., 1st Sess., 1969, pp. 10–11.

[23] *Congressional Quarterly*, July 18, 1969, pp. 1297–99.

[24] *Washington Post*, June 12, 1969.

[25] *Congressional Record,* June 9, 1969, p. S6137.

[26] Richard F. Fenno, Jr. *The Power of the Purse: Appropriations Politics in Congress* (Boston: Little, Brown, 1966), p. 312; Murray L. Weidenbaum and John S. Saloma III, *Congress and the Federal Budget* (Washington: American Enterprise Institute, 1965), p. 126.

[27] Aaron Wildavsky, *The Politics of the Budgetary Process* (Boston: Little, Brown, 1964), p. 55.

[28] House Committee on Appropriations, Labor and HEW Subcommittee, Part 7, 1969, p. 100.

[29] Lucille Eddinger, "Lobby Profile: Education Coalition," *National Journal,* November 1, 1969, pp. 48–51.

[30] *Congressional Record,* October 28, 1969, pp. H10109, H10111.

[31] *Ibid.,* pp. H10118, H10131, H10134–35; *National Journal,* November 1, 1969, p. 16.

[32] *Congressional Record,* October 28, 1969, p. H10139.

[33] *Ibid.,* p. H10122; *National Journal,* November 1, 1969, p. 16.

[34] *Congressional Record,* October 28, 1969, p. S13381.

[35] *National Journal,* November 22, 1969, p. 169.

[36] *Ibid.,* December 20, 1969, pp. 383–84; December 27, 1969, pp. 436–37.

[37] *Congressional Quarterly,* January 23, 1970, pp. 209–10; *National Journal,* January 17, 1970, pp. 117–18.

[38] *Congressional Quarterly,* January 30, 1970, pp. 256–57; February 6, 1970, p. 348.

[39] *Congressional Record,* January 28, 1970, p. S739.

[40] *Ibid.,* pp. H404, H456, H391–92.

[41] *Ibid.,* pp. H398, H455.

[42] *National Journal,* January 31, 1970, p. 216.

[43] *Congressional Quarterly,* February 6, 1970, p. 348; *National Journal,* January 24, 1970, pp. 159–62; January 31, 1970, pp. 215–16.

[44] *National Journal,* February 21, 1970, p. 381; February 28, 1970, p. 470; March 7, 1970, pp. 487–88.

[45] *Ibid.,* April 18, 1970, p. 1117.

[46] *Ibid.,* May 23, 1970, pp. 814–15; *Congressional Record,* August 17, 1970, p. S13638.

[47] *Newsweek,* July 13, 1970, p. 39.

[48] *Time,* August 24, 1970, p. 10; *Newsweek,* August 24, 1970, pp. 13–14.

[49] *Congressional Record,* August 18, 1970, p. S13640.

[50] *Ibid.,* p. S13638.

[51] *Ibid.,* p. S13641.

[52] *Ibid.,* pp. S13651, S13654.

[53] *Ibid.,* p. S13659.

[54] *New York Times,* April 8, 1971; *Washington Post,* April 8, 1971.

[55] *New York Times,* July 12, 1971.

[56] *Washington Post,* June 11, 1971.

8

WILL the FEDERAL ROLE BE REDUCED?

ESEA Again: Presidential Delays and Congressional Action

In March 1970, more than a year after he became President, Mr. Nixon sent Congress an education message. His central concern was for reform and "re-examination of our entire approach to learning." His major proposals were for a new organization to stimulate educational research and for a Presidential commission to study school finance requirements.

The President discussed the accumulating evidence from research on school achievement which indicated that readily measurable increases in achievement scores were not produced by increased school spending, curriculum changes, or even lower student-teacher ratios. The President described the learning process as a "mystery" and declared that a new National Institute of Education was required to develop "new measures of educational output."

> In the last decade, the Government launched a series of ambitious, idealistic, and costly programs for the disadvantaged, based on the assumption that extra resources would equalize learning opportunity and eventually help eliminate poverty. . . .

However, the best available evidence indicates that most of the compensatory education programs have not measurably helped poor children catch up.[1]

The President's major specific proposal was for the "Right to Read" effort proclaimed as a central goal by his Commissioner of Education. Here again he relied mostly on research, supporting only modest increases in library and innovative projects funds that he had earlier cut back sharply.

While citing research findings against expansion of existing compensatory programs, he ignored indications that what most clearly influenced learning was the composition of the student body. Evidence that children learned primarily from other children—evidence that supported efforts to produce economic and racial integration in the schools—was disregarded.

Nor did the President make any decision on the other key school issue—how to bear the fiscal burden of rapidly increasing local school costs. Clearly, increasing the federal role in meeting the largest single burden of many local and state governments had been a basic motivation, both in the long struggle for federal aid and in the annual battles over appropriations levels. A severe financial crisis was evident, with school systems in some major and smaller cities facing forced closings, frequent defeats of bond issues, and cutbacks in the quality of school programs. Mr. Nixon's answer was the creation of the President's Commission on School Finance, which would study the problems for two years.[2]

While the President proposed further studies and a White House commission—the classic devices for keeping options open and for avoiding any short-term budgetary impact while maintaining an appearance of action—Congress was busy already. In January 1970 the Senate Labor and Public Welfare Committee had reported out a massive $35-billion bill extending the Elementary and Secondary Education Act for four more years. The bill began a dramatic alteration of the impacted areas program by providing that all children in public housing be counted as creating federal "impacts" on the local school system—a change that could add as much as a quarter billion dollars to the impacted areas effort, and substantially alter its whole character. The Senate bill also broadened the base for assistance under the large Title I program for poor children, raising the income floor for those families counted in allocation formulae from $3000 to $4000.[3]

154   The greatly expanded Senate bill passed before the Presi-

dent's education message had even been submitted. The Senate endorsed the measure 80-0.[4]

While the House and Senate conferees worked on a final bill, the President's message went to Congress. The Congressional reaction was angry and the conferees continued their work. The message from the White House was, in Presidential Counsellor Daniel Moynihan's words, "We're busted." The President of the National Education Association responded that the message was "another example of how this Administration underestimates the intelligence of the American people," accusing Mr. Nixon of glossing over the fact that the federal share of the nation's school costs had declined from "8 per cent in fiscal 1968 to 6.6 percent in fiscal 1970." "Money is the important thing," affirmed an American Federation of Teachers spokesman. "Lack of money is what has caused the present deterioration of the schools." Representative Perkins (D-Ky.) suggested that the research proposal was "camouflage," and Representative Roman Pucinski (D-Ill.) decided that it "looks like he wants to duck the problem for another two years."[5]

Less than a month after the President's message, the conference committee bill came to the Senate. In place of the two-year, $12-billion authorization supported by the President, the conferees had substituted a three-year extension, permitting possible funding for a fourth year. The bill authorized future appropriations up to $25 billion. The conference bill also largely defeated the Administration's effort to consolidate categorical programs—the special-purpose, often overlapping programs with detailed federal administrative requirements. The measure accepted both the broadening of the base for Title I costs, and the provision of funds for public housing residents in the impacted areas program. The bill created an adult basic education program for adult training in high school subjects, and greatly expanded bilingual education programs primarily intended to deal with severe learning problems of Spanish-speaking children. After only minutes of discussion, the Senate adopted this bill 74-4.[6]

The House took up the bill a few days later. During the final debate, Majority Leader Albert reviewed the record of Congressional leadership in the shaping of this and previous ESEA measures:

> In all of these areas the initiative for these measures came from within the Education and Labor Committee rather than from the executive branch of the Government. . . .

155

H.R. 514 . . . was introduced by Chairman Perkins on the very opening day of the 91st Congress, January 3, 1969. Hearings commenced on January 15 but Secretary Finch was not prepared to testify until March 10, the last day of the hearings. The Education and Labor Committee promptly cleared H.R. 514 on March 18 and it was passed by the House on April 23.

At every stage of the legislative process, Chairman Perkins had to doggedly fight the efforts of the administration to reduce the duration and scope of this measure.[7]

The only significant opposition to the House bill was on racial grounds. Once again the conferees had eviscerated the House amendments against school integration. In spite of grumbling, however, opponents were unable to reverse the momentum of the legislation. The conference report was adopted by a massive 312-58 margin.[8] The basic education policy of the first Nixon Administration was set. The President had had very little to do with it.

The Budget Battle Escalates

The Election-Year Struggles Intense battles over the proper level of federal school aid had been a continuing feature of the Nixon period. It was not surprising that they reached their peak during the very ideological 1972 Presidential campaign and during 1973, when a President with a vast personal reelection mandate began to assert his domestic priorities with a new intensity.

The 1972 hearings began shortly after the President's State of the Union promise of a new approach to school finance and federal aid. In March the House's General Education subcommittee examined various school financing changes. The subcommittee chairman, Representative Pucinski, strongly urged federal assumption of one-third of the country's total school costs and the establishment of a national spending floor for all students. Pucinski agreed with the President's diagnosis about the inherent weaknesses of basing school budgets on the local property tax, which produced 53 percent of all funds for elementary and secondary schools, in contrast to less than 7 percent arising from the broad federal tax base.[9]

The struggle over national priorities emerged once again in a very concrete fashion during the debate on the HEW
156 budget for the 1973 fiscal year. Once again the Administration

submitted a standstill budget. Allowing for inflation, the proposal actually amounted to a cut in existing support for schools. Once again Congress rejected the President's recommendations and moved both to expand existing programs and to fund new efforts.

The HEW appropriation bill came to the House floor already carrying a substantial committee increase to the budget, and the education coalition succeeded in defeating the Appropriations committee and adding another third of a billion dollars for school programs on the floor. Appropriations Subcommittee Chairman Daniel Flood (D-Pa.) presented his committee's bill as an extremely generous one. "Now hold your hats," he announced, "it exceeds the budget by $912 million—exclamation mark."

> Now, everybody wants to hear this. Every man, woman and child in the country is affected by this next one. Everybody. Of course, the Department of Health, Education, and Welfare is where the big—and that is capital BIG—increases over the budget occur. Why? Because Flood wanted it. No. We can't kid the troops. . . . This is what the people want. That is why it is in there. Members know that. . . .
> . . . the committee has added—hold your seats—$915,836,-000. When we hear tomorrow, when amendments are being offered to this bill, about this penny-pinching, miserly Committee on Appropriations who could not care less about education, children, anything, put that in your pipes and smoke it.[10]

Even before the vote on the additional education package, there were rumors of a Presidential veto. The Majority Whip, Representative Tip O'Neill (D-Mass.), responded to these threats by reminding the members that the President's Defense budget request was already up $4.7 billion for the coming year, and that the Secretary of Defense had recently announced an additional $5 billion or more would be required to pay for accelerated bombing activities. "I trust," he said, "that our President will come down on the side of human life and human productivity." [11]

The next day Representative William Hathaway (D-Maine) introduced the amendment supported by the Emergency Committee for Full Funding. The largest part of the $364-million proposal was devoted to raising the average annual payment per child from a poor family from $133 to $150. The other significant increases were for library programs, impacted areas, adult education, and educational innovation projects. The amendment provided $10 million to initiate a program of impacted 157 area funding for public housing tenants—a sum that would be the first money actually put into a new program created in 1969.

The amendment was strongly opposed, both by the Appropriations Committee and the Administration. Representative Flood called it a "package" developed by groups that "meet in some hidden, mysterious place in the dead of night to concoct these amendments." It would only court a veto, he argued. Several members raised serious questions about the effectiveness of the compensatory education approach embodied in the large Title I program—questions based on extensive research findings. Representative O'Hara (D-Mich.), on the other hand, argued that failure to approve the modest program increases provided by the amendment, after the House had voted against desegregating urban schools, would show that "quality education will be nothing more than code words for racism."

On the decisive vote the education forces prevailed and the rarely defeated Appropriations Committee was again reversed. The House voted 212-163 to raise the education budget by another $364 million.[12]

As the bill neared final passage, the Republicans tried to give the President the right to cut $1.3 billion in expenditures from the massive bill, thus bringing it back to his original budget level. Minority Leader Gerald Ford called the amendment "the only way to insure that this loaded and bloated appropriation bill will not be vetoed." The GOP effort lost 137-209.[13]

When the bill got to the Senate, the Senate Appropriations Committee voted an additional $861-million increase, with most of the money going to health programs. Under the leadership of Senators Pastore (D-R.I.), Case (R-N.J.), and Percy (R-Ill.), education supporters campaigned on the Senate floor to raise school spending. Pastore obtained agreement on raising to the level of the House amendment funds for several programs cut by the Senate committee. Case fought unsuccessfully to add $50 million to the public housing provision of the impacted areas program, while Percy managed to win approval for $30 million more for this program, which the Administration intensely opposed. The Senate also sharply increased funds for the relatively new bilingual program, designed to serve some of the five million children whose learning was impaired by language difficulties.[14]

The debate was permeated by a sense of crisis in the educational system, particularly by those Senators whose states included large urban centers. Senator Hart of Michigan called the bill "the cutting edge of the debate over reordering national spending priorities." Detroit, he said, faced a deficit of $40 million in its public school budget. Senator Case of New Jersey spoke of the great problem of financing schooling for public housing children in cities with declining tax bases and rapidly increasing school costs. Senator Percy reported that broadening the impacted areas program was Mayor Daley's "No. 1 priority for Chicago schools and the 60,000 children there in public housing."

> We closed our schools in Chicago early this year because we ran out of money. We have a fiscal crisis there. There are over 80,000 children who would benefit . . . over the entire State.[15]

Senator Stevenson (D-Ill.) pointed out that Chicago had been forced to fire 630 teachers and cancel adult education, reading, and health programs to bring its deficit down to $68 million.[16] The Administration's only response to this crisis, however, was an assertion that education was really a local and not a national concern.

In the end, the Senate produced a bill $2.3 million over the President's budget for HEW. It passed handsomely 72-11.[17]

When the bill went to conference, the members agreed to a whopping $800-million increase in the President's education budget—a 24-percent rise in school spending. The increase was so sharp, however, that the usual bipartisanship in the conference committee broke down. In spite of loud veto threats and partisan division, the House adopted the bill, 240-167.[18]

President Nixon did indeed veto the bill, making an election-year attack on "reckless Federal spending that just cannot be done without more taxes or more inflation." [19] The President's veto was sustained in the House, receiving overwhelming GOP support and the votes of some Democratic conservatives, including the Appropriations Committee chairman.[20]

The House committee was back on the floor with another HEW bill just a month later. The White House threatened yet another veto unless Congress complied precisely with the President's spending ceiling. After the House and Senate reached agreement on a new bill exceeding the President's education spending request by $301 million, Mr. Nixon fired back another veto. Dramatically appealing for a fight against inflation, the President again held the GOP support necessary to sustain the veto.

Faced with a President unwilling to compromise, Congress had to surrender or come up with a new method to protect   159 its power. The President's opponents responded by refusing to pass a third appropriations bill and by operating for the entire year under a unique form of "continuing resolution." Continuing resolutions are normally used only to keep programs functioning at the level of the previous year's budget while the appropriation bill is pending. In its February 1973 resolution, however, Congress offered the President the choice between losing all authority to spend in his largest domestic department, HEW, and signing a resolution that imposed spending at least as high as the original House appropriation bill. In the end, the President signed this novel type of resolution calling for much more spending than the second bill he vetoed.

The Congressional triumph was short-lived. After signing the resolution, the President proceeded to ignore it, saying that no program would actually receive any more money than he had asked for in the first place. Administrators of some programs that Congress had expanded found themselves with nothing, since the President had recommended shutting down their programs. Under his theory of impoundment, the President attempted to make Congress's action meaningless.[21]

The President's Postelection Offensive After the President's massive reelection victory, following a campaign where he had harshly attacked government spending, things looked grim for education supporters. Within days of the election, the Administration's top education official, HEW Assistant Secretary Sidney Marland, Jr., predicted a "very spartan" school aid budget with no new programs. He hoped the budget wouldn't be "substantially lowered," and said attention would shift from budget levels to a renewed effort for revenue-sharing and antibusing legislation.[22] The President now had the advantage of a clear set of priorities and a strengthened hold on House Republicans. As a lame-duck President he need feel virtually no political incentive to compromise.

The President's leverage was enhanced by the fact that the Elementary and Secondary Education Act was due to expire within a few months of his second inaugural. If the President was adamant, the pressure for Congress to maintain the flow of school aid by adopting something he supported would be heavy.

The President's determination to fight was evident in a long interview with the *Washington Star-News* two days before his reelection. He pledged to stop "throwing dollars at problems" and to concentrate on "reform of existing institutions." Most of the programs of the 1960s, he said, "were massive failures" that the country should "shuck off" and "trim down." He saw the campaign as a contest between Democratic promises of spending additional billions, and his own determination to instill "a new feeling of responsibility, a new feeling of self-discipline."

> The average American is just like the child in the family. You give him some responsibility and he is going to amount to something. If, on the other hand, you make him completely dependent and pamper him and cater to him too much, you are going to make him soft, spoiled and eventually a very weak individual.[23]

In his inaugural address the President attacked the "condescending policies of paternalism—of 'Washington knows best.' " Americans, he said, had been "trusting too much in government." "Government must learn to take less from people so that people can do more for themselves." [24]

The new policy was very clear in his education budget. In spite of rapid inflation the budget actually called for a cutback in school spending. During a period when the average cost of educating a student was going up more than 10 percent a year, the President opposed even allowing a constant number of depreciating dollars for schools.[25] The day before he sent his drastic new budget to Congress, Mr. Nixon opened the political battle with a national radio address promising to hold down taxes by "keeping a tight lid on spending." He appealed for support against the "enormous pressure from special interests to spend your money for what they want."

> It is time to get big government off your back and out of your pocket. I ask your support to hold government spending down, so that we can keep your taxes and your prices from going up.[26]

The new budget was presented in a far more belligerent mood, including an open threat that even this level of funds would be denied unless Congress approved the President's education revenue sharing. Commissioner of Education Marland summed it up: "We stand on ERS, live or die." [27]

The response to the budget was hostile. Representative Perkins, the House committee chairman, said, "I'm really concerned that the Administration is backing away from support for education." The Senate chairman, Harrison Williams (D-N.J.), called it "an abdication of federal responsibility." 161

Senator Mondale warned that "we're not about to throw ESEA into the trashcan." Senator Stevenson dismissed it as a "gimmick" that ignored the need for more money. The education groups were sharply critical. Even the representative of the National School Boards Association, which had once supported revenue sharing, called the Administration approach "intellectually dishonest." Underneath all the "fanfare and promise," he said, "it's just the old shell game."[28]

The Administration's rigid commitment to cutting back the federal role in supporting education tended to draw together in common opposition a wide variety of education groups with very different interests. Refusing to deal seriously with the school organizations or to offer any incentives for change, the White House was unable to exploit internal differences or get rid of bad programs. Even representatives of groups with a very localized perspective, like the organization speaking for local school boards, now felt so little confidence in the Administration that they opposed a bill which was supposed to increase their power in spending federal funds.

Congress had rejected the President's proposed school budgets every year of his first term, and both houses soon set to work to repeat the pattern in the first contest of the second term. It became clear to HEW officials that they would have to make some compromise if any semblance of program consolidation was to be achieved. The pressure for compromise was increased by a number of court decisions challenging the President's power to impound funds, and by the erosion of the President's influence as the Watergate scandal developed. When the President changed his chief domestic advisor, replacing John Ehrlichman, an unbending conservative with thinly veiled contempt for Congress, by Melvin Laird, a former GOP House leader, conditions improved rapidly.

The White House released $77 million of the impounded funds, and HEW Secretary Frank Carlucci proposed a compromise whereby the Administration would accept only partial consolidation of some grant programs, and would offer $540 million in "forward funding" and thus allow administrators the luxury of more than a year's advance planning for at least part of their federal aid money. This resolution of the ruinous dilemma whereby school aid budgets remained wholly undecided until months after the school year began, seemed very attractive to education supporters.[29] However, even with this extra money, which could not be spent for more than a year, the President was still asking for $400 million less than the previous year's continuing resolution had provided. Representative Al Quie, the House GOP education spokesman, summed up the problem: "Consolidation is politically acceptable only if it carries the possibility of more money. The Administration approach appeared to mean less money.[30]

The House and Senate rejected the budget proposal. The conservative Senate Appropriations Committee leaders succeeded in holding off additional floor amendments, and sent to conference an HEW bill about 6 percent over the President's request. Senator Percy pointed out that it was barely enough to cover the 5.8-percent rise in the cost of living since the budget had been sent to Capitol Hill.[31]

The conference committee lowered the Senate bill a half billion dollars, leaving the total appropriations for HEW $700 million below the previous year, although the school budget was still up $946 million.[32]

When the bill returned to the House floor, however, it was assailed by members angry over the omission of a "hold harmless" formula that would prevent sudden loss of money for individual school districts. In an era of stagnant or declining appropriations, members were often more concerned about avoiding sudden drastic changes at the local level than about the overall equity of the distribution formula. Anyone who suddenly lost a lot of funds was sure to protest. The bill went back to conference on a 272-139 vote.[33]

The conservatives who dominated the appropriations conference committee took advantage of the extra round to lop off another $400 million. Emboldened by their first real success in years in fighting off floor amendments, and by a White House veto threat as well, the conferees presented the cut as the only alternative to another year of operation under a continuing resolution. The committee tried to justify the cuts by claiming credit for rejecting a White House request to exempt the President from impoundment litigation—litigation that threatened to free hundreds of millions he had refused to spend the previous year.[34]

Some liberal critics charged a sellout. Representative Frank Thompson (D-N.J.) called it "a $400 million collapse." Representative Herman Badillo (D-N.Y.) declared the conferees had "played ball" with the Administration and wanted to involve Congress in the "misguided and inhuman campaign to balance its budget at the expense of our most vital social programs."[35]

The committee had the tactical advantage, however. The 163

bill seemed the only alternative to another year of utter confusion, and the "hold harmless" proviso would spread the losses around thinly. Protest was useless and the conference bill swept to an overwhelming victory.

In financial terms the 1973 bill was a real triumph for the President. After years of discouragement and confusion produced by a series of Presidential vetoes, Congress was at last sufficiently demoralized for the conservatives on the Appropriations committees to successfully slash the HEW budget. While the cuts were not drastic, an inflation rate of more than 8 percent assured a substantial decline in real federal support for educational programs.

The education supporters' defeat in Congress, however, was partly repaired by a victory over impoundment. Facing loss after loss in the courts and confronting dozens of legal actions, the President agreed to release $466 million of impounded education funds.[36] Thus the end result of the 1973 session of Congress was a standoff between the two sides.

As 1974 began, the President continued his traditional approach to the school budget in spite of his increasing danger of impeachment. The President's budget again called for revenue sharing, and proposed substantial dollar cuts in spending for the education of poor children, for those not speaking English, for the impacted areas program, and for library services. He also proposed to sharply cut back the program of aid for desegregating school districts.[37] Yet another bitter battle had begun.

The New Pattern in the Appropriations Process Year after year after year the President had struggled to restrain Congressional majorities supporting increased federal aid funding. The President's clear preference would have been for a frozen or declining level of dollars turned back to the states to be used as they wish. During a period of rapidly increasing school costs, the result would have been a sharp reduction in the already modest federal role in school finance. Not only would the scale of the effort have declined, but the money would have been spread so widely, with so few controls, that its impact would probably have been virtually invisible.

Under incessant White House pressure and the rare circumstance of consistent vetoes against education spending, Congress could do little more than protect the existing effort and gradually expand its budget. The Great Society drive that had

dramatically increased the federal role in education now gave way to trench warfare over the basic framework of that role. Congress's achievement was to preserve that framework.

The long struggle over money undermined the traditional beliefs about the nature of the appropriations process. In elementary and secondary education, the President was no longer the progressive initiator, and the appropriations committees were no longer the burying grounds of good programs. The President was now the principal conservative force and the chief obstacle to more resources for the schools. The Appropriations committees increased his budgets with monotonous regularity. They responded to a broad coalition of committee leaders, of many members of Congress, and almost all the country's major education groups—a coalition that worked to consolidate the legislative heritage of the Johnson Administration. Time after time this coalition demonstrated its wide and broad support in Congress, and thus frustrated the President's program.

The Nixon Counterproposal: Revenue Sharing

In 1971, and repeatedly in the following years, President Nixon argued that the proper federal role in education called for abandoning existing categorical programs, and turning over to state and local authorities the federal aid funds for a few broadly defined purposes. He presented the idea in 1971 as a basic part of his New American Revolution. The federal government, he insisted, had grown "musclebound," while the states and cities were "caught between the prospects of bankruptcy . . . and adding to an already crushing tax burden." [38]

The Democratic reaction was openly hostile. One House education spokesman, Representative John Brademas (D-Ind.), called the proposal "pablum." Another influential member of the Education and Labor Committee, Representative William Ford (D-Mich.), observed that the President was doing "absolutely nothing" about the central problem of money, that "he simply intends to rearrange existing funds." [39]

Support for the President's plan to consolidate thirty-three programs into a package of five broad objectives was so thin that both houses put off hearings for most of the year. When the witnesses were finally called, their reception was frosty.

HEW Secretary Elliot Richardson told the Senate committee that it would end the "jungle of federal guidelines, regulations, 165 application forms and evaluation requirements." Administration officials, however, conceded that the bill would have no impact on the financial crisis in big-city education, and confessed that they had no position on the proper response of the federal government to the court decisions that were undermining the use of local property taxes to finance public education.

The proposed bill divided the education groups, but most were suspicious. The more conservative groups, including the state superintendents' organization and the National School Boards Association, supported the approach at first with reservations. The big teachers' groups, the NEA and the American Federation of Teachers, attacked it as a way of avoiding the real issue of coming up with more money for the schools. The national organizations representing special groups like handicapped children and parochial schools defended the existing categorical arrangements, strongly preferring guaranteed support to a situation where they would have to fight for funds within each state.

Congressional criticism of the plan was particularly intense in the House committee, where the hearing was held shortly after the President's veto of a large child-development program. Chairman Carl Perkins opened up with an attack on efforts to destroy the Elementary and Secondary Education Act. The schools, he said, were in "desperate shape" and the basic need was for more federal money. Subcommittee Chairman Roman Pucinski belittled the bill as a mere "consolidation" ignoring the "crushing burden" of local taxation, which would "imperil the very continuation of public elementary and secondary education in our country." Even Congresswoman Edith Green, usually a fervent supporter of state control, called the bill a "farce," and announced she would support consolidation only if a serious financial commitment was made. Representative Brademas asserted the plan would merely render federal aid totally inconsequential. "To spread that modest amount of Federal money more broadly, and not target it . . . seems to me to be pouring a glass of water on the Sahara." [40] The proposal was dead for that session.

The President tried to revive the idea in his 1972 State of the Union address, coupling it with a promise of a "revolutionary" response to court decisions attacking the property tax.[41] Although a Presidential commission reported later in the year that the federal government should assume about a fourth of school costs, the President's promised recommendations were never made. News leaks that the Administration was considering a European-style value-added tax that would tax goods at each stage of their manufacture and sale, produced a heated Democratic attack. The Democrats charged that it would be no reform to replace an inequitable and imperfectly progressive system of property taxation by a blatantly regressive type of national sales tax. After the Presidential election the idea was quietly shelved. No proposal at all was made.

Although the revenue-sharing idea went nowhere during 1972, and the Congressional commitees displayed virtually no serious interest in it, the President for the third straight year renewed the drive in 1973. In his March 1 State of the Union message, he called for "expanding State and local control" through combining thirty different programs into a "single flexible authority" dealing with a "few broad areas." He asked for no new programs at all, except tax help for parents of children attending private schools.[42]

The President's unambiguously conservative strategy in sending the revenue-sharing bill to the Hill with a budget actually cutting the dollar levels of the previous year, sorely tried even his most fervent supporters. Senator Peter Dominick (R-Colo.), a deeply conservative loyalist Republican and the ranking GOP member of the Senate subcommittee, made unusually brusque remarks when introducing the bill:

> . . . I am doing this as a matter of courtesy; a courtesy which I might add was not extended to any of the minority members of the subcommittee in the form of a request for suggestions, advice or guidance. . . .
> I seize this opportunity to indicate my disinclination to being the passive and grateful recipient of . . . priorities devoid of any congressional input.[43]

One thing nobody at the White House had noticed was that their draft bill would sharply cut the funds going to Dominick's home state of Colorado.

The basic problem was that the Administration's approach called for a drastic reshuffling of increasingly well-established relationships and understandings within existing programs, without providing any clear benefits for educators. In fact the proposed cutback in the budget seemed to confirm the arguments of those who claimed revenue sharing was just a way for the Administration to abdicate any federal responsibility for the problems of the schools. When HEW official Charles Saunders said that revenue sharing was opposed by those "who 167 have a vested interest in maintaining the status quo," he was saying more than he intended. Those who felt that they were better off under categorical .programs included those with a vested interest in money for poor children, for big cities, for crippled and disabled children, and a variety of other groups with special programs. One HEW planner told the *National Journal* that the state officials to whom the Administration wanted to give broad discretion, didn't really want it: "They argued that such a percentage of discretion opened them up to battles from educational interests they would rather not fight." [44]

Once again revenue sharing failed to generate any significant Congressional support. After Melvin Laird replaced John Ehrlichman as the President's top domestic policy advisor, the air of confrontation gave way to a calmer approach. Laird, who had long been the dominant GOP member on the House Appropriations subcommittee controlling the HEW budget, had no desire to go through another year without an appropriation bill. By mid-June the Acting Commissioner of Education informed state school officials that the drive for revenue sharing would be deferred until 1974. In September HEW Secretary Carlucci even offered to raise the education aid budget, if Congress would make a partial move toward "revenue sharing" by consolidating some segments of overlapping programs.[45] Congress's refusal to act in 1973 initiated an automatic one-year extension of the Elementary and Secondary Education Act.

As revenue-sharing proposals ground to a halt in the house, the Senate subcommitee began to move in precisely the opposite direction to the President's plans. The subcommittee chairman, Senator Pell (D-R.I.), introduced a new basic bill designed to channel large new sums into general aid, support school fiscal equalization plans adopted by the states, and provide some relief from excessive property taxation. In addition, the bill attacked the performance of the existing administrators by proposing the creation of new statistical reporting and evaluation agencies outside HEW—agencies intended to deal with growing Congressional anger at the executive branch's failure to implement programs and provide Congress with the information it needed. Pell dismissed the President's bill as "a cynical insult to those of us who have worked . . . in order to place a fair share of the responsibility for education on the shoulders of the federal government." [46]

The push began again in January 1974, when the President 168 sent Congress an education message listing revenue sharing as his first priority. A President now facing an impeachment investigation no longer took so threatening a tone with Congress. "Last year," said Representative Perkins, "the administration told us to enact its special revenue sharing proposal or there would be no aid for elementary and secondary education. This year, there is no such threat." [47] Another opponent commented: "We'll give him something—maybe more form than substance—and he'll take anything he can get." [48]

The House committee took the initiative by reporting out a new bill early in the 1974 session, only to run into disputes over school busing and a formula that redistributed substantial funds from New York to a number of other states. The bill consolidated the administration of some programs, but left the basic structure of the largest ones intact. One principal defense of the compromise was the report that the President was apparently prepared to sign it and to negotiate in what Representative Al Quie, the GOP education spokesman, described as a "conciliatory mood."

> After 2½ years of no action on a 1971 bill to create special revenue sharing for education, the administration did abandon that effort and last fall began to work with us in a very cooperative way to gain enactment of what was realistic. . . . Our former colleague Mel Laird was of course a key factor in achieving this spirit of compromise.[49]

In place of consolidation of some thirty programs into a single fund, the House committee offered only a move to combine seven programs into two broader programs. While this change hardly amounted to the development of revenue sharing, and might well have been denounced as inadequate in the more strident period of the Nixon Administration, it was now gratefully accepted.

In a national radio speech shortly before final House action, President Nixon hailed the measure as "an important first step" toward more state and local control. He was willing to accept this but warned against the Senate bill, calling the committee draft a move "in precisely the wrong direction" that would create a "bureaucratic nightmare" producing "miles of red tape." If the bill came to him in that form, he announced, he would definitely veto it.[50]

Congress completed action on the Elementary and Secondary Education Act and the other basic school programs in the final days of the Nixon Administration. In late July 1974, Congress sent to the White House a $25 billion authorization bill setting 169 the nation's basic education policy until mid-1978. The bill rejected the President's antibusing proposals and made no significant move in the direction of revenue sharing. In fact, the measure established a series of new and expanded federal responsibilities, including schooling for handicapped children, development of community schools used for a wide variety of local functions, special efforts in reading instruction, larger bilingual programs, and an aid formula for the impacted areas program that accepted additional federal responsibility for financing the education of children living in federal housing projects. The legislation preserved and strengthened the basic structure of the Great Society education programs.

When President Ford took office he found the education bill on his desk, awaiting action. Three days after he was sworn in, in his first speech to a joint session of Congress, he announced he would sign the measure: "Any reservations I might have about its provisions—and I do have—fade in comparison to the urgent needs of America for quality education." Later, in signing the bill, Ford said his decision illustrated "a new spirit of cooperation and compromise . . . between the legislative and executive branches." He said he would soon submit advance funding requests for some programs so that local school administrators could have the uncommon convenience of rationally planning how to spend federal funds before a school year began.

Although the new President yielded to Congress' initiative in maintaining the basic structure of school programs, his early statements made it clear that battles on other major fronts were far from over. "I must be frank," he told Congress. "In implementing its provisions, I will oppose excessive funding during this inflationary crisis." When signing the bill he again underlined his commitment to hold down the school aid budget in spite of very rapid inflation in education costs.[51] Ford brought to the Presidency a long and deeply conservative House record on this issue and his early statements suggested that the annual White–House-Congressional contests would continue. The transition from one conservative President to another might moderate the harsh tone of the previous struggles because of Mr. Ford's more positive view of Congress' policy role, but the executive branch was likely to remain the principal obstacle to expansion of federal education programs.

Busing had been the most explosive and divisive issue in the school bill. A large number of House members had been willing to risk destruction of the entire bill unless the Senate would accept the Administration-backed efforts to restrain court-ordered desegregation. President Ford had strongly supported both the Administration plan and a proposed antibusing Constitutional amendment in the House. This issue too would recur.

Four years of Presidential pressure for Congressional enactment of the basic goal of Mr. Nixon's educational policy—revenue sharing—had proved an exercise in futility. This part of the President's New American Revolution ran squarely into determined resistance of the Democrats on the committees controlling education legislation. By neither threats of ending all federal aid, nor promises of budget compromises if they went along, nor conciliation, had he succeeded in producing any real change in the basic structure of education programs inherited from President Johnson. President Ford simply recognized this reality when he signed the ESEA bill.

Extending the structure of elementary and secondary school aid was a major Congressional victory. The programs had originally been enacted by a very liberal Congress in 1965 with powerful Presidential support. They represented a massive departure from the tradition of American education, and their implementation produced such serious controversy that they were almost converted into revenue sharing just two years later, in 1967. At that time all the energies of the Congressional leadership and the White House were exerted to protect the program. Now, in the face of five years of intense White House resistance, bitter and continuous funding battles, and two expirations of the basic statutes establishing ESEA, Congress held firm.

NOTES

[1] Congressional Quarterly, *Nixon: The Second Year of His Presidency* (Washington: Congressional Quarterly, Inc., 1971), p. 31-A.
[2] *Ibid.*, pp. 31-A–32-A.
[3] *National Journal*, February 14, 1970, pp. 338–39.
[4] *Ibid.*, February 21, 1970, p. 379.
[5] *Ibid.*, March 7, 1970, pp. 484–85.
[6] *Congressional Record* (perm. ed.), April 1, 1970, pp. 10020–21.
[7] *Ibid.*, April 7, 1970, pp. 10612–13.
[8] *Congressional Quarterly*, April 10, 1970, p. 947.
[9] *Ibid.*, March 11, 1972, p. 559.
[10] *Congressional Record*, June 14, 1972, pp. H5585–86.
[11] *Ibid.*, p. H5610.
[12] *Congressional Record*, June 15, 1972, pp. H5672–81.
[13] *Ibid.*, pp. H5711–12.
[14] *Congressional Record*, June 27, 1972, pp. S10331–62.

15 *Ibid.*, p. S10343.

16 *Ibid.*, pp. S10349–51.

17 *Ibid.*, pp. S10426–27.

18 *Congressional Record*, August 9, 1972, pp. H7397, H7413–14.

19 *Ibid.*, August 16, 1972, p. H7742.

20 *Ibid.*, p. H7743.

21 Robert W. Frase, "Five Years of Struggle for Federal Funds," *Publishers Weekly*, January 21, 1974, reprinted in *Congressional Record*, February 28, 1974, pp. E1000–03.

22 *Washington Star-News*, November 10, 1972, p. A-7.

23 Reprint of interview in *New York Times*, November 10, 1972.

24 *Congressional Quarterly*, January 27, 1973, p. 135.

25 "The Cost of Education Index, 1957–72," *School Management* (January 1972), pp. 24–25. The data for the 1966–72 period show that the cost per pupil had increased 56 percent in five years.

26 *Congressional Quarterly*, February 3, 1973, pp. 233–34.

27 Karen De Witt, "Education Report: Administration Revenue-Sharing Plan Unlikely to Get Passing Grade from Congress," *National Journal*, March 24, 1973, p. 418.

28 *Ibid.*, pp. 421–25.

29 *Washington Post*, September 20, 1973; *New York Times*, June 18, 1973.

30 *Congressional Quarterly*, September 15, 1973, p. 2424.

31 *Congressional Record*, October 4, 1973, p. S18620; October 9, 1974, p. S18840.

32 *Ibid.*, November 13, 1973, pp. H9916–19.

33 *Ibid.*, p. H9928.

34 *Congressional Record*, December 5, 1973, p. H10659.

35 *Ibid.*, p. H10664.

36 *New York Times*, December 20, 1973.

37 *Congressional Record*, February 6, 1974, p. H577.

38 *New York Times*, January 23, 1971.

39 *Ibid.*

40 *Congressional Quarterly*, November 6, 1971, p. 2287; November 13, 1971, p. 2359; House Committee on Education and Labor, *Hearings, Oversight Hearing on Elementary and Secondary Education*, 92d Cong., 1st Sess., 1971, pp. 10, 11–14, 15, 24, 27–29, 34.

41 *Congressional Record*, January 20, 1972, p. H147.

42 *Ibid.*, March 1, 1973, pp. H1271–72.

43 *Ibid.*, March 22, 1973, p. S5377.

44 De Witt, "Education Report: Administration Revenue-Sharing Plan . . . ," pp. 419–20.

45 *New York Times*, June 18, 1973; *Washington Post*, September 20, 1973.

46 Karen De Witt, "Education Report: Senate Bill to Extend Current . . . ," *National Journal*, May 5, 1973, p. 665.

47 *Congressional Record*, February 6, 1974, p. H577.

48 Evan Jenkins, "Turning Point for U.S. Education," *New York Times*, February 14, 1974.

49 *Congressional Record*, March 12, 1974, p. H1652–53.

50 White House Press Release, "Address by the President on the Future of American Education," March 23, 1974.

51 *Congressional Quarterly*, August 17 and 24, 1974, pp. 2211, 2321.

9

DESEGREGATION AID
and the POLITICS
of POLARIZATION

The Emergency Education Act

The Initial Nixon Goal   It is one of the ironies of the Nixon period that a President striving earnestly to slow or reverse the momentum of school desegregation should build his only proposal for substantial new aid to elementary and secondary education around the desegregation process. In a long policy statement of March 1970, the President strongly opposed recent court-ordered desegregation plans for big cities. The one favorable element, in a statement openly hostile to the basic goal of the civil rights groups, was a call for a new federal aid program providing as much as $1.5 billion to help districts forced by the courts to desegregate.

After the President's pledge a Cabinet Committee on School Desegregation, chaired by Vice President Agnew, worked out the details of a program with some help from consultants, including the country's best known desegregation researcher, James Coleman. A close White House observer, John Osborne, explained the politics of the program:

> The South's remaining segregated schools had to desegregate, the Supreme Court and the lower federal courts had made further delay impossible, and the Administration had no practicable choice but to make the process as acceptable and rewarding as it could. Most of the requested $1.5 billion in special funds . . . is earmarked, Congress willing, for Southern school districts that are integrating now or have integrated in the past two years. . . . the chief and declared objective is to reward while helping the white South in its enforced surrender to integration.[1]

The basic idea had broad appeal across a political spectrum that ranged from local Southern educators hoping to hold white students by upgrading programs, to ardent civil rights supporters in Congress. The problem was that the goals of the various supporters were incompatible. Eventually a serious division developed between the Administration and Congressional civil rights advocates. The Administration wished to ensure that the money went to districts forced to desegregate by the courts, and that none was used for busing students. Congress—particularly the Senate—insisted on a program where funds were more available to Northern districts, and refused to deny local authorities the right to implement court orders or voluntary local plans requiring pupil transportation.

When the Administration first sent the legislation to Capitol Hill, almost two-thirds of the earmarked funds were to be reserved for Southern districts. In a very important decision, the President himself altered HEW's draft bill to forbid spending the funds for busing "to overcome racial imbalance." The measure was built around providing massive rapid temporary aid to districts experiencing the educational "emergencies" produced by sudden desegregation. Not only did the bill try to prohibit subsidies for busing, but it also proposed to put some additional money into compensatory education in segregated ghetto schools. The program was conceived as a two-year effort, not a long-term commitment.

Congressional hearings opened within weeks, and the Administration asked the Appropriations committees for $150 million to be channeled through existing programs to school systems while Congress was considering the new legislation.[2]

Administration witnesses were closely questioned in both houses about ambiguities in the program. On the House side there was pressure for a more explicit stand against busing. On the Senate side civil rights supporters expressed their fears of local abuse of the program, unless it was strictly monitored from

Washington. Civil rights organizations had recently published an exposé of the misuse of ESEA money—sometimes when school systems practiced open discrimination and sometimes when local authorities were in fact unofficially aiding segregated private schools. The liberals also pressed the Administration to change the bill from one merely responding to an "emergency" to one favoring integration. In both chambers Northerners pressed for modifications of a funding formula so as to provide more money for desegregation efforts in the North.

Senator Walter Mondale (D-Minn.), chairman of the Select Committee on Equal Educational Opportunity, reflected liberal worries in his questions to the HEW Secretary:

> Wouldn't it be better to just come out and declare clearly and unequivocally a national policy that it is fundamental to this country that we begin to be educated and live together. Wouldn't it be better for this legislation . . . to state that purpose, and quit dancing around about when busing could be used. Wouldn't it be better to pursue a funding allocation which required and creates an incentive for quality integrated education wherever it is found?[3]

Among the civil rights witnesses, Washington Research Project Director Marian Edelman was perhaps the most forceful in outlining what she saw as deficiencies in the bill. Although strongly supporting federal aid for desegregation, she testified against this legislation. Its problems included "a lack of a defined goal . . . , a lack of a well-developed mechanism for review of project applications and dispersal of money, the lack of an established monitoring system of evaluation."

> Minimal criteria should be drafted which would spell out which districts would be eligible for funds and which not, to insure that priority will be given to those districts who will use it best based on a record of decent effort toward desegregation and to discourage recalcitrant districts from submitting applications.[4]

Long before Congress could act on the substantive legislation, the Administration was granted temporary funding to provide emergency aid for September 1970. The experience with the early grants was to deepen liberal criticisms and reinforce Congressional pressures for much tighter controls.

The money became available in late August. Under strong White House pressure for rapid action without red tape, HEW allowed its civil rights staff only thirty-six hours to examine a district's application before sending out money. Local officials threw together plans to get some money before schools opened, and HEW made only a cursory review. The frenzy to send dollars south was epitomized by the decision of the acting Commissioner of Education to give $1.3 million to Jackson, Mississippi, four days before HEW received the city's formal application.[5]

Very serious errors were made. Civil rights organizations reported that more than half the districts examined were continuing illegal practices of segregation while receiving the desegregation money. Much of the money was diverted to normal school operations rather than special desegregation efforts. In Mississippi the very districts that were busiest firing black teachers and finding new ways to maintain segregation within schools nominally desegregated got the most federal money.[6]

After the General Accounting Office, Congress's auditing and investigatory arm, examined the program, it issued a bleak report. The GAO found that the applications did not explain how the money would be spent and did not relate the new funds to integration. Often the program became little more than a form of general aid, operating in favor of the most segregationist systems in the country. The money made virtually no impact on the North and West, since more than 90 percent of the initial funds were allocated to Southern districts.[7]

The Liberals Fight Back   The dismal results of the initial effort left liberals in Congress so skeptical of the Administration's intentions that in late 1970 they blocked passage of the President's bill. Senator Mondale proposed an alternate bill reserving specific sums for various approaches to integration. Mondale's bill encouraged litigation by providing some money for attorneys' fees of successful litigants. Congress, the Minnesota Senator argued, should not give "vast sums of money to the discretion of an Administration whose negative and highly political approach in this area has been documented time and again." [8]

The skepticism was deepened in 1971, when the President announced a policy of maximum HEW and Justice Department opposition to busing. Pupil transportation was obviously appropriate under the unanimous rule of the Supreme Court in the 1971 *Swann* case, which upheld a court order requiring massive busing to desegregate a large school system in the South. Yet in July HEW Secretary Richardson told Congress that HEW was already giving requests for federal money for busing "very low priority," and that the Administration would accept an absolute prohibition on the use of funds for pupil transportation even when it was wholly unrelated to race.[9] The President then openly endorsed the antibusing proposals, and the White House threatened to fire any federal officials who did not respond to the President's position.[10]

Even so, compromise between civil rights forces and the White House had still seemed possible early in the year. The Administration had accepted several changes in its bill. Mondale's plan of reserving definite sums for particular desegregation activities was retained in weakened form, and the Minnesota Senator's administrative safeguards were largely left intact.

The compromise bill, now named the Emergency School Aid and Quality Integrated Education Act, was reported to the Senate floor by a unanimous committee vote. Two-thirds of the money would be used for project grants; $225 million for metropolitan area desegregation efforts; and substantial sums for bilingual education, integrated educational television programs, and attorneys' fees.[11] While the bill would not require desegregation, it was a definite progressive step toward federal support for successful integration.

The debate brought before the Senate a major effort to make the federal government the central positive force in a movement for desegregating Northern urban areas. Senator Abraham Ribicoff (D-Conn.) began a spirited debate with his proposal that each metropolitan area be required to develop a plan for comprehensive integration over a period of a decade. This plan went in exactly the opposite direction from the President and was light years in advance of public opinion on the issue. It failed, of course, 35-51. What was interesting, though, was the fact that it was supported by a substantial majority of Northern and Western Democrats, including all seven Democratic Senators then considered possible 1972 Presidential candidates: McGovern, Muskie, Humphrey, Kennedy, Jackson, Hughes, and Bayh.[12] The amendment fight was a classic example of how a Congressional minority far in advance of public opinion begins to develop a new issue.

When the final vote on the Senate bill came, it passed 74-8. Senators had rejected a series of weakening amendments by substantial margins.[13] To the extent that the bill had been converted into an effective tool for real desegregation, and for major new solutions to severe persisting problems of Northern urban school segregation, the credit belonged not to the President but to Congressional liberals and moderates, the great bulk of whom were Democrats.

177

The Democrats Split over Busing   When the bill went to the House, however, it faced considerable resistance from busing critics. House Subcommittee Chairman Roman Pucinski, who represented a largely Polish district in Chicago where busing was immensely unpopular, had little enthusiasm for the Senate measure. He wanted to substitute a much larger program of general aid to school districts.[14]

As action proceeded in the House, it was increasingly apparent that a substantial number of urban liberals with previously strong civil rights records now believed that they had to oppose busing, or anything that looked like it might be used for busing. This development badly split the Democrats and created a coalition in the House sympathetic to the President's position. The polls showed that public opposition to busing had sharply increased since the beginning of the Nixon Presidency, and many House members responded. The President escalated the pressure on Congress with a major appeal for a prohibition against using the money for busing. The request produced an open division between Pucinski and Chairman Perkins.

When the full committee reported out the bill without the White House antibusing provision, there were signs of a deep split within Democratic ranks. A New York City Congressman and two liberal Michigan members called the bill the "Back Door School Bus Financing Bill of 1971." A number of other committee Democrats failed to vote on the bill.

Congressional Democrats had a very long history of North-South division over the race issue. As lawsuits now began to affect some Northern cities, there were new schisms. Some House members from affected areas abandoned their traditional support for desegregation, thus joining the great majority of Southerners and Republicans following the President's leadership.

The committee bill lacked the specific focus and controls of the Senate legislation. It did retain, however, the Mondale requirement that each district receiving special funds must have at least one model integrated school.

When the measure got to the Rules Committee, the Democratic majority stalled. The Republicans charged that the House leadership was behind this maneuver to protect House Democrats from the necessity of voting on a divisive issue. That issue became vastly more explosive when in September a federal court found the city of Detroit and the state of Michigan guilty of intentional school segregation. The possibility of a decision ordering desegregation of the entire 3.5-million metropolitan area stirred a public reaction so intensely hostile that many Michigan politicians suddenly became fervently opposed to busing.

Although the House had voted for the bill by more than a two-thirds majority the previous year, now only 135 members voted to force the bill to the floor under a special procedure.[15] Searching for a way to pass the program, Representative Pucinski worked with the GOP leadership and the White House in devising a plan to tack the program, together with the antibusing amendments, onto the pending higher education bill. It worked, but at the price of incorporating the most sweeping antiintegration provisions yet into the bill.

The House went wild in a late evening session on November 4, 1971. Members showed that they would pass anything labeled antibusing by giving whopping margins to a whole series of drastic limitations on both the courts and executive-branch civil rights officials. The first proposal, sponsored by a suburban Michigan Congressman and six of his Michigan colleagues, directed the courts to delay execution of all desegregation orders until local officials had a chance to appeal it all the way to the Supreme Court, or until the time for appeal was exhausted. Although the measure was an extraordinary infringement on the autonomy of the judicial system, it passed almost two to one. It tried to delay not only controversial decisions like that in Detroit, but also cases based on settled law. There were serious doubts about its constitutionality.

A second major change was proposed by John Ashbrook (R-Ohio), who was running in the GOP Presidential primaries as a more conservative alternative to President Nixon. Ashbrook's amendment forbade use of federal funds from any source, including the previously unrestricted impacted areas money, for buying or operating buses. This also passed almost two to one.

Congresswoman Green (D-Ore.) then came forward with a further elaboration: an amendment that forbade federal administrators to even *suggest* to state and local officials that they employ busing for desegregation purposes. Federal agencies were also forbidden to condition federal aid on the use of state or local funds for busing. This amendment passed by an almost identical margin.[16]

In adopting the Ashbrook and Green amendments, the House had supported partial repeal of the 1964 Civil Rights Act. The 1964 law required withholding of federal funds from

179

school systems defying Constitutional desegregation requirements. The amendments not only forbade such a policy, but also denied bureaucrats even the right to advocate compliance with the Constitution, which their oaths of office required them to uphold. In the space of a very brief debate, the House had taken extremely drastic action in its eagerness to respond to the busing issue.

A Compromise Is Found   When the bill reached the Senate, GOP Leader Hugh Scott joined with Majority Leader Mansfield to frustrate the President's goals. Many Senators shared the desire of their House colleagues to record their opposition to "forced busing," but the leadership crafted an artful compromise that avoided serious damage to civil rights. In spite of strong and escalating Presidential pressure, further restrictive amendments were beaten back.

The Senate amendment retained much of the language of the House amendments, but added crucial qualifying phrases. Thus, for example, use of federal funds for busing was forbidden "except on the express written request of appropriate local school officials." Since local school superintendents were clamoring for money to comply with desegregation orders, and had testified to this effect, obviously there would indeed be busing. Similarly, federal officials were forbidden to withhold funds to force busing or to recommend busing plans "unless constitutionally required." The moratorium on implementation of court orders was limited to cases requiring consolidation of two or more districts, and would automatically expire in a year and a half. While the Scott-Mansfield amendment represented a step backward for the Senate, it was vastly less damaging to school desegregation than the House position.

Attention then focused on the President and on the effort of a conference committee to hammer out an agreement between the House and Senate positions. President Nixon made his position clear in a nationally televised address calling on Congress to take drastic action to forestall busing.

Two days after the March 1972 Florida primary, where George Wallace defeated other Democratic contenders largely through his emphasis on busing, the President told the nation that Congress should pass a bill delaying all busing orders, and another measure designed to make separate schools more equal. On March 17 he submitted a message to Congress outlining the "Student Transportation Moratorium Act" and the "Equal Educational Opportunities Act." The bills not only delayed court orders, but also prescribed what remedies the courts could employ and in what order of preference they must be adopted. They permitted the reopening of existing busing cases in the South.[17] The equalization bill offered no new money.

In the wake of the President's statement, HEW Secretary Richardson announced that the Administration supported the Ashbrook amendment and the House moratorium proposal, and he called on the conferees to include both these amendments and the President's new freeze on court orders in the higher education bill.

Earlier the Administration had quietly supported a House move to "instruct" the liberal House conferees to insist on the House antibusing proposals. The House had responded by passing such a resolution 272-139.[18] Later, after a Republican conferee indicated some disposition to compromise, the House took the extraordinary step of voting for yet another resolution insisting that the House representatives be unyielding on the three amendments. The vote was still more lopsided 275-124, even after warnings that the issue might jeopardize the whole higher education package.[19] Facing fall campaigns, House members were in a frenzy to get on the safe side of the busing dispute.

Eventually, however, a compromise was found. The House version of the moratorium bill, a masterpiece of poor draftsmanship, was agreed upon, while the Ashbrook proposal was rendered harmless. The House moratorium requirement was both sweeping and unclear, and some liberals accepted it in the hope that the courts would find it meaningless or unconstitutional (as they soon did). The conferees ignored the President's proposals.[20]

The Emergency Education bill came out of the conference with a mixture of House and Senate proposals. The bill dropped the idea of requiring a single model integrated school, but retained the requirement of a district-wide plan for ending minority-group isolation. The reservation of funds for voluntary metropolitan desegregation efforts was retained but the amount sharply decreased. The bill kept the Senate list of activities eligible for funding, but dropped some of the Senate controls. The desegregation aid provisions remained much more definite than those originally supported by the Administration, but far weaker than the Mondale proposal. Because the debate had been on busing, neither house paid much attention either to the monumental higher education changes or to the desegregation assistance bill—this last by far the largest new categorical 181 program of the Nixon Administration for elementary and secondary education. On busing once again liberal seniority on the conference committee had produced a bill ignoring the position supported by the House and the President.

The Senate resoundingly defeated an attempt to send the bill back to conference for more antibusing language, and adopted it overwhelmingly.[21] The House followed suit, in spite of attacks by GOP Leader Gerald Ford and Congresswoman Green, who wanted harsher antibusing action and other changes.[22]

Even after the bill passed, the President continued his strident criticism on the busing issue. Eventually he signed the bill, but only with an angry statement: "Not in the course of this administration has there been a more manifest congressional retreat from an urgent call for responsibility."[23]

More Antibusing Measures

Under intense White House election-year pressure for action, yet another antibusing measure was pushed through the House and onto the Senate floor. The President's ironically named "Equal Educational Opportunities" bill simply attempted to nullify recent Supreme Court busing decisions by legislation, to forbid the courts to issue similar orders in the future, and to allow school districts already desegregated to go back into court to "reopen" their cases. The House adopted the measure 282-102, after further limiting the narrow circumstances under which the White House bill would have permitted busing to the nearest school.

The measure then went to the Senate. The debate began October 6, a month before a national election. Lacking the votes to defeat this bill, Senate liberals began a filibuster. Loaded down with long arguments about the unconstitutional character of the legislation, its drastic infringement both on courts and on the responsible local administrators, and its false assumptions about the results of desegregation, the liberals held the floor for several days. After failing three times to shut off debate through cloture motions, the bill's supporters gave up.[24]

Under President Nixon the roles had been reversed. As the 1960s began, black Americans looked to the White House for the protection of their rights, and legislation backed by the

President faced its mortal danger from filibusters by conservatives in the Senate. Now the President was leading the assault on court-ordered desegregation and pressing incessantly for action restricting the courts. His bill too died in the Senate, but through a filibuster by liberals.

In the post-election year 1973 there was no great Congressional excitement about busing. The fear of metropolitan desegregation was lessened by the Supreme Court's failure to uphold a district court decision that would have consolidated the school systems of the Richmond metropolitan area.

The fight became intense again in 1974, during the battle on the new elementary and secondary education bill. Once again members of the Michigan delegation sponsored the sweeping amendments the House had adopted in 1971.

While the amendments were pending, President Nixon devoted much of a nationally broadcast speech to the issue, and in it made misleading and incorrect statements. He asserted that neighborhood schools are more effective educationally, although research shows this is not true. He said that the courts were "acting on the basis of complicated plans drawn up by far-away officials in Washington, D.C.," to order children out of their neighborhoods, although the local school officials or local federal district judges generally devise the plans. Finally, he claimed that segregated schools could be desegregated without busing, in spite of spreading ghettos in many urban communities. He endorsed the Michigan amendments.[25]

The House speeches were pointed but the debate was brief. An effort by a bipartisan group of moderates to work out a compromise bill was assailed by both sides in a polarized House and defeated on a voice vote. Liberals declared the compromise still involved tampering with the courts, while conservatives said it would be "pro-busing."

As the final vote neared, both Quie and Perkins futilely tried to calm the passions of the members. Quie, handling his last major school bill before retirement, expressed serious doubts about the constitutionality of the busing proviso:"I wish the House would not complicate the future of a good education bill with these amendments." Chairman Perkins warned that "we are just fooling ourselves" if we try "to reverse Supreme Court decisions." Near the end of the debate a South Carolina Congressman, William Jennings Bryan Dorn, told his Northern colleagues that desegregation in his district had brought "a new day of better education and improved community relations." He assailed the amendment:

It is yet another attempt to set up a special arrangement for the northern metropolitan areas. It is yet another attempt to return to the old dual system. Those days are gone forever, Mr. Speaker. We cannot go back.

For the Congress to continue to tack on the so-called anti-busing amendments to every conceivable piece of legislation is an exercise in futility. There is simply no way for us to return to the outmoded, outdated, segregated neighborhood school system of the past.[26]

The admonitions were useless. The House passed the amendment 293-117, thus rejecting the advice of its experts and ignoring the committee's vote against including the antibusing section in its bill. Before action was finished, the House also wrote in an amendment refusing the use of any federal funds for busing costs, even if local officials wanted to use them for this purpose. A great many advocates of local control of the schools now voted to prevent local school officials from spending public funds to implement rights provided by the federal Constitution.[27]

Once again the House sent to the Senate a major education bill with White House–supported amendments intended to drastically curtail school desegregation, and greatly limit the ability of the courts to enforce a major constitutional right. Once again it was an election year. This time, however, the bill came to the Senate not just before adjournment but in early May, making a filibuster strategy difficult if not impossible.

When the bill reached the Senate floor, civil rights supporters were seriously frightened. With strong White House pressure on the issue, in an election year, there was no way to avoid a public vote. More and more Northern school cases were being filed and some liberals in affected areas, like Senator Haskell (D-Colo.), switched their positions. Others were under heavy pressure to record themselves against busing before facing the electorate in the fall. In a series of close votes, however, the Senate defeated the Administration proposals by a single vote. Once again the bill went to conference and once again the central dispute in the shaping of the country's basic structure of aid to elementary and secondary schools was over desegregation. The President threatened a veto unless the Senate yielded.[28]

As the country was absorbed in the spectacle of the House impeachment proceedings, the most closely fought battle in recent Congressional history came to a head. After the razor-thin one-vote decisions in the Senate, the giant school bill went to a conference committee charged with compromising the irreconcilable positions of Senate civil rights supporters and the large House majority intensely opposed to busing. The conference committee dragged on for six weeks. House busing opponents underlined both their suspicion of the liberal conferees and their determination through the extraordinary step of three successive resolutions insisting that the House delegates stand fast. Each carried by a huge margin. President Nixon's veto threat intensified the problem. One hundred and forty-six House members, more than enough to sustain a veto, wrote a letter to the President urging him to reject any compromise. They promised they would sustain his veto.

The conference committee, however, eventually compromised away most of the House position. The resulting bill declared Congress' strong support for the neighborhood school system. In a typically contradictory and confusing fashion, the bill contained language forbidding the courts to order busing of students beyond the next closest school but modified the prohibition with a proviso specifying that the new law was "not intended to modify or diminish the authority of the courts of the United States to enforce fully the fifth and fourteenth amendments to the Constitution of the United States." The bill also emasculated the section most strongly supported by the Southerners, a section that would have authorized reopening of all the existing school desegregation cases in the South. The bill did restrain the spending of most federal school aid for busing and severely restricted HEW civil rights enforcement powers. By and large, however, the bill was a victory for those who wished to avoid a direct confrontation with the courts over desegregation. In signing the bill, President Ford praised the new restrictions but said it was "unfair" and a "double standard" not to let Southern communities reopen court orders in the hope of obtaining a plan requiring less desegregation.

One feature of the bill Ford signed attracted virtually no attention but was an ironic reflection of the changing role of the President and Congress. The Emergency Education bill program was extended through Congressional initiative. The Nixon Administration, which had originally conceived the idea of desegregation assistance, had lost interest, calling for virtually no new money in 1975 and refusing to spend much of the available funds the previous fiscal year. Congress persisted. As a result, a program originally designed as a temporary transitional effort aimed at assuaging school officials forced to desegregate in the Deep South had now been transformed by Congress into

185

a commitment to help desegregation for a longer period of time in a broader geographic area. Thus, while the executive branch would continue to fight urban school integration in the North and West, it would also continue to administer an assistance program intended to help make the desegregation process work successfully. Since the Supreme Court in a 1973 decision had belatedly begun to require urban desegregation outside the South, the aid program might well be of great importance in the growing number of cities facing desegregation.

One very interesting but little noticed fact about the shaping of the new ESEA bill was the fate of the Emergency School program, so proudly announced by the Administration four years earlier. In his 1974 budget message the President reported that the Administration hadn't given out a substantial fraction of the money available the past year. For the next year he proposed a drastic cutback of more than two-thirds in new funds for the effort.[29] The idea of helping school districts desegregate had lost its priority. The Nixon Administration's interest was now firmly focused on the politics of polarization through the support of antibusing legislation attempting to restrict the Constitutional powers of the courts. Congress rejected the effort to phase out the program.

Summary: The Threatened Programs Are Preserved by Congress

Throughout the entire Nixon Administration, very difficult issues about financing education and desegregating the nation's schools posed extremely important questions of national policy. These questions were raised in pointed fashion by a series of critical court decisions on each issue. The dramatic nature of the money question was underlined by the inability of a growing number of urban systems even to operate for a normal school year. Annual statistics on the segregation issue showed intensifying urban segregation, while polls showed mounting white resistance to busing remedies required by the courts. Decisions on national policy were urgently needed.

The President chose to assume a conservative stance on each issue, cutting back the federal role in financing the schools and attempting to use federal power to roll back urban desegregation efforts. In each case Congress successfully defeated most of the President's initiatives during the period of this study. Congress reversed its traditional role in the appropriations process, while the President, in his drive to hold down education funds, repeatedly employed, or threatened to employ, his ultimate weapon, the veto. The Congressional achievement was considerable. A relatively fragile education program based on delicate compromise was preserved and expanded in the face of strong and determined executive opposition. Significant new programs for Spanish-speaking children, for adult education, for American Indian education, and other purposes were supported. After a long struggle the President's school desegregation bill was enacted in a manner that aided the desegregation process rather than outlawed it. None of these changes offered sweeping answers to the fundamental problems of the educational system, but all were moves forward. By comparison with any period of American history except the Johnson years, it was a record of very substantial success.

During these years the President did not have a set of coherent educational goals, nor did he assign the problems of elementary and secondary school systems a high priority. With rare exceptions the Administration's policy in education and other major domestic programs was preoccupied with budgetary questions, reorganization and decentralization proposals, and the politics of race. Faced with a drastic lowering of the priority of school funds in the budgetary calculus of the Nixon Administration, Congressional education supporters turned around the normal appropriations procedures and forced a significant reallocation of resources into the schools. In the face of vigorous Presidential leadership and intense public pressure to act against urban desegregation plans requiring busing, Congress refused to approve the President's drastic antiintegration measures.

Divided government did, however, have costs. Although everyone recognized critical problems in local school systems, there were no major policy breakthroughs. While education supporters strongly preferred divided government and preservation of the Great Society programs, to a united government that would follow the President's lead in cutting back the federal commitment to education and desegregation, most educators felt an urgent need for positive new initiatives. The President attacked the education budget and the courts with a pickax, while the Congress tried to shield the courts and trowel on more money. Neither could make sensitive adjustments of emphasis, or confront successfully controversial but important new issues. Likewise, neither could command the political 187 power and unity of purpose necessary to get rid of ineffective but very popular programs. Education programs lumbered forward, thanks to Congress. At least they did not lurch backward.

NOTES

[1] John Osborne, *The First Two Years of the Nixon Watch* (New York: Liveright, 1971), pp. 85–86.

[2] Senate Committee on Labor and Public Welfare, Subcommittee on Education, *Hearings, Emergency School Aid Act of 1970*, 91st Cong., 2d Sess., 1970, pp. 2–51.

[3] *Ibid.*, p. 55.

[4] *Ibid.*, pp. 148, 151.

[5] Earl Browning, Jr., "Emergency School Assistance: Financing the Desegregation Retreat," unpublished manuscript (1971).

[6] *The Emergency School Program—an Evaluation, 1970*, reprinted in *Congressional Record*, December 29, 1970, pp. S21434–35; Luther Munford, "Black Gravity," unpublished senior thesis, Princeton University (1971).

[7] *Congressional Record*, March 16, 1971, pp. S3293–94.

[8] *Washington Post*, December 17, December 23, December 29, and December 30, 1970.

[9] *Congressional Quarterly*, August 28, 1971, pp. 1829–30.

[10] *Ibid.*, p. 1829.

[11] *Congressional Quarterly*, April 23, 1971, pp. 933–34.

[12] *Congressional Record*, April 21, 1971, p. S5317.

[13] *Washington Post*, April 27, 1971.

[14] *Ibid.*, July 2, 1971.

[15] The foregoing account is based on reports in *Congressional Quarterly*, October 30, 1971, pp. 2239–41; and November 6, 1971, p. 2276.

[16] *Congressional Record*, November 4, 1971, pp. H10407–27; *Congressional Quarterly*, November 13, 1971, p. 2310.

[17] The text of the message appears in *Congressional Quarterly*, March 25, 1972, pp. 642–48.

[18] *Congressional Record*, March 8, 1972, p. H1860.

[19] *Ibid.*, May 11, 1972, pp. H4420–24.

[20] *Congressional Quarterly*, May 27, 1972, pp. 1242–43.

[21] *Congressional Record*, May 23, 1972, pp. S8292–93; and May 24, 1972, p. S8403.

[22] *Congressional Quarterly*, June 10, 1972, p. 1371.

[23] *Ibid.*; *Congressional Quarterly*, June 24, 1972, p. 1566.

[24] Michael Wise, "Congress, Busing, and Federal Law," *Civil Rights Digest* V (Summer 1973), pp. 28–36.

[25] White House Press Release, "Address by the President on the Future of American Education," March 23, 1974.

[26] *Congressional Record*, March 26, 1974, pp. H2170–77.

[27] *Ibid.*, March 26, 1974, p. H2177; March 27, 1974, pp. H2240–42.

[28] *Congressional Quarterly*, May 25, 1974, pp. 1334–35.

[29] *The Budget of the United States Government, 1975*, p. 199.

part four

CONGRESS
and JOBS

10

A PUBLIC JOBS PROGRAM: THE FIRST ATTEMPTS

Nothing is more important as a measure of worth in American society than one's job. Nothing becomes a more important and explosive political issue in modern American politics than rapidly rising joblessness. Many of the major domestic policy innovations of the past generation have been directly or indirectly intended to prepare poor people for decent jobs. The issue is peculiarly crucial for minority groups, many of whom live in communities that never escape the crushing impact of depression conditions. Real social progress, many argue, is absolutely dependent upon changing the employment situation.

The striking fact in recent political history is the degree to which Congress has dominated the shaping of policies in the manpower field. Nowhere is Congressional initiative more unambiguously clear than in the contemporary development of the idea of government as the employer of last resort—an idea that received its first successful legislative expression in the Emergency Employment Act of 1971. The next two chapters will assess and explain the role of Congress in the creation of this major policy breakthrough.

A Public Jobs Chronology

1962   The Manpower Development and Training Act (MDTA).

1964   President Johnson's War on Poverty program establishes the Job Corps, the Neighborhood Youth Corps, and the Community Action Program.

1965   The Nelson amendment is passed, initiating Operation Mainstream: the hiring of hard-core unemployed for conservation projects.

1967   Johnson's opposition kills Senate public jobs bill.

1970   A Senate-initiated manpower bill is killed by Nixon's veto.

1971   The Emergency Employment Act of 1971.
Nixon vetoes a House-initiated job-creation bill, but signs a smaller version of it.

1972   A massive job-creation bill dies on the House floor.

1973   Nixon tries to eliminate the public jobs program; the program is reduced, but survives.

1974   Ford endorses public jobs program.

Prelude: The Government and Unemployment

Since the Great Depression it has become a commonplace that the government has some responsibility for preventing major dislocations of the economy and cushioning the impact of joblessness on individuals. Unemployment compensation, for example, has become a fixed principle of American government. Many of the other emergency Depression programs, however, died with the end of the economic crisis. The massive public works programs that had given jobs to as many as four million Americans at one time were no longer necessary once the economy revived.

Not until the Kennedy and Nixon years did the national government even embrace the Keynesian idea of large deficit spending to stimulate the economy when recessions or depressions threatened. In the 1950s President Eisenhower devoted great energies to fighting for a balanced budget, even at the price of politically damaging recessions, when the economy was in obvious need of a fiscal policy designed to stimulate buying power. Only in 1962 did President Kennedy announce his determination to use deficit financing to stimulate the economy and create jobs. Kennedy's proposal to cut taxes and intentionally increase the federal deficit to bring the economy out of its doldrums was a decisive political advance. President Johnson enthusiastically followed the same course of action, pushing the

Kennedy proposal to final enactment and insisting on massive domestic commitments even in the face of deficits produced by ballooning expenditures for the Vietnam War. President Nixon took office with simultaneous promises to cut taxes and balance the budget, but ran historic deficits. Eventually he himself announced he was a "Keynesian," and argued that his budgets were actually balanced "full employment" budgets.

Poverty amid Prosperity The economic policies of the Kennedy and Johnson Administrations succeeded in producing a remarkable period of economic growth and falling unemployment. During these years joblessness fell from almost 6 percent of the labor force to less than 3.5 percent—well under the economists' definition of "full employment" in the American labor market. The social impact of prosperity was striking: an average of two-thirds of a million families moved out of poverty each year.[1]

However, even in the early 1960s, it was obvious that economic growth would not in itself solve the whole problem of poverty and joblessness. Particular areas of the country, and even particular parts of cities, suffered from exceptionally poor labor markets. Discrimination remained a chronic and extremely serious problem, and many jobless workers lacked qualifications for most job openings.

High as the jobless figures frequently were, they substantially understated the problem. There were millions of working families earning less than poverty-level wages. The official unemployment statistics didn't even count several million workers so discouraged that they were no longer actively looking for work. By definition, these people were described as "not in the labor force." Ghetto unemployment levels were frequently 30 percent or more, with astronomical levels for teen-age blacks and workers on Indian reservations.

Growing awareness of these problems was reflected in the Democratic Congresses of the late 1950s and early 1960s, when liberals began to talk of reviving some of the New Deal job programs. Already, during the 1957–58 recession, Congressional Democrats had pressed for enactment of a billion-dollar community facilities program, clearly inspired by the New Deal's Public Works Administration. The Civilian Conservation Corps rural camps for jobless city young people who did conservation work in the countryside were also fondly remembered, and Senator Hubert Humphrey began a battle to revive them late in the Eisenhower Presidency. Prior to his election as President,

John Kennedy had represented the depressed New England region in the Senate, and had served as floor manager of the first unsuccessful area redevelopment bill during the 1956 session. Within two weeks of taking office, he asked Congress for depressed area assistance.[2] The measure, similar to a bill Eisenhower had vetoed twice, became law in 1961.

The Training Approach While Kennedy supported a relatively small program of subsidies for private development, he was reluctant to accept the public works approach supported by Congressional liberals led by Senator Joseph Clark (D-Pa.). In 1961 the White House opposed a bill intended to generate $2.2 billion of new public building activity, in spite of substantial support for the measure among Presidential advisors. The next year the President requested mere "standby authority" for such activities, changing his position only under mounting pressure. Congress approved a $900-million Accelerated Public Works program, an appropriation 50 percent over the President's belated request.[3] This was strictly a temporary commitment, intended to help diminish joblessness during the current recession.

The major White House economic proposals were intended to stimulate demand and upgrade worker qualifications—an emphasis that would persist throughout the Johnson Administration. The training approach was a solution compatible with the general American tendency to seek educational answers to social problems. Since it did not attack any of the basic assumptions of a private business economy, but merely provided supporting governmental services to make more skilled workers available, it raised few difficult issues likely to embroil liberals and conservatives. As the 1960s began there was broad agreement about the need for an educational approach. As one scholar observed:

> By 1961, politicians who disagreed on every other subject were in consensus on one point: The unemployed must be retrained. Liberals who favored government spending to create jobs looked on retraining as a necessary supplement to enable the unemployed to fill the jobs. And conservatives who preached "fiscal responsibility" tended to seize on retraining as a *substitute* for vigorous spending measures. . . .
> . . . If the fault were not in the economic system, as the conservatives had been contending, it must be in the people.[4]

The belief that various forms of training were critical in solving the job problem was at the center of the 1962 Manpower

Development and Training Act (MDTA) and all its subsequent amendments, the 1964 tax-cut bill, the Economic Opportunity Act, the Appalachia program, and related pieces of legislation. There were successful efforts to raise the growth rate, new vocational programs, action against job discrimination, an effort to create concentrated training programs adapted to ghetto conditions, and finally a variety of incentives to private industry to train and give jobs to the hard-core unemployed. Almost everything was attempted except direct provision of jobs, and very severe problems remained.

When the War on Poverty proposals of the Johnson Administration were being assembled, the President received a proposal from Sargeant Shriver, coordinator of the poverty effort, and from the Labor Department, that direct job creation be incorporated in the program. The job proposal called for a new cigarette tax to finance public employment. Although this idea went to the Cabinet, the general belief within the executive branch was that the pending tax cut was itself "a job creation measure of unprecedented boldness." The reigning hope was that with economic expansion opening up jobs and the training programs upgrading workers, the problem of large-scale chronic joblessness would very rapidly decline. The President saw no political sense in simultaneously pressing for a general tax cut to produce jobs and for a tax increase to do the same. His firm opposition doomed the idea.[5] But the wave of economic prosperity that was to wash over the nation served only to further emphasize the isolation and poverty of the nation's urban and rural slums.

The War on Poverty got into the public employment business by indirection and a number of half measures, most of which were usually described as training programs. The poverty program package contained several such efforts. In 1963 the Senate had passed a Youth Employment Opportunities Act, modeled on New Deal programs for jobless young people. Though the measure had been pigeonholed by the House Rules Committee, a similar approach was reflected in the Job Corps and Neighborhood Youth Corps sections of the 1964 bill. The Job Corps included rural centers clearly related to the old CCC model, and urban centers functioning essentially as residential vocational education programs. The Neighborhood Youth Corps, which created by far the largest number of new jobs, was intended to provide part-time and summer jobs to help young people stay in school, and also to provide them some temporary work if out of school. The bill included as well a 195 small program designed to provide "work experience" for welfare recipients. Finally the Community Action Program, the core of the bill, provided for the hiring of thousands of local subprofessional community workers to staff the new neighborhood poverty organizations.

While the poverty program produced a number of jobs, the whole effort was built around using public employment as a temporary device to prepare and qualify workers for jobs in the private sector. Most of the jobs were for teen-agers. They were intended to reduce delinquency, diminish the likelihood of ghetto riots, give kids from jobless families a conception of the "work role," and make members of the most severely unemployed groups in the population more attractive to potential employers. Even the jobs in the poverty program itself were mostly low-paying, and were conceived as training grounds for more regular employment. Nowhere in the legislation, or in the administrative apparatus that the new law created, was there an effort to face up to the uncomfortable fact of persisting very high levels of unemployment and underemployment.

Public Employment: Congressional Beginnings The two small programs that during the Johnson Administration focused explicitly on provision of public service jobs were initiated by Congress. In 1965 Senator Gaylord Nelson (D-Wis.) sponsored an amendment to the poverty bill authorizing employment of adult poor people for conservation and beautification projects. In 1966 the Nelson program was expanded by an amendment sponsored by Representative James Scheuer (D-N.Y.) permitting employment of subprofessional aides. Finally, also in 1966, Congress wrote into law an amendment sponsored by Senators Robert Kennedy (D-N.Y.) and Jacob Javits (R-N.Y.) for a small "special impact" program to employ poor people in areas suffering from unusually high levels of poverty.[6]

The most important of these new programs—early trials for the major legislation of the 1970s—was the Nelson program, which eventually became known as Operation Mainstream. Senator Nelson had initiated the battle for this legislation within weeks of Senate passage of the President's 1964 poverty bill. Although Nelson was not yet even a member of the Labor and Public Welfare Committee, his bill to authorize a billion dollars a year for reducing unemployment through "needed conservation work at the Federal, State, and municipal levels" was given a friendly hearing. Senator Joseph Clark, the Senate's leading manpower expert, argued that there was slack in the economy because large defense commitments had prevented "increased public expenditures in fields such as community renewal, resource development, transportation, and education." He concluded that the "country is plagued with community resource, and worker obsolescence . . . which must be corrected through a proper arsenal of public investment programs."[7]

Senator Nelson had written to state and local officials across the country and found almost unanimous favorable response. Hundreds of letters detailed local needs for additional manpower and enthusiastically endorsed the idea. "I don't think," Nelson testified, "we have a serious problem on so-called WPA or make-work projects because every agency at local level, and every State agency, has needs and important work to be done that they just don't have funds to do." He estimated that the bill would create from 100,000 to 125,000 jobs.[8]

There was no chance for action in 1964. The Senate had just passed a poverty bill, and the one-day hearing came too late in the session for serious action. The bill lacked powerful sponsorship and the Administration had rejected the job creation strategy.

The following year, however, a scaled-down version of the Nelson proposal became part of the poverty program. With a $10-million appropriation, the proposal had been reduced by 99 percent. The money was given to the Office of Economic Opportunity (OEO) to employ chronically unemployed people in beautification programs, forest and wildlife conservation, and related purposes. Those hired were to receive either the federal minimum wage or the prevailing local wage for similar work, if that was more.

During its first full year of operation, 1966, the program provided jobs for 14,000 adults. The bulk of the money went to rural areas for popular projects such as Green Thumb, a program that offered rural senior citizens the chance to work on conservation projects. The Nelson program was so well received that Congress had almost tripled the initial appropriation to nearly $30 million by 1967.[9]

During the 1967 fiscal year, however, the Nelson amendment program was still operating on a tiny scale and the Kennedy-Javits "special impact" was far smaller. The total number of public service employment jobs generated by these programs was only 33,000.

To the extent that there was a public service employment commitment, it was still principally for temporary teen-age jobs. The great majority of the jobs were in the Neighborhood Youth 197

Corps, which during the year generated 165,000 summer employment positions. There were many rationales for providing work for teen-agers, especially those living in the ghettos, during the "long, hot summers" of the 1960s, but political leadership was not yet ready to face the implications of accepting public responsibility for the economy's persistent failure to produce decent jobs for a great many adults.

The first major Congressional initiative on the issue came in 1967, in the midst of a fierce battle over the future of the poverty program. During its first years the poverty program had become highly controversial, enraging many city officials by its attempts to organize the poor, and the election of a much more conservative House in 1966 threatened the program's existence. In the Senate the criticisms were examined in exhaustive hearings by a subcommittee of the Labor and Public Welfare Committee. In a rare example of Congressional oversight, the subcommittee commissioned dozens of reports by consultants and produced some twenty-six volumes of hearings and reports. The result was not merely a defense of the existing program, but a move to add a massive second title to the bill. The Senate committee supported a two-year, $2.8-billion "emergency employment" effort. The bill, supported by such powerful national organizations as the U.S. Conference of Mayors, the AFL-CIO, and the National Education Association, was intended to create a half million jobs for the hard-core unemployed. It was endorsed by 251 economists, and a poll taken just a month before the Senate debate showed that 69 percent of the public supported "large-scale Federal work projects to give jobs to the unemployed."[10]

It had become clear, by this point, that no expansion strategy would solve the job problems of those at the end of the waiting lines. Reducing joblessness much below 4 percent through general stimulation of the economy, it seemed certain, would produce unacceptable inflation. The eminent economists Samuelson and Solow had concluded that output levels sufficient to maintain 3-percent unemployment would probably require from 4 to 5-percent inflation each year. The tendency was to define as "full employment" the situation where four out of every hundred workers were without jobs. Unless these people were simply to be forgotten, there was an urgent need for a program to give them jobs without overheating the economy. Economists estimated that from 1.0 to 1.5 million jobs for employable poor people were needed—jobs that could be created to fill unmet needs for governmental services.

In 1965 a study commissioned by the poverty program had concluded that various governmental agencies needed as many as 4.3 million additional employees. The study called for payment of new public workers at the minimum wage level for the subprofessional jobs, most of which would involve helping out in schools or health facilities. In early 1966 the National Commission on Technology, Automation, and Economic Progress recommended that the national government become the "employer of last resort." Later in the year the widely publicized White House Conference on Civil Rights made a similar recommendation.[11]

The job program proposed by the Senate committee in 1967 tried to deal with this recognized need, and enjoyed a broad base of Senate support. A leading moderate GOP spokesman, Hugh Scott (R-Pa.), for example, attacked President Johnson's opposition to the bill. While conceding that the approach was no "panacea," Scott said that a measure that would rapidly produce 200,000 jobs and eventually reach a half million would respond to a "desperate" need and dwarf the accomplishments of the various existing manpower programs. Scott found the President's attitude "difficult to understand."

> Instead of accelerating efforts to alleviate the most immediately desperate conditions in our big city slums and other deprived areas, this administration has seen fit to rest on the laurels of the last Congress . . . and try to sabotage the efforts of the members of the Committee on Labor and Public Welfare to report to the Senate the Emergency Employment Act.[12]

While the committee was considering the bill, the Administration sent a memorandum to members calling for deletion of the jobs section. Secretary of Labor Willard Wirtz testified that the "most immediate problem is a training problem, not a job development problem." The Administration memo pointed out that the President had given close personal attention to the bill, and was trying to just keep the poverty program alive and win a tax increase to meet mounting war costs without killing domestic programs.[13]

The debate found the President in a tacit alliance with Congressional conservatives opposing a policy change. Both GOP conservatives and the Johnson Administration preferred the alternative of providing additional subsidies to private companies to train the hard-core unemployed for jobs. Secretary Wirtz had described the possibility of increasing the role of private business as the "most underdeveloped aspect of the 199 manpower program (and possibly of the poverty program as well)."[14]

Senator Robert Byrd (D-W.Va.), the leader of the opposition, said that the President didn't want the program, and insisted that there was "no shortage of jobs in the United States today." He claimed the committee's program would create "makework" jobs, "unskilled jobs with no future." The President himself would use very similar arguments in his 1968 Manpower Report. "In our thriving economy," he wrote, "where jobs in a rapidly growing private sector are widely available and the unemployment rate is low, the 'make work' programs of the 1930s are not the answer." The President insisted that "the jobs are there," and argued that "government-supported on-the-job training is the most effective gateway to meaningful employment."[15]

The program's supporters argued that it was an overdue and urgently needed response to the terrible urban conditions that were even then producing the worst ghetto riots in American history. "Everywhere our subcommittee went," said Senator Javits, "we heard the same judgment—'Jobs are first,' 'What we need are jobs.'" Providing jobs, he said, would be the most important step the Senate could take to "avert a replay of this summer's outbreaks." Senator Robert Kennedy argued that "the people of the ghetto and the barrio live today with an unemployment rate far worse than the rest of the Nation knew during the depth of the great depression." By the Labor Department's own figures, Kennedy pointed out, slum residents were not participating in the national growth of family income, and young blacks were not getting their share of the new jobs the economy was generating. He called unemployment the "most critical of our failures," and stressed that "providing jobs is the one step that is in everyone's interest." The program would, he argued, use wasted resources, cut crime, lower the cost of welfare, and help create "new kinds of public service careers."[16] Nor were the slums cited by Kennedy the only problem areas: unemployment was high in some depressed rural districts, too.

The Administration further undermined the chances of the new program by announcing a commitment to an alternative approach two days before the final votes. The White House announced a $40-million effort that the President described as a "major test program to mobilize the resources of private industry and the Federal Government to help find jobs and provide training for thousands of America's hard-core unemployed." Taking funds from a variety of existing programs and centralizing government contacts with private business, the President expressed great confidence that the program would "help provide every American the opportunity for a good job at a good wage."[17]

Shortly before the final vote, supporters of the program realized that it was impossible to pass the committee bill. Committee Democrats threw their support to a compromise measure authored by Senate conservative Winston Prouty (R-Vt.). Prouty's amendment would have reduced the two-year, $2.8-billion authorization to a one-year, $875-million effort with a substantial fraction of the money going to private industry and other training programs. At least a half billion dollars would still have gone into the first-year jobs program.[18]

The Prouty proposal was defeated by a close 42-47 vote. The program would have been adopted easily, had the Northern wing of the Democratic party been united. The measure was supported by sixteen Republicans and twenty-six Democrats, but opposed by thirteen Northern Democrats including Majority Leader Mansfield and several strong liberals. All but two Southern Democrats had voted against the jobs plan. Since two Senators had told Senator Clark that they would switch their votes if it would make the difference, it was obvious that Presidential support, or probably even White House neutrality, would have permitted Senate passage.[19] As it was, several years would pass before the Democrats united behind the new approach. A Democratic President had forestalled a Senate policy initiative.

The 1967 Senate defeat marked the last time in the 1960s that the public jobs approach would receive serious Congressional consideration. In the face of White House resistance, the drastic break with previous policy was impossible. The economy was still buoyant; therefore joblessness was a real issue only to those groups largely cut off from the rest of the society and lacking political power. Not until unemployment rose drastically and a broader spectrum of Americans was affected would there be another major Congressional initiative.

The Fight over the Manpower Approach

The Nixon Goal: Consolidation, Decentralization The Nixon Administration arrived in office to find a confusing array of overlapping manpower programs that weren't working very well. The President rapidly made reform of the programs a

201

central goal of his domestic policy. The manpower message was one of three basic related domestic proposals that President Nixon sent to Capitol Hill in August 1969.

In his message the President described the principal difficulties in manpower programs as "duplication of effort, inflexible funding arrangements, and an endless ribbon of red tape." His bill, he said, would "pull together much of the array of federal training services and make it possible for state and local government to respond to the needs of the individual trainee." The Nixon proposal called for sweeping change, consolidating the various existing programs into a "cohesive manpower services system," while decentralizing administration and delegating a good deal of policy-making to the state governments. Aside from a "trigger" provision that would release an extra 10 percent of manpower money when unemployment was over 4.5 percent, and a call for a computerized "job bank," there was little that was substantively new.[20]

The whole emphasis of the President's recommendations was on organizational rationalization. The basic assumptions remained that the private market could provide the needed jobs and that training would make the difference for jobless people. The President's consolidation proposals responded to serious and generally recognized organizational problems created by the array of conflicting programs. In fact, one observer has commented, it contained the "consensus views about manpower organization that had been developing for several years."[21]

Much more controversial was the recommendation to give the governors a major administrative role in the program and to make the state employment services central agencies. These proposals were hotly contested by city officials and minority-group spokesmen, who pointed to the state government's inability or unwillingness to deal with urban problems, and to the poor record of the state employment services in helping the hard-core unemployed. As a result, this approach produced intensive Congressional criticism. It would be significantly changed.

More disturbing to public employment supporters was the failure of the President's proposal to recognize the need for a different approach to deal with rapidly rising unemployment. President Johnson's major policy initiative during the final year of his Administration had been the Job Opportunities in the Business Sector (JOBS) program. The President hoped to find a half million jobs for the hard-core unemployed by mid-1971. President Nixon picked up this emphasis on subsidizing private training programs and made it an even more prominent feature of his manpower budget, at the expense of other existing programs.[22]

The JOBS program ran into a variety of problems. It was very difficult for federal officials to monitor strictly the practices of companies without endangering the cooperative relationships on which the program was based. The tendency was therefore simply to take the companies' word, even in the absence of specific reports. Some firms merely used the federal subsidy to lower their labor costs, while others trained workers at government cost in fields where there were very few openings. In some cases no training at all was provided. There was a high turnover rate, with many workers rapidly leaving the program. Most important, however, was the lack of evidence that the program was creating any additional jobs in a contracting economy. If a company was hiring subsidized ghetto residents while laying off other workers directly or through attrition, there were just as many jobless people, and the prospects for permanent post-training employment of workers without seniority were poor. The fact was that the JOBS program only made sense during a period of economic boom, but it became the centerpiece of manpower strategy just as that period was ending.

Congress Initiates Its Own Bill Even before the President submitted his manpower bill to Congress, the labor movement and liberals in the House had begun work on a bill emphasizing public employment. Representative James O'Hara (D-Mich.) introduced a comprehensive Manpower Act that provided for strong centralized administrative standards, a program to help workers upgrade their jobs, and a major commitment to public service employment. The O'Hara program's objectives were to "guarantee every American willing and able to work, an opportunity for a meaningful job and for training." The bill was supported by the AFL-CIO and cosponsored by a hundred Representatives. The Administration criticized the idea of "job invention" and warned of the potential costs of such an approach. Even the academic experts, organized in the National Manpower Policy Task Force, suggested only experiments and warned of "unknown and possibly large risks" in a major program.[23] Academic enthusiasm would come after the Congressional initiative.

At the same time Senator Nelson, who was now chairman of the Subcommittee on Employment, Manpower, and Poverty, was working with his staff on a public jobs proposal. Shortly 203 after the submission of the President's bill, he issued a Labor Day statement promising hearings on the measure across the country, and committing himself to a battle to develop public support for "a major program to create hundreds of thousands of public service jobs."[24]

When the hearings opened in November 1969, the President's bill faced attack on several fronts. Democrats were acutely unhappy about the major roles reserved for state officials, and about the uncertain positions of mayors and local community action agencies in the operation of manpower programs. They were deeply concerned about the future of some of the categorical programs they believed to be highly successful. Most important, however, they pressed an attack on the basic assumptions of the whole approach and continually raised the alternative of public jobs.

The difficulties of the President's bill were increased by strong labor opposition. AFL-CIO President George Meany called public jobs "the best avenue for those who cannot find a place in the private sector of our economy." He emphasized labor's support for the O'Hara approach.[25]

At the hearings the public jobs issue was immediately raised. In his opening statement, Senator Nelson questioned the "overall adequacy" of existing manpower programs, and said that "rational discussion of our performance" was impossible until the question of how many jobs were needed and the role of public service employment were faced. Both Nelson and Senator Jacob Javits, the most active GOP member, argued for public jobs before Administration testimony even began.[26] Nelson criticized continued reliance on "job training, rather than job-creating programs," and argued that the loss of 800,000 jobs for each 1-percent increase in the unemployment rate required a new approach. Labor Secretary George Shultz responded that there were "regular jobs" available and that "the economy is producing more and more jobs at a very rapid rate." He argued that there were "a lot of job openings right now."[27]

The Senate subcommittee held sessions in cities across the country, hearing repeated tales of vast problems of joblessness. In Los Angeles a county official testified that the county had 661,000 people on welfare and expected an additional 110,000 during the next year. The local welfare rolls carried more people than lived in the entire state of New Hampshire.[28] After the 1965 Watts riot, a state commission had concluded that the most basic cause of the upheaval was ghetto joblessness, and the unemployment rate was still high. Income in some black and Chicano neighborhoods had actually gone down an average of 8 percent between 1959 and 1965.[29] One twenty-four-year-old black resident illustrated the failure of existing training programs in testimony by describing his enrollment in four successive training efforts without qualifying for any available job paying as much as $2 an hour.[30] Similar stories came from city after city.

As the hearings proceeded, the unemployment rate continued to climb month after month, and there was a mounting demand for programs that did more than just redistribute growing unemployment. By March 1970 Senator Nelson was denouncing the Administration for the highest unemployment rate since 1965, and urging rapid help for the 900,000 additional people without jobs, two-thirds of whom were blue-collar workers. He called the JOBS program "completely unrealistic," and condemned the diversion of funds from the Neighborhood Youth Corps to a program that so far had produced few placements in permanent jobs.

Two months later, in May, the attack on the whole Nixon strategy intensified. Senator Cranston (D-Calif.) declared the JOBS program was failing so badly that the Labor Department had been able to use only about a fourth of the appropriations. Senate Subcommittee Staff Director William Bechtel said that the JOBS program was both expensive and far less successful than expected in actually finding jobs. Senator Nelson asserted that both JOBS and the Nixon manpower bill had been designed for a period of "almost uniquely low unemployment" and thus were very vulnerable to recession. Since the Administration bill was drafted, Nelson said, "more than 1 million additional people have been thrown out of work."[31]

By mid-May Nelson and seven other Senators had introduced an alternative bill intended to force a head-on confrontation regarding most of the major controversial issues in the bill. Nelson's public challenge to the Administration came as the end of the hearings was approaching and the time for committee decisions was nearing. The Nelson bill was an amalgam of contradictions that attempted to provide a base for administrative flexibility while also preserving popular categorical programs. It even wrote into law new measures reflecting the special causes of various subcommittee Democrats. The new bill increased the powers of both local governments and community action agencies—these last the local spokesmen for the poor—at the expense of state authority. Most significantly, however, it added a massive new public jobs program.

205

Two days before the bill was introduced, the Urban Coalition and the Urban League issued a call for public jobs to cope with the worst crisis of joblessness since 1962. The burden of the Administration's drive against inflation, they said, was being felt most heavily by the poor and the black, while the country was ignoring a "backlog of real needs in the public sector."

Introducing the new proposal, Nelson insisted that seven months of hearings had revealed virtually unanimous support for public service jobs around the country. Existing small-scale programs, he declared, had demonstrated the feasibility of the approach, but had met only a trivial fraction of the national need. For thirty years, he said, polls had shown strong public support for federally subsidized work programs for those without jobs; the time had therefore come to face the fact that "there simply are not now enough jobs in America for all her citizens . . . jobs that pay enough to support a man and his family at even the poverty level—and offer hope of advancement." At the same time, the country faced "an extraordinary crisis" of "wholesale neglect," and "starvation of the public services that alone can make a modern industrial society a livable habitat for man."[32]

With both bills on the table, a solid Democratic majority opened up negotiations with the Republicans over the bill to be reported out of the Employment subcommittee. Since Senators serve on several subcommittees simultaneously, most discussions were actually between Nelson, who held the authorized proxy votes of the other six Democrats, and Javits, who tried to use four GOP proxies, and his own sense of persuasion and bargaining, to win acceptance of as many as possible of the Administration's goals. A clearly unified majority, the subcommittee preserved the basic structure of the Democratic proposal. The subcommittee measure, reported to the full committee in mid-July, provided at least $1 billion for 150,000 new jobs. These jobs, the committee staff reported, would restore some of the credibility of job-training programs that currently had little relationship to a situation where "the unemployment rate for black teenagers is over 41%, and when many depressed rural areas simply have no jobs to offer to graduates of training programs."[33]

When the bill went to the full committee, most Republicans were ready to accept it as the best that could be obtained. On the first committee vote the tally was 12-0, with five members absent. Later a handful of GOP members voted against the measure, and three influential Republicans expressed some reservations.

As reported to the floor, the 1970 bill reserved one-third of the basic $2-billion authorization for public service jobs. In addition the committee provided $1 billion under a separate heading, exclusively for producing jobs. If Congress were to appropriate the full amount, then, there would be $1.66 billion to put people to work.

The Administration Response: The Dominick Amendments
When the bill reached the Senate floor, the Administration attempted to win a measure it could accept by working for a series of Labor Department amendments offered for the White House by Senator Peter Dominick (R-Colo.).

The position of the Administration and Senate conservatives was outlined in the minority report signed by three GOP committee members. "We strongly disagree," they wrote, "with the concept that manpower funds should be used to finance either mere job creation or a permanent expansion of public services." They were concerned about what they saw as "a permanent submarket in the public sector characterized by minimum wages and poor advancement opportunities." They did not wish to promote a situation where the government would guarantee everyone work.

In his effort to change the nature of the bill, Senator Dominick sponsored amendments intended to reinstate governors as key program administrators, and to require that any public jobs be both temporary and low-paying. The amendment, however, was soon defeated by a huge 19-55 margin. The real fight focused on the public jobs section.

Senator Dominick sought to lessen the attractiveness and permanency of public jobs. A staunch conservative, he was firmly opposed to government tampering with the job market. His proposal called for maximum wages equal either to the minimum wage, or to 80 percent of the normal wage for comparable work not under the minimum-wage law. Rather than allowing states and localities to make commitments to long-term augmentation of their staffs, he favored legislating a maximum term of two years for anyone holding a job created by the bill. These changes, he said, would ensure that the jobs program be part of a coordinated manpower strategy built around the objective of private employment, rather than an end in itself.

207

The difference in approach was very clear and it was underlined by Senator Nelson's response. Nelson said that there were five million public jobs that needed to be done. He insisted it was fundamentally unfair to pay the new workers 20 percent less than what existing staff doing the same work was receiving. "The question is," he said, "do we establish public service jobs to perform these necessary jobs, or only to serve a training function?" The Senate's answer was clear. The Dominick-Administration plan failed 29–43.[34]

With the strong Senate showing against the Dominick approach, effective opposition to the bill collapsed. The Colorado Senator took to the floor again to denounce what he saw as a $4-billion effort to "inject the Federal Government into every city and county and State in the country," but his appeal was wasted. Now that it was clear the Senate was going to pass a popular program dealing with the very visible national problem of unemployment in a Congressional election year, there was a rush to get on the bandwagon. Final passage came by a 68-6 vote on September 17, 1970. Every Democrat who voted, including all the Southerners, favored the measure. Only a small hard core of Republicans persisted in their opposition to the bill.[35]

The Importance of the Senate Victory The Senate triumph was a dramatic example of Congressional initiative in domestic policy. In the face of strong opposition from two successive Presidents, and divided counsel from the academic oracles of economists who play such a significant role in generating new issues, Senator Nelson and his allies had rallied broad support for a new approach to one of the most fundamental questions in the society. Cutting through the explanations of the poor records of many established manpower programs, they concluded that some of the assumptions underlying a decade of thought and experimentation with federal programs were wrong. Except in unusually prosperous conditions, they decided, there could not be a rational approach to employment policy until public authorities recognized that there were simply not enough decent jobs to go around, and accepted a responsibility to create job opportunities.

Special circumstances had enhanced the possibility of Congressional creativity. The jobs issue was close to the heart of the whole Democratic coalition, and had been ever since the 1930s. It was an issue on which there was broad public support for action. Developed in a manner emphasizing state and local authority, it had sidestepped the traditional ideological battles over the role of the federal government and the danger of federal interference in local affairs. The program simultaneously addressed several crises—unemployment, the chronic need for funds for state and local public services, and the mounting welfare mess. Finally, it was an election year when both parties were battling for control of the Senate, and when both knew the economy was the leading domestic issue.

The Sequel in the House: Compromise and Criticism
Earlier in the year House liberals had been deeply pessimistic about the chances of putting a public jobs bill through the more conservative chamber. After Senate action, however, the imminent approach of the November election and the continuing growth of the unemployment statistics began to improve prospects. Some GOP support was needed, but a good many House Republicans were disposed to look favorably on a compromise on the sensitive issue. The crucial question was the attitude of the Administration, since House Republicans were more orthodox and united, and less ready to oppose the President than were some of their Senate counterparts.

At this point, signs of possible flexibility from the Labor Department led to negotiations. After a young Labor staff member "unofficially" gave a leading Democrat's staff a document outlining possible compromises, Democratic leader James O'Hara (D-Mich.) went into negotiations with leading GOP committee members and the Assistant Secretary of Labor. The group worked hard to put together a compromise measure before the Congressional recess in mid-October, and finally brought a bill to the House floor on the last day before the election recess.

The negotiations produced a compromise acceptable to both sides, embodying some of the restrictions the Senate had rejected. A House committee staff member described it:

> In the end, they gave us our public service employment program but exacted language in return that required the Secretary to set "objectives" for the movement of persons employed under this program into "non-subsidized" employment within certain periods of time.[36]

The compromise bill also contained provisions about sponsorship of programs that met some of the Administration's goals by decreasing the number of local authorities eligible to run independent programs. The House bill also differed from the 209

Senate bill in moving away from the narrow categorical emphasis of existing manpower programs.

When, in a drafting session lasting most of the night, an agreement had been reached, Democratic and Republican leaders were so eager to obtain final passage before adjournment that they rushed the package through committee and onto the floor with virtually none of the carefully detailed committee work that often takes place in House committees. An opponent of the compromise bill, Congresswoman Edith Green (D-Ore.), bitterly attacked the process:

> This 71-page bill, reported out by the full Committee on Education and Labor the same day it was introduced, is the "late-into-the-night" product of a coalition of a Democratic and a Republican member of the committee, some committee staffers, and administrative spokesmen for the Labor Department.
>
> They labored . . . until 3:30 a.m. on the day the bill was approved. . . .
>
> . . . when the chairman called the committee together on September 30 at 10:30 a.m., the members did not know what was in it. . . .
>
> Yet demands were made that the bill be reported out by 11 a.m. Only a parliamentary squabble delayed the session to later in the afternoon.[37]

The same day the committee acted, the Secretary of Labor pledged the "full support of the administration" for the bill. He praised the measure as "a responsible response to President Nixon's request for comprehensive manpower legislation."[38]

When the bill was brought to the House floor on October 14 —the last day before the recess—Mrs. Green confounded the effort to win rapid passage by raising parliamentary objections that forced a delay until after the election.

The battle resumed in mid-November, but pressure on the President and on Congressional Republicans had greatly diminished. With the election over and the status quo largely maintained on Capitol Hill, the political urgency of the jobs issue had declined.

On November 17 the House took up the measure again. Some conservatives now argued that the state governments had been downgraded in the compromise, and even claimed that regarding public jobs the Labor Department had made a "Potsdam agreement" (referring to the much criticized agreement with the Soviet Union near the end of the Second World War). But a leading GOP spokesman, Al Quie (R-Minn.), assured the members that the bill "has the complete support of the Nixon Administration." He said it achieved the President's "most important objective" by consolidating many overlapping programs.[39]

The main test of sentiment on the jobs issue came on an amendment that attempted to kill the entire new program. The jobs program won easily 69-31. Two other amendment battles, however, did have a significant impact on the ultimate shape of the program. The House rejected an effort to guarantee "special consideration for the placement of qualified individuals who are unemployed, unskilled, or underemployed," responding to the argument that the program should remain a flexible part of a comprehensive manpower package with few rigid legislative limitations. When the question of a veterans preference came up, however, the same argument for a broad program was rejected. Responding to national concern in late 1970 about the failure to find work for Vietnam veterans, the House wrote into law an explicit veterans preference—a provision absent from earlier manpower and job-related poverty programs.

These votes showed something about the nature of the coalition supporting the bill, and are useful in understanding the emphases which would later emerge in the administration of a public jobs program. It was not—as in the late 1960s—a program aimed at a residual category of hard-core unemployed, but one intended to provide benefits for a broad spectrum of people confronting economic frustration. Moreover, this program for jobless and inadequately employed people was seen from the beginning as a major way to deal with the critical situation of hundreds of thousands of disillusioned young war veterans. In view of the limited scale of the program, a major commitment to giving veterans special consideration was certain to have a strong impact. At any rate the program did not suffer the liability of identification in Congress as an effort for only the poor, the powerless, and the black. Inability to find a decent job was a much broader problem now, and the bill drew strength from this fact.

After a short debate, the House indicated strong support for the compromise bill. An effort to kill it by sending it back to committee was defeated 80-275, and the bill was shouted through on a voice vote.[40]

The bill's outlook seemed promising as supporters of public service jobs from both houses were appointed to the conference committee. With huge favorable majorities and Administration commitment to manpower reform, it appeared that the conferees had considerable latitude. The committee substantially increased the percent of manpower funds that the House version gave to the jobs program, and allowed smaller localities to take over program administration.

Conservatives were highly critical when they saw the extent to which the more liberal Senate version had prevailed over the House-Administration compromise. The criticism did not assume serious proportions in the Senate, but did become a real threat in the House.

Leaders of both parties in the Senate united behind the conference bill. Both Nelson and Javits presented the measure as a compromise with the Administration. They emphasized that they had given up one-fourth of the public jobs money the Senate had originally authorized (though Senator Nelson conceded the unlikelihood that the Appropriations Committee would have provided this "add-on" money anyway). Javits appealed to the President against a veto, calling the bill "the very best that can be done," substantially increasing flexibility in the administration of manpower programs, providing an important state planning role, and providing safeguards against the creation of permanent "make work" jobs. In spite of storm signals from the White House, the Senate consensus in favor of action was still operating. Final passage came by a 68-13 vote, with only five Republicans opposing the measure.[41]

The Outcome: Veto When the bill reached the House side, the weight of Administration resistance began to be felt. The huge margin of support for the bill, more than three to one in November, melted away to a bare eighteen-vote victory in December. Bipartisanship vanished and GOP support evaporated. As a result the division was close enough to encourage White House beliefs that a veto could be sustained.

Not only did the President choose to veto the bill, but he sent it back to Capitol Hill with a stinging message attacking the whole concept of public service jobs. "W.P.A.-type jobs," he asserted, "are not the answer for the men and women who have them, for government, which is less efficient as a result, or for the taxpayers who must foot the bill." The Emergency Employment program, said Mr. Nixon, "represents a reversion to the remedies that were tried 35 years ago." He claimed it would "relegate" many workers to subsidized "dead end" jobs.[42]

This harshly ideological message from an Administration that before the election had been willing to compromise provoked bitter Congressional reaction. Representative O'Hara saw the veto as "a grim Christmas present to the Nation's unemployed." Charging that the sudden shift was transparently political, he attacked the President's slighting reference to "W.P.A.-type jobs." Jobs, O'Hara said, were "a whale of a lot better for the spirit and for the stomach than a Hoover-type breadline."[43] Cooperation had vanished. Both parties were reviving clichés from the 1930s.

The attempt to override the veto focused first on the Senate, where the margin of victory had been huge. Four days before Christmas, in the expiring hours of the session, the debate took place. Lame-duck Senator George Murphy (R-Calif.), speaking for the Administration, interpreted the bill as saying that "where a problem arises, just throw some of the taxpayers' money at it and it will go away." While Murphy had earlier voted for public jobs, he now agreed with the President about the dangers of "make-work" and "widespread abuse."[44]

Senators defending the bill repeated once again the old arguments, and lashed into what they saw as basic distortions in the President's description of the bill. Senator Edward Kennedy declared the President was assuming that states and localities had no useful work to be done even though their officials unanimously spoke of inability to provide basic services.

> The President's attack . . . becomes even more incomprehensible when we consider that the family assistance legislation which the administration is now supporting provides $150 million for public service employment and does not even contain the safeguards found in the manpower bill.[45]

Senators Nelson and Cranston (D-Calif.) accused the President of displaying insensitivity to the critical employment problems of veterans, and of opposing the most popular and best answer to public criticism of welfare handouts to employable adults. Nelson observed that the President seemed most upset about the very provisions his spokesmen had tried to make even worse. The President claimed the new jobs would not be good jobs, and yet, said Nelson, the Labor Department had tried to enact a provision paying workers only 80 percent of the prevailing wage, thus creating "a new 'poverty corps' of substandard public jobs." The President complained about possible "make-work" jobs, but his spokesmen had fought to make all the jobs temporary. "Temporary jobs," Nelson argued, "by their very nature are make-work jobs."[46]

The arguments had little impact. The President's veto, and his pressure on Republicans no longer facing elections, brought 213 a very strong GOP shift against the bill. Although the Senate had voted eleven to one for a more far-reaching bill in September, supporters could not now obtain the required margin to override the veto. Republicans now split three to one in favor of the President. While there was a 48-35 majority in favor of overriding the veto, it was far short of the required two-thirds majority.[47] The veto was easily sustained.

In the aftermath of the President's victory, criticism continued to swirl. Newspapers, including even the conservative *Washington Star*, accused Mr. Nixon of insensitivity to people thrown out of work by the Administration's economic policies. "Also victimized by the downturned Presidential thumb," said the *Star*, "are the financially beset cities, where hard times simultaneously have worsened problems and sapped the resources for dealing with them."[48]

Worst of all, from the President's perspective, economic figures continued to show that Administration strategy was not working. By mid-1970 the JOBS program was at least 100,000 short of its employment target. By the end of the recession-ridden year, even National Alliance of Businessmen officials were conceding that the plan was not really workable during a period of severe economic contraction.[49] The jobless rate remained very high.

NOTES

[1] Joseph A. Kershaw, *Government against Poverty* (Washington: Brookings Institution, 1970), p. 73.

[2] Arthur M. Schlesinger, Jr., *A Thousand Days* (Boston: Houghton Mifflin, 1965), pp. 622, 628; James L. Sundquist, *Politics and Policy; The Eisenhower, Kennedy, and Johnson Years* (Washington: Brookings Institution, 1968), p. 92.

[3] Sundquist, *Politics and Policy*, pp. 93–96.

[4] James L. Sundquist, ed., *On Fighting Poverty* (New York: Basic Books, 1969), p. 16. The importance of education solutions throughout American history is effectively described in Rush Welter, *Public Education and Democratic Thought in America* (New York: Columbia University Press, 1962).

[5] Adam Yarmolinsky, "The Beginnings of OEO," in Sundquist, *On Fighting Poverty*, p. 50; Sundquist, *Politics and Policy*, pp. 243–44.

[6] Garth L. Magnum, "Guaranteeing Employment Opportunities," in Robert Theobald, ed., *Social Policies for America in the Seventies* (New York: Doubleday, 1968), pp. 35–37.

[7] Senate Committee on Labor and Public Welfare, Subcommittee on Employment and Manpower, *Hearings, Conserve Human and Natural Resources of the Nation*, 88th Cong., 2d Sess., 1964, pp. 15.

8 *Ibid.*, pp. 48, 52–55.

9 Office of Economic Opportunity, "The Unemployed and Community Betterment: A Guide to Projects under the Nelson Amendment," 1966, pp. 2–5; Senator Gaylord Nelson, "Legislative Memo," April 20, 1967.

10 *Congressional Record*, September 25, 1967, pp. 26687–88; October 3, 1967, p. 27634.

11 Kershaw, pp. 82, 90–92; Lee Rainwater and William Yancey, *The Moynihan Report and the Politics of Controversy* (Cambridge: MIT Press, 1967), p. 285.

12 *Congressional Record*, September 25, 1967, pp. 26805–06.

13 *Congressional Quarterly Almanac, 1967* (Washington: Congressional Quarterly, Inc., 1968), p. 1065.

14 *Congressional Record*, September 26, 1967, p. 26824.

15 *Ibid.*, October 3, 1967, p. 27623; U.S. Department of Labor, *Manpower Report of the President*, 1968, p. xiii.

16 *Congressional Record*, September 27, 1967, pp. 27062, 27084–86.

17 *Ibid.*, October 2, 1967, p. 27428.

18 *Ibid.*, October 3, 1967, pp. 27612, 27618.

19 *Ibid.*, October 4, 1967, p. 27833; *Congressional Quarterly Almanac*, 1967, p. 1070.

20 Text in Congressional Quarterly, *Nixon: The First Year of His Presidency* (Washington: Congressional Quarterly, Inc., 1970), pp. 78-A–79-A.

21 Roger H. Davidson, "Rule Making, Trouble in the Manpower Subgovernment," unpublished manuscript (1972), p. 13.

22 Sar A. Levitan, Garth L. Mangum, and Robert Taggart, III, *Economic Opportunity in the Ghetto: The Partnership of Government and Business* (Baltimore: Johns Hopkins University Press, 1970), pp. 19–20, 28.

23 Davidson, pp. 15–16; Austin P. Sullivan, Jr., "Public Service Employment—A Congressional Perspective," unpublished paper prepared for Industrial Relations Research Association, December 28, 1971, pp. 2–4.

24 William J. Spring, "Congress and Public Service Employment," unpublished manuscript, December 28, 1971, p. 21.

25 Senate Committee on Labor and Public Welfare, Subcommittee on Employment, Manpower, and Poverty, *Hearings, Manpower Development and Training Legislation*, 1970, 91st Cong., 1st and 2d Sess., 1969–70, pp. 75–78.

26 *Ibid.*, pp. 80–82, 123.

27 *Ibid.*, pp. 123–24.

28 *Ibid.*, pp. 285, 287.

29 *Ibid.*, pp. 290–91.

30 Spring, p. 23.

31 Statements by Senator Gaylord Nelson, March 24 and May 11, 1970; Employment Subcommittee Press Release, May 8, 1970; statement by William Bechtel, May 13, 1970.

32 *Congressional Record*, May 20, 1970, S7505–06.

33 Davidson, p. 25; Employment Subcommittee Press Release, July 15, 1970.

34 Employment Subcommittee Press Release, August 5, 1970; Davidson, p. 25; *Congressional Record*, September 17, 1970, pp. S15856–76.

35 *Congressional Record*, September 17, 1970, p. S15892.

36 Sullivan, p. 6.

37 *Congressional Record*, October 14, 1970, p. H10114.

[38] *Ibid.*, November 17, 1970, p. H10362.

[39] *Congressional Record*, November 17, 1970, pp. 37676–77.

[40] *Congressional Record.*

[41] *Ibid.*, December 9, 1970, pp. H11403–06; December 10, 1970, pp. S19953–58.

[42] *Washington Post*, December 11 and December 12, 1970; *New York Times*, December 17, 1970.

[43] *Congressional Record*, December 17, 1970, p. H12032.

[44] *Ibid.*, December 21, 1970, p. S20966.

[45] *Ibid.*, p. S20967.

[46] *Ibid.*, pp. S20974–86.

[47] *Ibid.*, p. S20990.

[48] Reprinted in *Congressional Record*, December 30, 1970, p. E10833.

[49] *New York Times*, December 26, 1970.

11

THE PUBLIC
JOBS BREAKTHROUGH

The Emergency Employment Act of 1971

Yet Another Senate Initiative The Congress had hardly convened when Senator Nelson and thirty-one cosponsors submitted a new bill. Among the sponsors were Senate GOP Leader Hugh Scott and a number of other prominent Republican moderates.[1]

The committee supported the new bill 15-2 and the issue was back on the floor by early April. The new bill, the Emergency Employment Act, was designed both to meet some of the President's objections and to force a clear political decision on the jobs issue, unencumbered by the general manpower reform provisions the earlier bill had carried. The new bill was intended to create a "temporary" program that was triggered whenever unemployment reached 4.5 percent and that increased as the problem worsened. It was presented as "emergency stopgap legislation" that would expire after two years.[2]

The Administration had in the meantime developed a new approach to the whole manpower field. In place of its old reform package, it now supported "special revenue sharing" that would turn manpower money over to state and local governments with very few controls. This bill was part of the strong central drive of the President's second term to turn over control of federal programs to state and local officials. There could be no public employment effort now, Administration spokesmen said, unless this new strategy was adopted.

The Senate bill expressed a broad consensus that action was urgently necessary. The major state and local government associations were pushing the bill. There were almost five and a half million people unable to find jobs, including nearly a tenth of all black workers, a ninth of the construction workers, a sixth of out-of-school teen-agers, and about a third of all black teen-agers in the job market.[3] Senator Javits said that the situation was "horrendous and alarming in the poverty neighborhoods," while there was "work crying to be done" in the cities. The new bill, he stressed, met the President's requirement that public service employment be "transitional and short-term." He tried to reassure his fellow Republicans that they were no longer opposing the President.[4]

Senator Dominick, however, warned that the bill would "face the strong possibility of another veto," since it added another categorical program when the Administration was trying to eliminate such programs. Senator Taft (R-Ohio) said that since localities needed help, Congress should concentrate on revenue sharing rather than "putting the cart before the horse" with what amounted to an inefficient method of transferring resources.[5]

The bill's supporters responded with a series of very different justifications for the bill, expressing varying objectives that would later confuse the program's administrators. Senator Thomas Eagleton (D-Mo.), for example, saw the program as a preferable form of revenue sharing:

> It is the federal government lending a helping hand to the local governments, but it is also not an abrogation of the responsibility by the federal government. . . . Rather this bill indicates in broad areas how the money should be spent and then says to the local governments: "You pick out which needs are of the greatest concern to your community and go hire the people you need."[6]

Others pointed to the way the bill directed special attention at such politically important groups as unemployed engineers, scientists, and Vietnam veterans. The committee report had highlighted the importance of getting jobs to specialists whose "idle talents constitute a scandalous waste of valuable national

218

resources." The committee had strongly directed administrators to help veterans, particularly those with combat experience. Special attention was also directed to Indians, migrant workers, jobless senior citizens, and welfare recipients. In the case of welfare families, supporters suggested the bill would give some useful experience with one of the policies contained in the President's hopelessly bogged-down welfare bill. The strategy was to assemble a broad coalition for the bill, including members not particularly concerned with providing good jobs for traditional welfare recipients.[7]

The real test of strength on the bill came, as often happens, on a procedural vote. Senator Prouty (R-Vt.) moved to send the bill back to committee for a month, hoping to gain consideration of the President's revenue-sharing proposal. Senator Humphrey responded to the motion with a passionate speech that concluded, "It is a capital crime to permit unemployment when this Nation needs men and women on the job."

> I hear about the program for reorganization. . . .
> . . . Maybe reorganization is needed. But I tell you . . . what is needed more . . . is jobs—j-o-b-s. . . .
> This emergency act is desperately needed. It should have been signed into law a year ago. The unemployed people should have been at work. The country has suffered. The people have suffered. The economy has suffered.[8]

The recommittal motion was defeated 29-44. It was a substantial margin, but not enough to override a veto. After the key test, the bill sailed through on final passage 62-10. Only eight of the most conservative Republicans and two Southern Democrats recorded themselves in opposition.[9]

The Fight to Win the House After the successful drive to power a skillfully constructed bill through the Senate, supporters faced the much more difficult challenge of the House. Even before the Administration had capped its resistance with the 1970 veto, the House had been closely divided. Some Republicans had probably been influenced to vote for the 1970 manpower bill by the major changes it incorporated in the operation of manpower programs—changes excluded from the simple jobs bill now passed by the Senate. There was a great deal of GOP support for the revenue-sharing approach, whereas this bill not only ignored the President's proposal, but took a significant step toward an alternative strategy that relied on continued heavy federal involvement. Finally there was the 219 problem of the veto, whose impending menace discouraged advocates and threatened to reduce the whole battle to meaninglessness.

A House staff member summed up the situation. Having seen "a year of hard work down the drain," he recalled that "many of us wondered if it was worth the effort to repeat the exercise, just to be vetoed again." [10] The problem was compounded by the smashing defeat that the program's leading advocate, Representative James O'Hara, had suffered in his effort to win the position of Majority Leader.

Within the House a key development was the decision of the new Speaker, Carl Albert (D-Okla.), to make jobs a central Democratic issue and commit his prestige very strongly to moving along a package of legislation. The economy was always the best Democratic issue, and one that brought together all the party's factions. By concentrating on a program including jobs, public works to create more jobs, higher minimum wage and social security retirement benefits, the Democrats could help millions of people and claim a good deal of political credit, while avoiding the passions associated with questions of racial change and guaranteed incomes for welfare recipients. Although the public service employment program was a major policy innovation, it was one with powerful and long-term public and union support, and compatible with party tradition.

The Speaker's support gave new hope to House proponents. Leadership now passed from O'Hara to Subcommittee Chairman Dominick Daniels (D-N.J.), who was better able to work with the erratic Mrs. Green, and who cooperated well on the bill with Chairman Carl Perkins. This broad base of support from the Democratic establishment was to become decisive when the old conservative coalition seemed, for a time, to put the bill in mortal danger.[11]

The House subcommittee hearings that began in late February served primarily to provide a forum for repeated attacks on the failure of the Nixon economic policies and for praise of the public jobs plan. Once again the hearings underlined the intense desire of local officials for help. A Mobile, Alabama, city commissioner reflected the general attitude when he said he would be happy to accept anything the committee could agree on that would help pay the costs of providing city services. "If you can't get the whole chicken," he said, "then you buy part of it."[12]

Much of the committee's work revolved around the dispute over whether the program should be temporary or permanent.

The old argument continued between those who saw it as a transitional aid for people down on their luck in a basically healthy economy, and those who insisted that there just weren't enough jobs, and that the best way to provide them would be by meeting long-standing needs for public services. One academic witness told the committee that the Nixon unemployment projections had been widely off target, and that optimistic predictions could not be credited. Another urged members to consider the fact that government employment should be regarded as a normal rather than as an anomalous situation, since a fifth of all Americans already worked for some public agency, and a fourth of all new jobs in the economy were in public service.

The Secretary of Labor finally appeared on the last day of the subcommittee hearings, just as the Senate was moving rapidly toward final passage of its bill. Secretary Hodgson tried to shift attention to the Administration's manpower revenue-sharing measure, introduced just the day before. He pointed hopefully to a slight decline in the month's unemployment statistics, and predicted that the "rate will fall off markedly as the pace of the economy quickens." In his view, the main problem with existing programs was not the absence of jobs, but the failure to allow enough local control and state government influence. The jobs proposals, he said, had two fundamental defects. First, they did not permit consolidation and decentralization of the programs. More importantly, however, the bills did not "unequivocally assure" that the new jobs would not be permanent. The bills, he concluded, were "well-intentioned," but they "detract from the needed early effort to achieve lasting reforms."[13]

The Administration position came under fire from several directions. Congresswoman Ella Grasso (D-Conn.) asked Hodgson whether his position was that nothing should be done for chronically unemployed people now "falling into deeper despair," until the whole controversial Administration domestic program was enacted. He answered that "temporary measures . . . would detract from the attention that we feel is necessary for an overall restructuring of manpower reform." [14]

The leading GOP manpower expert, Representative Steiger (R-Wis.), was openly puzzled by what he saw as contradictions in the President's position. How, he asked, could the President zero in on the danger of make-work jobs in his veto message, and then turn around and insist that the jobs be temporary? Steiger pointed out that the jobs proposed for welfare clients 221 in the latest version of the Administration welfare and revenue-sharing plan had no guarantee at all to prevent make-work assignments.[15]

The Secretary warned that passage of the Democratic bill would invite a veto. He conceded that the Administration was changing the rules of the game after the Democrats were ready to meet most of the old objections. "I can understand," he said, "how some people, like yourselves, . . . could feel that you had finally learned to play ball in our court and by the time you did that we moved the court."[16]

The Administration's basic strategy to defuse the movement for public jobs was to concede the possibility of change on this issue within some of its program proposals, while maintaining very strong pressure against any major new jobs effort whose popularity might soon give it permanent status. The welfare proposal was partially modified, but the welfare bill was bogged down in fundamental disagreements between the House and the Senate, so that its passage seemed highly unlikely anyway. Similarly the proposal to grant state and local officials the right to make some limited use of temporary public jobs—among other approaches—under the manpower revenue-sharing bill, had to be discounted by the bill's slim chance of enactment.

The Democatic bill was easily reported out of the Education and Labor Committee, whose membership—particularly on labor issues—was more liberal than the House as a whole. The committee vote, however, was highly partisan. All but three GOP committee members signed a minority report attacking the bill as just another narrow categorical program.[17] The real question was whether the Republicans could carry the support of their frequent allies, the Southern Democrats.

The approaching showdown shaped up as the first major test of the ability of the new House leadership to carry out the Democratic economic program announced by Speaker Albert in early April. The Speaker had called on the House to fill "the void left by the inactivity of the Nixon Administration," arguing that severe unemployment and the highest level of unused plant capacity since the 1957–58 recession meant that Congress couldn't afford to "wait longer for the President to take the lead."[18]

Democratic anger had increased when President Nixon announced in January that he was using his administrative authority to provide a $3-billion tax break for business, in the hope that it would stimulate investments and eventually produce more jobs. Liberals who had encountered repeated vetoes on economic grounds found the President's decision to make this large and dubious sacrifice of federal revenues infuriating. The President, they felt, was insisting that there was no money for social programs, or even jobs, while finding billions for a trickle-down approach with little possibility for fast results.

When the bill first reached the House floor, however, the Speaker's plan appeared to be mortally threatened by the conservative coalition. After a divided Rules Committee sent the emergency jobs bill to the floor with a rule that made it impossible for the Republicans to offer the Nixon manpower revenue-sharing proposal as a substitute, the rule was challenged on the House floor. The Democratic leadership was shocked when the challenge carried by a healthy 210-182 margin.[19] Now there would be a vote on the Administration plan, and the margin on the procedural test suggested an excellent chance for enactment of the entire GOP package.

On the first vote the conservative coalition seemed effectively in control. The Republicans had managed to win almost unanimous support of party members for the change, and the winning margin had been provided by forty-five Democrats, mostly Southern and Border state conservatives. There were even racial overtones, since some reports indicated that Rules Committee Chairman William Colmer (D-Miss.) had mobilized Southern votes in exchange for GOP assurances of support in the Mississippian's battle against strong job discrimination legislation.[20]

Worried about losing the bill, the House Democratic leadership pulled it off the floor for two weeks while they and supporting organizations worked to recover the lost votes. One observer has described the intense effort to unify the Democrats:

> Labor and urban lobbyists swung into action to assure that their friends were solidly behind the public-jobs bill. But the decisive push was made by Speaker Albert and Majority Leader Hale Boggs (La.), who personally made the rounds of southerners' offices to shake loose their support. . . . The leaders made it clear that local government officials were solidly behind the public-jobs concept, and that the vote would present a chance to embarrass the Nixon administration.[21]

When debate resumed, Democratic spokesmen were ready with a barrage of criticism of the President's proposal. Representative Daniels (D-N.J.) saw it as an "unexamined idea" that was "utterly inconsistent with what the administration recommended last year." Representative Pucinski (D-Ill.) **223** viewed it as a "cruel hoax" that wouldn't create "one new additional job." Pucinski claimed that restrictions in the Administration bill would give preference for work to welfare recipients and deny help to others out of work. Representative Scheuer (D-N.Y.) insisted there was nothing in the record of state response to unemployment problems to justify the Administration's confidence in state direction of manpower.[22]

The choice, declared Representative O'Hara (D-Mich.), was between reshuffling existing programs and a basically new approach to "meet the needs of the 2.5 million people who have been added to the unemployment rolls in the last 2 years." The executive branch, he said, had now become rigidly committed to revenue sharing as an end in itself, even if it failed to solve any problems. It would imperil those existing programs that were working, and create bitter battles among the various affected groups for parts of the state and local appropriations. The bill wouldn't prevent states from simply financing existing programs and lowering their taxes, nor would it ensure any more public employment. His speech climaxed:

> We cannot cure unemployment by pretending it does not exist —or that it is "merely transitional" or "local" or any of the other excuses that Schultz and Hodgson and Nixon have advanced to conceal the havoc they have wrought upon the lives of the nearly 3 million Americans they have added to the unemployment rolls. . . . We cannot cure unemployment by "training" people for jobs that do not exist. We can cure unemployment by creating jobs.[23]

The Democrats time after time returned to the unemployment figures: the level was going up again and nothing seemed to be working.

Speaker Albert took the floor with a strong plea for reversing "the cumulative drain on the energies and abilities of millions of willing but hopeless Americans." He asked members to look at the growing list of towns with substantial long-term joblessness and consider the massive governmental, labor, and academic support for the public service jobs plan.[24] Yet more important than the Speaker's words were the efforts of leading House Democrats to win back the errant Southerners.

The fate of the bill was determined on a vote to substitute the Administration approach for the committee bill. Restored Democratic unity showed as the twenty-eight-vote loss of two weeks earlier now gave way to a twenty-two-vote victory for the public jobs bill. After this key vote, and defeat of the Republi-

Figure 11-1

Unemployment Levels at Time of House Passage of 1971
Emergency Employment Act

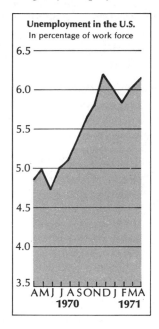

Unemployment in the U.S.
In percentage of work force

SOURCE   New York Times, *May 8, 1971.*

can proposal to make the jobs "transitional" only, the House
quickly passed the bill.[25]

The President's About-Face   As the House and Senate conferees met to work out a compromise bill, the prospects for a
veto seemed very high. The Congressmen who had once again
beaten the Administration in each House met in an atmosphere
of general gloom. Senator Javits thought a veto likely, and
Representative Al Quie put the chances of it at nine to one.
Once again months of legislative work seemed about to go up
in smoke.
At this point, however, things began to change, in part because Congress was presenting the President with what he saw
as an even more objectionable approach to job creation: a
large public works bill. The President was facing the serious   225

Table 11-1

Public Attitudes about the Economy in July 1971

*Ratings of "the job President Nixon is
doing in keeping the economy healthy"*

Positive	22%
Negative	73%
Not sure	5%

Beliefs about whether "the country is in a recession or not"

Is in recession	62%
Is not	25%
Not sure	13%

*Feelings about changes in unemployment in
home communities during past year*

Unemployment has increased	70%
Unemployment has decreased	5%
Stayed the same	22%
Not sure	3%

SOURCE *Harris Survey of July 10–16, 1971, published in* Washington Post, *August 9, 1971.*

political problem of what to do about two popular job bills at a time when confidence in his economic policy was at a low ebb. A June 1971 poll found that only a fourth of the public thought the President was doing an excellent or "pretty good" job of managing the economy, while 70 percent rated his record as poor or only fair. Even the chairman of the President's Council of Economic Advisors, Paul McCracken, admitted that unemployment was not going away and conceded publicly that new approaches might be required. The success of Democratic Congressional candidates in exploiting economic issues in the 1970 election made the political problem all the more urgent.

Faced with these difficulties, the President changed his mind again. In mid-June the White House signaled its readiness to negotiate a compromise. After determining that the initiative was serious, the Congressmen abandoned normal conference proceedings to meet with Administration spokesmen in the search for common ground.[26]

There were substantial differences between the Senate bill, the product of a bipartisan compromise, and the more extensive House measure produced by House Democrats. The Adminis-

226

tration pressed for legislation closer to the Senate measure. The Senate had authorized a two-year "transitional" program, to be phased out when the jobless rate fell to 4.5 percent. The House supported a five-year, $5-billion program that could provide permanent jobs. Under the House plan, programs serving localities with high unemployment would continue even after the national figures fell.

The compromise bill was designed to meet the President's basic concerns, with at least reassuring language, while preserving some of the important House innovations. The conference committee and the Administration agreed on a two-year, $2.25-billion program with language describing the program as transitional. The House spokesmen, however, won the point of continuing programs in localities with more than 6-percent unemployed even after the national jobless level declined. The Administration wanted an explicit veterans preference, but settled for "special consideration" for former servicemen.[27]

Now that the Administration supported the bill, the whole atmosphere changed. In the House, GOP members awkwardly searched for explanations why they were now supporting a bill they had recently denounced as a danger to the republic. Representative Quie praised the "significant changes" that made the measure "an excellent compromise." Representative Steiger declared the measure was "vastly superior" to the House version. The GOP members were pleased to report that they had won the battle for a temporary program.[28]

Things looked much different on the majority side of the aisle. Chairman Perkins told the House that while the conferees had used the word "transitional" in the bill, it referred only to the fact that the bill authorized the program for just the first two years, and not to any limitations on the type of jobs. Perkins pointed out that the conference report clearly stated: ". . . it is the intention of the conferees that public service employment jobs lead wherever possible to permanent positions in the public or private sector." [29]

With the basic political arrangement made, there was no passionate interest in sorting out all the ambiguities contained in the bill. The final vote was a rout. The measure passed the House 343-14.[30]

The country had at last a public service jobs program. Seven years after the first Congressional proposals and four years after losing the first serious Senate effort, proponents had won over the executive branch. In fact, in signing the measure into law, the President even adopted some of the arguments used by

Capitol Hill critics after his earlier veto. "America needs more jobs," said Mr. Nixon, "and it needs them now."

> The employment will be real and steadying. It will not be dead-end entrapment in permanent public subsidy. Local programs will be designed with a view toward career advancement and toward developing new nonsubsidized careers for the worker.[31]

A half year earlier, the President had vetoed a manpower bill providing extensive reform of the various existing programs, largely because of fundamental disagreement with the whole idea of public service jobs. The President had sacrificed rationalization and better administration of the training programs, which he had defined as one of his most primary domestic objectives, to forestall a major step toward official recognition that the government must serve as employer of last resort. Now the President accepted the program in a bill that gave him nothing else. Placed at a disadvantage by Congressional initiatives and concerned about the political consequences of continued recession conditions, a conservative Republican President found himself approving the first substantial job creation program since the New Deal. (The next month the irony would deepen when the President responded to a intensifying economic crisis by resorting to price and wage controls authorized by the Congress over his strong initial objections.)

With the enthusiasm of a new convert, the President now pressed Congress for rapid appropriations, asking for the full $1 billion authorized. Bipartisan support brought the full amount out of the House Appropriations Committee with rare speed. Even Appropriations Chairman Mahon, who initially said the program "opens the gate for all kinds of mismanagement and even possible scandal," was talking about the "very serious unemployment problems" and supporting the appropriations.[32]

The money bill sailed through the House, and the Senate Appropriations Committee rushed it to the floor of the upper body two days later. The Senate saw the extraordinary spectacle of the Appropriations chairman on the floor asking full funding of a once-controversial program, almost immediately after House action, without changing a word in the House bill. The measure was receiving emergency treatment.

The only significant dissent came from a man who had been left behind by the President's sudden shift—Senator Dominick.

He had led the White House battle against the measure and now was upset. The new program, he warned, "is no more temporary than the Senate is." He expressed his concern that political leaders were being "bamboozled into trying to make a totally federally controlled economy out of this country."[33]

Dominick and most other Senators were well aware that "temporary" programs had a way of becoming permanent governmental commitments, if they were popular enough in their early years to develop a strong local constituency. Since the new program was aimed directly at a problem everyone opposed—joblessness—and since it also provided valuable resources, with few strings attached, to local and state governments, it had a good chance of survival and expansion. If the program grew and affected substantial percentages of unemployed Americans, it would indeed be a very important change in the American economic system. For the moment, though, there was general satisfaction about the compromises, whatever they might portend, and eagerness to get the people to work. Within weeks, people were working.

Another Battle Front: Welfare Reform

The debate over the necessity for government creation of jobs focused most intensely on the Emergency Employment Act, but Congressional leaders were also raising the issue very strongly in the maneuvering over the President's welfare reform proposal, and in House efforts to generate jobs through large public works bills. In the end the public works strategy provoked a veto and helped pressure the President into signing the Emergency Employment Act, while the criticisms of the welfare program led to substantial change in the Administration's proposal.

The demands for greater emphasis on work in welfare programs sprang from two different sources, one conservative and one liberal. Congressional conservatives held to the belief that welfare programs were becoming so attractive as to encourage people to quit low-paying jobs. Liberals argued that incorporating work-training programs into the welfare system was absurd, unless jobs were provided after the training was complete. The conservatives generally called for required work at pay levels about the same as the welfare money the recipient would receive anyway. Liberals commonly called for wage levels over 229 the poverty level, sometimes for wages equal to those paid to regular workers doing similar work.

Congress had first made a small appropriation for a welfare work-and-training program in 1962, and the effort was expanded in the 1964 poverty bill. In most cases it turned out that the money actually was spent on hiring people for menial work at menial wages; there was little training and little help in finding better jobs.

Congressional enthusiasm for the idea, however, produced an expanded effort—the Work Incentive Program (WIN) that was part of the 1967 Social Security amendments. The WIN program, which enjoyed strong conservative support, produced a screening of some 1.6 million welfare cases that found about a tenth of these people eligible for the work program. Only about a fifth of those who had completed the training effort by early 1970, however, had been placed in jobs. A major study by Leonard Goodwin of the people enrolled found that welfare clients did indeed share the general desire for work. They recognized that jobs could be the central element in reaching their goals.[34]

The WIN program selected out those poor people the Labor Department thought most likely to succeed, put them through training programs, and then usually left them still jobless. The result was to first raise their hopes and increase their self-confidence, then confront them with failure, then finally plunge them into deeper feelings of dependency on welfare. Even those who did find jobs, the Goodwin study showed, did not usually obtain the kind of good secure employment that might rapidly increase their confidence.[35]

As the Nixon Administration took over, the WIN program, like the JOBS program, was showing defects. The President, however, chose to make a much bigger version of the WIN effort a centerpiece of his welfare bill.

During the first year of his Administration, President Nixon announced welfare reform as the top priority of his domestic program. The President's bill was a complex mixture of liberal and conservative impulses, and he presented it as substituting "workfare" for welfare. The bill adopted the liberal argument for a national floor under welfare payments, and for payments to the working poor whose income was below welfare levels, but it attempted to satisfy Republicans through harsh work requirements forcing welfare mothers with school-age children out of their homes. In discussing the bill, the President appealed strongly to conservative stereotypes about lazy welfare recipients, and declared there was nothing wrong with menial jobs.

When the bill got to Capitol Hill, liberals focused criticism on three issues in particular: the inadequacy of the income levels, the lack of realism about work requirements, and the impossibility of mounting a decent program without providing day-care facilities for children. The basic premise of the Nixon plan was that welfare mothers could be pushed into private economy jobs through a combination of strict requirements and a financial incentive created by subtracting only part of their earnings from their welfare payments. Congressional critics insisted that the jobs weren't there, and that a decent work plan would require not only creating jobs but also facing up to the scandalous lack of child-care programs. So far, the mothers enrolled in WIN were getting neither jobs, nor decent care for their children. In mid-1970 HEW reported that it was two-thirds behind its target of providing day care for 188,000 children. It was providing for only 61,000 youngsters across the United States, 60 percent of whom were being cared for in their own homes or a relative's home.[36]

The Administration proposal was harshly criticized by the leading spokesman for welfare families, George Wiley, the executive director of the National Welfare Rights Organization. Wiley said that "only the stupidest person would put emphasis on work when there are no decent jobs paying a decent wage." He insisted that a decent welfare program must both "protect the right of a mother to be with her children," and provide "a guarantee of a good job at the end of the training," when the children are old enough to be left on their own.[37]

The leading critics of the welfare bill on the Senate Finance Committee, Senators Harris and Ribicoff, took note of widespread criticism of the failure of the Administration to propose a serious effort to create jobs, and tried to help rectify the failing with an amendment to the bill. The Secretary of Labor told the committee that the bill would require 2.5 million people to register for job training, but would create only 225,000 training positions. The AFL-CIO called for a large public service employment program for welfare recipients, a position echoed by spokesmen for the major urban organizations and the national religious groups. "The program," said Oregon's Republican Governor, Tom McCall, "cannot succeed without availability of jobs."[38]

The Ribicoff-Harris amendment proposed shifting $180 mil-   231

lion in the President's package from job training to job creation. The amendment was intended to create 30,000 jobs and
serve as a "partial supplement" to Senator Nelson's jobs bill.
Without the change, its authors argued, the work approach
would rest on a vain hope that private business would generate
jobs for great numbers of people in the middle of a recession.
Training people for jobs which simply didn't exist would only
magnify their frustration.

In the last days of the 1970 session, with the Senate deeply
divided over the welfare bill, the Administration attempted to
break through the stalemate by accepting several of Ribicoff's
proposals. Among the changes was an agreement to set aside
$150 million for public service jobs.[39] But it was too late and
the Senate divisions were too deep to reach any compromise in
1970. During the coming years, however, the idea of such
employment was to grow in importance.

When the Administration submitted its 1971 welfare bill,
it actually included a provision setting aside $800 million for
200,000 public service jobs.[40] Obviously the widespread Congressional support for the Emergency Employment Act, and the
powerful evidence of failure in the existing training programs,
were beginning to make a real impact on executive-branch
planning.

Even so, the Administration's policy modification was not
sufficient to satisfy its critics that enough public jobs were provided, or that the type of private jobs projected for welfare
mothers would be adequate. George Wiley, the National Welfare Rights Organization spokesman, charged that both HEW
and the Labor Department had stacks of studies showing welfare families wanted work, and insisted that the jobs did not
exist. The 200,000 jobs wouldn't meet the needs of welfare
parents alone, he said, and they ignored the millions of other
unemployed families who were potential welfare clients.

Senator Ribicoff was incensed at the Administration's continuing determination to rely strongly on private jobs well below the minimum wage level. He attacked the policy for forcing
people to take $1.20-an-hour jobs. "I think," he said, "it's a sad
day for the country when the Labor Department takes the position that people should stay in poverty and we should subsidize
slave labor." HEW Secretary Richardson argued that any
higher wage standard would be unfair to five million workers
in the country who were then receiving $1.20 or less for regular
jobs.[41]

232   When the welfare reform bill, including the Administration's

public jobs proposal, reached the floor of the House, it came from the powerful Ways and Means Committee under a rule that forbade substantive floor amendments. The House couldn't change the bill, but only vote it up or down. For the second straight year, it passed it.

When the bill reached the Senate, it went once again to the hostile Finance Committee, where both the conservative and liberal members had strong objections to the package. Under these circumstances the measure's fate would have been dim at best. Within weeks of the opening of hearings, however, the reform was killed by a Presidential decision to scuttle the bill for the time being. The President's New Economic Policy, announced on August 15, 1971, included a cutback on federal expenditures. Part of this reduction was to be accomplished by delaying implementation of welfare reform for a year, even if Congress passed it.[42] After two years of describing the welfare bill as his top domestic priority, and after exerting considerable pressure to win House passage, the President set the measure aside. It was dead for the rest of the year.[43]

The significance of the welfare bill's evolution did not lie in the creation of jobs, since the continuing Senate stalemate precluded enactment of any welfare reform bill during the Nixon presidency. The bill's importance lay rather in affording Congress an opportunity to expose elemental weaknesses in the President's "workfare" program. These critiques first produced a 1970 agreement to a small public jobs program, and by 1971 a major transfer of resources from training to job creation, within the Administration proposal. This was a very considerable shift for a government intensely committed to the idea of nongovernmental solutions.

New Bids for a Public Works Program

The 1971 Bill As economic conditions remained unfavorable and discussions of unemployment strategies intensified, Congress revived the New Deal idea of generating jobs through massive public works programs. Major bills were launched in the House in both 1971 and 1972. Each time the Administration was strongly opposed and the Democratic leadership strongly committed.

Public works acceleration was a basic part of the alternative economic approach supported by Speaker Albert in 1971. The basic vehicle that year was a cleverly concocted blend in   233 one bill of two very popular programs and a $2-billion Public Works Acceleration Act: a package that would be hard to veto. The new money was intended to help communities where joblessness exceeded 6 percent. Since much of the money would go toward meeting a backlog of water and sewer projects, the bill had a real ecological appeal as well.[44]

Intended to produce as many as 170,000 more jobs, the measure passed overwhelmingly in spite of GOP opposition. The closest vote was more than two to one in favor of the bill, as worried House members tried to make a record on the jobs issue. Final passage came by a huge 319-67 margin. On the closest test—a motion to send the bill back to committee—every single Northern and Western Democrat supported the bill, while only ten Southerners joined with GOP opponents. The Republicans even lost a fourth of their own members, in spite of talk of a veto.[45]

Although the corresponding Senate bill had no public works employment program, when the bill went to conference, the Senators accepted the House program. House members had insisted that the works program be pushed, in spite of Senate veto fears.

The conference bill touched off a Senate debate over the value of this approach for cutting unemployment. Much of the discussion revolved around the smaller program run in 1962 by the Kennedy Administration.

The bill's opponents argued that the public works approach was slow, expensive, and inefficient in helping unskilled workers. They attempted to exploit the institutional pride of Senators, charging that the Senate conferees had given in to the House members in a way that threatened the power of the Senate itself. Senator Norris Cotton (R-Vt.) described the bill as "a highly discredited relic of the past," while Senator Howard Baker (R-Tenn.) saw it as a "pork barrel" approach that would "produce very few jobs too late, at a cost of approximately $20,000 per job." Even the GOP's leading progressive, Senator Javits, saw little sense in creating more demand for construction, an industry where skilled labor was required and where there was already little joblessness in some areas.[46]

The Democrats countered with arguments that the Republicans had their figures wrong and that the money would meet very urgent local needs. Senator Montoya (D-N.M.), the subcommittee chairman, said that President Kennedy's program had cost only $8,000 per job, and had left a legacy of 1,500 waste treatment plans and 300 new hospitals. He asserted that one construction worker in nine was unemployed, and that each construction job had a "multiplier effect" that produced 1.5 jobs in the private sector. Senator Muskie (D-Maine) affirmed the existence of a massive backlog of applications for environmental and health projects.[47]

The arguments, however, seemed to have little impact. The Senate vote produced an almost straight party-line division and the bill carried 45-33. Only three Republicans voted for it; only one Democrat was opposed. As partisan pressure on the issue grew, the Republican split in the House gave way to almost monolithic opposition. The Senate vote suggested easy success for a Presidential veto. As it happened, House passage of the conference report by 275-104 proved anticlimactic.[48]

As expected, President Nixon vetoed the bill, cushioning the political impact by simultaneously announcing his support for the public service jobs program. The President said the measure would have little rapid impact in creating jobs, and would intensify existing inflationary pressures in the construction business. It was a "costly and time-consuming method of putting unemployed persons to work."[49]

The veto provoked heated Congressional criticism, but the Democratic efforts to override it failed. Speaker Albert declared there was "no more important bill" to end joblessness, and Representative Blatnik (D-Minn.) observed that millions of people in families without work were being told to "eat optimism."[50] When the issue came up for a vote in the Senate, the President was sustained by a safe margin. For the fifth time, President Nixon had succeeded in killing a Congressional initiative; for the second time he had successfully ended a job-creation program.

The defeat was not quite total. In order to hold GOP forces together against a program with some real popular appeal, Senator Howard Baker announced that he would propose an emergency "disaster area" plan for regions suffering particularly acute joblessness.

Within two weeks a much smaller version of the original bill was on the President's desk. Accelerated public works funds had been cut from $2 billion to $0.5 billion. Republican Congressional leaders now warned the President that a second veto would not only create damaging political criticism, but might well be overridden. The smaller bill had been worked out by leading committee members from both parties and passed with very wide support, 88-2, in the Senate. Mr. Nixon signed the bill. For the first time since the early 1960s, there was at least a 235 small effort to speed up public works so as to lessen unemployment.[51]

Five months later, as one powerful Senator noted ironically, the Administration was taking credit for the Congressional program and suggesting that it would request some more funds. After vetoing the big public works bill on the grounds that it could not have a rapid impact on unemployment and that it would raise "false hopes," the President now was raising hopes about a much smaller program and planning fast action on labor-intensive projects. The Commerce Department announced that the President had directed immediate action to create 7,000 jobs through spending $27 million of the appropriation— a much higher ratio of jobs to dollars than the Administration had found possible during the debate.[52]

Election-Year Escalation: The 1972 Proposal   During 1972, as the Presidential and Congressional campaigns heated up, Congress pressed the Administration to expand the public service jobs program and to support a much larger public works commitment. When a high level of unemployment persisted— even after a variety of efforts to stimulate the economy, and after the President's drastic reversal of economic policy in August 1971—support grew for lowering unemployment levels through direct government intervention. The Democrats took the lead with "Jobs Now" legislation intended to create 500,000 public jobs. The measure was introduced by sixty-three House Democrats in December 1971 and by twenty-one Senators in January 1972.[53]

This bill was supported by Walter Heller and other leading economists. Heller praised the plan to spend an additional $6 billion on public jobs during the next two years as particularly useful because it could tailor jobs to fit the growing numbers of teen-age, female, and black workers on the unemployment rolls. It would avoid the inflation caused by general stimulation to the economy, which produced skilled labor shortages while indirectly helping unskilled workers. Andrew Brimmer of the Federal Reserve Board also supported increased emphasis on public jobs. His analysis showed that merely increasing demand at the end of a recession often generated increased productivity, but not large numbers of new jobs.

The most ambitious bill was introduced in March 1972 by Senator Cranston and other Democratic liberals. The bill, whose supporters included all three of the party's leading Presidential candidates, aimed to provide 1,150,000 new jobs. It

236

called for spending $3 billion the first year and $7 billion the second.[54] Cranston argued that it was no more unrealistic than Senator Nelson's first jobs bill when introduced in 1970.

As the campaign unfolded, the jobs issue was widely discussed. The 1972 Democratic platform promised jobs to all who wished to work, and this pledge was repeated by the party's nominee, Senator George McGovern (D-S.D.). The platform called "a guaranteed job for all" the party's "primary economic objective."[55]

While the stage was being set for decisions about the scope and nature of future public employment efforts, Congress made a tangible decision to expand the existing Emergency Employment program as much as the current law allowed. When the Labor and HEW appropriations bill came to the House floor in June 1972, the normally parsimonious Appropriations Committee had allowed the full $250-million increase. The subcommittee chairman pointed out that this was "by far the largest increase" in the department's budget, and that committee members had encountered a great deal of pressure on its behalf in their home districts.[56]

When the bill came to the Senate, there was no conflict over the public jobs money. There was a little chafing, however, over the Administration's request for $450 million to expand the tarnished Work Incentive Program (WIN). In late 1971 Congress had adopted the proposal of Senator Talmadge (D-Ga.) that forced all welfare recipients over sixteen to register for job training, and required that 15 percent of all employable people on the rolls be promptly put in training or given jobs. The 1971 law had made some progress toward public jobs by setting aside one-third of WIN funds for jobs and on-the-job training in private business.

Response to the Administration's request produced evidence of growing doubts about the wisdom of the WIN program. Senators Magnuson (D-Wash.) and Norris Cotton (R-N.H.), the dominant figures on the Labor-HEW Appropriations subcommittee, said the results had been poor. Nonetheless, the Senate accepted the Administration's proposal, at least for the time being.

A more interesting and obviously political fight came up over the public works issue. With only a single day of hearings, and with the strong support of the Democratic House leadership, the Banking and Currency Committee sent to the floor a bill intended to stimulate creation of as many as a million jobs, primarily through construction of water and sewer proj- 237 ects. The measure required speedy action, with all the money to be committed within six months and two-thirds of the $5 billion actually spent within a year.

The bill was a direct challenge to the President; the committee had not even waited for the formality of listening to Administration views. The bill was also a challenge to the Appropriations Committee, since it permitted backdoor spending directly obligating the Treasury to make payments without annual appropriations bills.

Supporters said the bill would produce 500,000 jobs directly and at least an equal number indirectly, wiping out about a fifth of existing unemployment. If the states and localities matched part of the federal money, the impact would be even greater. At the same time it would finance desperately needed antipollution facilities.

The Republicans called the program expensive, and saw in it a duplication of existing efforts and "an outrageous, irresponsible political power play." Congress, they pointed out, had just finished greatly expanding the antipollution programs. Representative John Anderson (R-Ill.), head of the House GOP Conference, ridiculed the legislative tactics. "I must say that never in my years in Congress—including the salad days of L.B.J.'s famous automated legislation mill during the 89th—can I recall an occasion when a serious matter has been treated so lightly, so cavalierly by a standing committee of the House."[57]

Defeat of the proposal came on a very close vote. Representative Ben Blackburn (R-Ga.) proposed an amendment freezing grants whenever the projected federal budget deficit exceeded $20 billion—an amendment that he termed an "automatic deflation clause." Although the House was warned that this would render the bill useless during the recession, the amendment carried 197-194.[58]

After suffering this defeat, the Democratic leadership brought the issue up again on a roll call vote. Speaker Albert told his colleagues that the bill had strong leadership support, and his statement was underlined by a strong appeal from the Majority Leader. Appropriations Chairman Mahon, however, said the bill would make the House appear "ridiculous," since Congress had already given the Administration 250 percent of its request for water and sewer facilities. On the new vote the Democrats splintered and the Blackburn amendment was again approved, this time by a thirteen-vote margin. The House then moved quickly to defeat the entire bill.[59]

238

Once again the jobs issue had produced a very clear partisan division. On the final vote all but fourteen non-Southern Democrats supported the huge bill, while only twenty-three Republicans voted for it. The key to the outcome was the decision of forty-four Southern Democrats, including a number of Appropriations Committee members, to oppose the bill.[60]

The defeat was a severe blow for the Democratic leadership, and a major victory for the harried Appropriations Committee and the President. Hitherto the Democrats had shown unusual unity on the job issue, and there was a powerful political incentive to confront the President with a huge bill, forcing him to either accept it or bear the political costs of vetoing a measure aimed at two very popular goals—jobs and a better environment. The leaders had confidently predicted victory.

In retrospect one can see many reasons for the difficulties. The bill was very big—far larger than the bill the President had easily vetoed the previous year—and there were serious questions about the capacity of contractors specializing in such work to expand fast enough. The measure had been rushed through committee too precipitously in a house that prided itself especially on careful committee work. There were serious questions about both the wisdom of a public works strategy and the real backlog of needed projects, and the bill's proponents sometimes had no convincing answers. The legislation's obvious political purpose made it even more difficult to win over substantial numbers of Republicans. Given the grave weaknesses of the Democratic strategy, the President prevailed, although the victory was a narrow one.

Congressional Job Action: An Appraisal

Congressional leadership, during four years of the Nixon Administration, helped to redirect thinking about the nature of unemployment and to create an important new approach to the solution of joblessness. Previously, most manpower programs had been based on the assumption that people were out of work because something was wrong with them. The programs assumed that training the unemployed would make them eligible for available jobs. The new approach involved a very different understanding of the economy and of public responsibility. It assumed that, even with the best of training programs, there were not sufficient jobs available—especially during periods of recession. It further assumed that it was a

239

poor investment and a damaging course of action to force people into training programs and then confront them with failure when their training proved worthless in obtaining work. The new program assumed that money was better spent creating public jobs, thus meeting public needs while giving the jobless person what he required most.

It was a considerable achievement to legislate a new approach to one of the most important national issues, in the face of a hostile Administration and severe budgetary constraints. It did not, however, prove possible to expand the program sufficiently to help a major portion of the unemployed. By combining the jobs created under the Emergency Employment Act, the accelerated public works program, and the amendment to the WIN program, perhaps a quarter of a million new jobs could be created. Given the traditional limited reach of manpower programs, this was a major accomplishment. Viewed against the backdrop of some five million unemployed, however, the limits of its impact are clear.

Within these limits the results were rapid, particularly in the Emergency Employment Act effort. Once the President changed positions and the Appropriations Committee sped through the necessary funding, great emphasis was placed on hiring people quickly for the jobs. Early reports showed that by the spring of 1972, 140,000 people had been employed.

Since the act had so many conflicting objectives, and was designed to permit great amounts of local discretion, it was very difficult to clearly evaluate its success. An early analysis based on available national statistics and a series of local studies by manpower experts, however, did permit some tentative conclusions.

First of all, the act had produced jobs rapidly—jobs that were usually not menial and that represented a response to real public needs. The jobs had not been concentrated at the lowest levels, and had mostly involved ordinary kinds of public work and relatively normal recruitment procedures. Both minority workers and veterans—two groups of special concern to the authors of the legislation—did in fact obtain large numbers of positions. Contrary to some fears, there was little evidence that the program was being exploited for patronage purposes.

The researchers characterized the program as a "major departure" and the most significant change since manpower training became part of national policy. The program went into effect with breakneck speed, under heavy and continued pressure from Administration leadership and from the President himself for rapid hiring. In the rush, efforts to reform hiring procedures or job classification systems usually were lost sight of. The program functioned much better as a tool to put people to work than as a mechanism for helping those with the most acute problems. While in a certain sense all people without jobs are in need of help, manpower programs had frequently been criticized for "creaming"—for aiding those most qualified for jobs in the private market anyway, rather than the hardcore unemployed with little education, little work experience, and special personal problems. When the public employment idea had first been broached in the mid-1960s, it had been aimed especially at these people. As unemployment rose, affecting millions of workers who could normally have expected jobs, the proposal became broader and less precise. When the final bill was written, it was conceived of as helping veterans, unemployed aerospace workers, various minority groups, and others, without any sharp focus on provision of special opportunities to those with the weakest backgrounds. The discretion given to local agencies, and the law's expressed intention that agencies find some way to put the new employees on the permanent payroll in the long run, favored selection of the most qualified workers in many cities. In practice, the strongest preference was given to veterans—a decision that limited the aid to those not possessing the educational or health qualifications for service, and that constricted the opportunities for poor women.

The program served mostly high school graduates; only a fifth of those getting jobs were dropouts. It helped relatively few welfare families, since only about one job in ten went to a public aid recipient. The person hired tended to be "an average, stable worker forced into idleness in a 6 percent unemployment economy." For most of the workers, the new jobs paid better than their previous employment. Blacks received "at least proportional representation" in most of the local programs, and received a very heavy share of the jobs in some communities. Veterans received several times their share of the jobs.

Although the bill signed by the President emphasized that the program was transitional, most communities treated it as a straight employment effort, and did not try either to do much training or to restructure jobs and career patterns so as to bring a great many of the workers into permanent city-financed jobs. Expert observers pointed out that communities were going to be hard-pressed to meet the Labor Department's 241 goal of 50-percent retention. Localities were acting as if the money from Washington would continue to flow. Although the "transitional" language in the bill suggested otherwise, and the Administration was opposed to anything like a permanent program, local officials were obviously getting the message that many Congressional liberals were intending to send. The program was having something of the revenue-sharing impact that was desired by many Congressional supporters. Most of the new jobs were jobs in agencies that the agencies had not been able to fill because of budgetary problems. Thus the program was enhancing the ability of local and state officials to meet local requirements.[61]

The deficiencies in the program related to its lack of clear priorities and strong leverage over local practices. Early reports showed that the national goal of giving half the jobs to workers in "disadvantaged" categories was not being met. Good coordination with existing manpower programs was lacking in many areas. There was a danger that local officials would use the funds to replace rather than increase locally financed efforts, thus holding down local taxes but producing no more jobs. National policy-makers lacked good data about the number of additional worthwhile jobs as they contemplated expansion of the program.

Many of the problems arose from the contradictions between the Administration's restricted view of the program and the expansive plans of its Congressional supporters. These conflicts were thinly papered over in the measure that the President finally signed. The Senate committee had built consensus by including everyone's special concern—from Indians to aerospace workers—in the bill, with little effort to sort out relative priorities. In the end, the consensus reached only the general conclusions that public money should be used to create jobs for some unemployed workers, and that the localities should have broad discretion in deciding what to do, so long as they gave some attention to the designated target groups.

When the National Urban Coalition evaluated the program in 1972, it underlined the limits of the effort and called for a large expansion. It praised the "exceptionally high" record of employing minority workers, but argued that there was not enough concentration on the hard-core jobless and the neighborhoods with the most crippling levels of unemployment. The Coalition charged that the Administration's hurry to hand out funds, and its reluctance to monitor local decisions, had diminished the possible impact of the program on disadvantaged workers. Basically, however, the Coalition enthusiastically supported the public jobs approach. It called for a tripling of the effort—thus creating jobs for a tenth of the nation's unemployed—and urged a sharper focus on ghetto communities and workers with special problems.[62]

The 1973 White House Attack

Congressional liberals succeeded in creating the first large public employment program since the Depression by agreeing to obscure the nature of the change, and by accepting a compromise that defined the program as transitional. While Democrats made a major theme of the concept of the government as the employer of last resort in their 1972 platform, the program was an obvious anomaly in a conservative Administration. After his sweeping 1972 election victory, President Nixon decided to eliminate it. Buoyed by rising employment figures, he recommended no new funds at all for the program in his January 1973 budget message, and authorized diversion of much of the existing money from financing jobs for adults to providing temporary summer jobs for teen-agers.

In both houses of Congress, however, committees controlled by strong supporters of public jobs began the struggle for renewal early in 1973. With both the Emergency Employment Act and the Manpower Development and Training Act due to expire in midyear, Congressional advocates faced massive problems. Administration officials knew that they could accomplish their objective of eliminating the program merely by delaying or vetoing enactment of new legislation. With the jobless rate dipping below 5 percent for the first time in years, some of the urgency was going out of the issue. The President created a crisis in the manpower training programs when he announced that new enrollments would be curtailed until the Labor Department implemented revenue sharing by administrative order, without Congressional approval. This bland announcement that the public jobs program was no longer necessary deepened the predicament of the committees.[63]

Encouraged by broad local and state support for their program, House Democratic leaders tried to force the issue by bringing to the floor in April a public jobs bill doubling the size of the effort. The Rules Committee supported the Democratic leadership by sending the measure quickly to the floor with a favorable rule. There, however, it faced intense and 243 overwhelming GOP opposition, and the defection of certain Southern conservatives. Under the threat of a Presidential veto, the House voted by a narrow majority to table it.[64]

The setback in the House didn't stop Senate supporters. In July Senator Gaylord Nelson brought two major bills to the Senate floor, directly challenging the President's priorities, and each was decisively passed. The manpower training bill rejected the President's effort to reduce effective resources by more than a third, and substantially altered the Administration's unstructured revenue-sharing plan. The bill authorized localities to use the training funds for direct job creation if they wished. It passed by a huge 88-5 margin.[65]

The next day the Senate began debate on extending the public jobs legislation for two more years. After a relatively brief discussion, studded with favorable comments about the experience in several states, the Senate decisively rejected an effort to sharply cut back the program. Final passage came by a 71-24 vote.[66]

In the House the battle dragged on for months, with the Administration refusing to accept public employment and the committee rejecting the effort to enact the President's manpower revenue-sharing approach. Finally, as the end of the session neared, a compromise was worked out. The House adopted a bill that moved toward the revenue-sharing approach but specifically set $250 million aside for public jobs. The bill also authorized localities to spend the revenue-sharing money for jobs instead of training, if they wished.

When the bill went to conference with the Senate, an agreement was reached specifying that a minimum of $250 million be spent the first year and $350 million the second year. The legislation extended the public jobs program for four years, and authorized the appropriation of however much money Congress judged desirable. Part of the compromise was an agreement from the President to accept restoration of funds he had earlier tried to cut out of the manpower training budget. The legislation also reserved management of a variety of special purpose programs (for Indians, migrant workers, etc.) to the federal government, and gave the Labor Department broader responsibility for supervising local plans than the Administration wished.[67]

While the program had been cut back very seriously, it survived. The legislative framework would be available through the 1977 fiscal year to permit a liberal Congress or a new Administration to make public employment a major component

244

of its manpower policy. An idea that had been dismissed as radical and unnecessary even during the social experimentation of the Great Society was now on the way to becoming an accepted instrument of economic policy. Moreover, this breakthrough had been accomplished and sustained in the face of strong ideological opposition from the President. It was totally an accomplishment of Congress.

The 1973 struggle ended on an ironic note. After a year of fervent Administration assurances that public jobs were unnecessary because of rapid economic growth, the dislocations threatened by the Arab oil boycott suddenly threatened to produce a very high level of joblessness. Searching for a response, some Administration officials embraced the very remedy they had been fighting so stubbornly. Spokesmen now told the press that public jobs might be a good remedy.[68]

Years are usually required before a new social policy developed by liberals becomes sufficiently familiar and develops sufficient public support to win conservative endorsement. Often it never happens. In the case of the public employment program, however, the economic difficulties of mid-1974 brought a sharp and sudden executive-branch movement to embrace a Congressional initiative strenuously resisted for years.

The change was striking during the final days of the Nixon Presidency and the beginnings of the Ford Administration. Three days before Nixon resigned, Federal Reserve Board Chairman Arthur Burns proposed that the government meet increased joblessness by creating 800,000 public employment jobs at a cost of $4 billion. Burns, Nixon's appointee as the nation's chief banker and formerly a top White House aide, was strongly conservative. Climbing joblessness and a desire for a solution with the minimum inflationary consequences were bringing some conservatives to the point of endorsing a solution that liberals were advocating largely for social reasons.

President Ford, in a comment at his first press conference after taking office, indicated his willingness to consider a significant expansion of the program:

> ... we have a public service employment program on the statute books which is funded right today, not for any major program but to take care of those areas in our country where there are limited areas of unemployment. . . . There is a recommendation from some of my advisors saying that if the economy gets any more serious, that this ought to be a program, a broader, more expensive public service program.

245

We will approach this program with compassion and action where there is a need for it.[69]

The President's statement quickly produced a response within the executive branch and intensified the already substantial Congressional interest in the jobs legislation. Labor Secretary Peter Brennan promptly announced that his department was considering a $680 million program to start when joblessness reached 5.5 percent.

In the Senate, Senator Jacob Javits (R-N.Y.) was leading the effort to enact a $4 billion program. The idea was to quickly pump significant funding into the program structure Congress had successfully sought to maintain in the recently completed manpower bill.

The leading public jobs spokesman in the House was a freshman member from a heavily Republican district in Michigan, Representative Richard VanderVeen (D-Mich.) who had scored a great upset by capturing the seat Gerald Ford vacated when he left the House to become Vice President. VanderVeen and forty other Congressmen had introduced legislation to create 900,000 public service jobs in July. Many other leading members of both houses supported the public jobs approach.

Public jobs were also strongly endorsed as a basic economic remedy by a broadening array of liberal, labor, and civil rights organizations and activists. Fifteen major national organizations, including the AFL-CIO, the Leadership Conference on Civil Rights, national Catholic and Protestant church organizations, and others endorsed a statement urging a broad jobs program in September 1974. After a conference of black leaders, NAACP Executive Director Roy Wilkins urged that top priority be given to creating 1 million public jobs. The Congressional initiative had created a major new economic tool.

Summary: Congress, the Government, and Jobs

Poverty and hopelessness in American society are closely connected with the inability of the economy, even in boom times, to provide jobs for everyone who wants to work. There are always millions of men and women shut out and the number rapidly soars when the economy turns down. Before the New Deal this devastating experience—which sharply contracts millions of families' opportunities, wastes manpower, and destroys the confidence of those excluded—was considered beyond the reach of government. Over the next several decades the nation's political leadership came to accept responsibility for ensuring prosperity through governmental stimulation produced by deficit spending.

Concern about those still unemployed when the government is following a Keynesian fiscal policy was reflected in a whole series of Congressional initiatives in the 1950s, and in legislation during the early 1960s. The legislation relied on training.

The problem was that the manpower programs depended upon familiar and popular, but often false, assumptions. The executive branch stubbornly clung to those assumptions, whereas Congress challenged them. While there were problems with the Congressional solution, the early evidence showed it was achieving the broad, if vague, goals of the law. Surely the program was far more successful and vastly better adapted to the Nixon recession period than the major Presidential alternative of two successive Administrations: job training when there weren't any jobs.

No one thought public service employment was a panacea, and it certainly wasn't—especially on the limited scale the political circumstances permitted. The program did show, however, that a drastically different approach to joblessness was feasible and would be well received. It helped create a major issue in the 1972 Presidential election campaign. A significant departure in public policy, it moved beyond the assumptions of manpower training, the War on Poverty, and the other approaches that shared a common reliance on the private economy. It would become more important soon.

What factors permitted Congress to assume a continuing initiative on this issue? In the first place, Congressional innovations on social policy are usually Democratic innovations, and this issue appealed to the deepest levels of agreement among the Democratic factions. Prosperity and jobs have been the classic Democratic issues. The two Eisenhower recessions and the Nixon recession, together with continuing efforts to keep alive the memory of the New Deal response to the Depression, have been central to the Democratic campaigns. The recession of 1958 produced the large Congressional victory that began to erode conservative control of Congress, and the economic boom of the Johnson years helped consolidate Democratic strength. Subsequently, the deepening recession of 1970 was a major factor in the failure of the President's strong effort to build GOP forces in Congress.

247

Although public service employment was a new policy approach, the job creation experiments of the New Deal were fondly remembered by many Congressional Democrats, who introduced modified versions of them throughout the late 1950s and early 1960s. In fact, the first of the public jobs bills, Senator Nelson's 1964 measure, bore a strong resemblance to the Civilian Conservation Corps.

The 1971 bill was structured to avoid the most sensitive issues that divide Northern and Southern Democrats. There was no federal control problem, since the jobs were given to state and local governments without any major restrictions. Civil rights was not an issue since federal law already contained a prohibition on discrimination in such programs, and a nondiscrimination policy was now generally accepted. The public opposition to welfare spending was countered through reliance on the most popular alternative to welfare programs—work.

With the Democrats unified, the Republicans threatened by a poor economic performance, and the leadership and committee chairmen in both houses united behind the approach, conditions were optimal for a Congressional initiative. Legislation promoting social change is usually highly controversial, but in this case the essence of the innovation was finding a simple, popular, and retrospectively obvious answer to a very serious social problem. The change was one of the most important since the government recognized unemployment as a legitimate official concern. Its potential impact on future policy was very great. Its origin was almost wholly Congressional.

NOTES

[1] *Congressional Record*, January 26, 1971, p. S165.
[2] *Ibid.*, April 1, 1971, p. S4307.
[3] *Ibid.*, p. S4308.
[4] *Ibid.*, pp. S4312–13.
[5] *Ibid.*, pp. S4316–20.
[6] *Ibid.*, p. S4326.
[7] *Ibid.*, pp. S4322–24.
[8] *Ibid.*, p. S4332.
[9] *Ibid.*, p. S4333, S4345.
[10] Sullivan, p. 10.
[11] *Ibid.*, pp. 10–11.
[12] House Committee on Education and Labor, *Hearings, Emergency Employment Act of 1971*, 92d Cong., 1st Sess., 1971, p. 83.

[13] *Ibid.*, pp. 240–47.
[14] *Ibid.*, p. 260.
[15] *Ibid.*, pp. 252, 273–75.
[16] *Ibid.*, p. 274.
[17] House Committee on Education and Labor, "Emergency Employment Act of 1971," Report No. 92–176, 92d Cong., 1st Sess., 1971, pp. 11–18.
[18] *New York Times*, April 9, 1971; *Washington Post*, April 9, 1971.
[19] *Congressional Record*, May 18, 1971, p. H4047.
[20] *New York Times*, May 19, 1971.
[21] Roger H. Davidson, *The Politics of Comprehensive Manpower Legislation* (Baltimore: Johns Hopkins University Press, 1972), p. 89.
[22] *Congressional Record*, June 1, 1971, pp. H4463–64, H4469.
[23] *Congressional Record*, June 2, 1971, pp. H4505–06.
[24] *Ibid.*, p. H4526.
[25] *Ibid.*, p. H4538.
[26] *Washington Post*, June 18, 1971; *New York Times*, June 18, 1971.
[27] *New York Times*, June 23, 1971.
[28] *Congressional Record*, July 1, 1971, pp. H6225, H6228.
[29] *Ibid.*, p. H6225.
[30] *Ibid.*, p. H6229.
[31] *Washington Post*, July 13, 1971.
[32] *Congressional Quarterly*, August 17, 1971, p. 1741.
[33] *Ibid.*
[34] Leonard Goodwin, *Do the Poor Want to Work? A Social-Psychological Study of Work Orientations* (Washington: Brookings Institution, 1972), pp. 32–52.
[35] *Ibid.*, pp. 113–15.
[36] Gilbert Y. Steiner, *The State of Welfare* (Washington: Brookings Institution, 1971), p. 73.
[37] *New York Times*, August 23, 1970.
[38] *Congressional Quarterly Almanac*, 1970, pp. 1035–41.
[39] *Ibid.*, p. 1041; *Washington Post*, December 7, 1970.
[40] *New York Times*, February 24, 1971.
[41] *Ibid.*, July 28, 1971.
[42] *Ibid.*, August 16, 1971.
[43] See Daniel P. Moynihan, *The Politics of a Guaranteed Income* (New York: Vintage, 1973) for an analysis from a Nixon Administration perspective.
[44] *New York Times*, April 23, 1971; *Congressional Quarterly*, April 30, 1971, 967–68.
[45] *Congressional Quarterly*, April 30, 1971, p. 1010.
[46] *Congressional Record*, June 8, 1971, pp. S8541, S8546.
[47] *Ibid.*, pp. S8548–49, S8552.
[48] *Ibid.*, p. S8554; *Congressional Record*, June 15, 1971, p. H5180.
[49] *Washington Post*, June 30, 1971.
[50] *Ibid.*; *Minneapolis Tribune*, June 30, 1971.
[51] *New York Times*, July 1, 1971; *Congressional Record*, July 30, 1971, p. S12558.
[52] *Congressional Record*, December 9, 1971, pp. S21041–42.
[53] The bill was S. 3092, 92d Cong., 2d Sess., 1972.
[54] S. 3311, 92d Cong., 2d Sess., 1972.
[55] *Washington Post*, July 9, 1972.
[56] *Congressional Record*, June 17, 1972, pp. H5585–86.

[57] *Washington Star-News*, July 20, 1972; *Congressional Record*, July 19, 1972, p. H6678.

[58] *Washington Post*, July 20, 1972.

[59] *Congressional Record*, July 19, 1972, pp. H6694, H6698.

[60] *Ibid.*

[61] Sar A. Levitan and Robert Taggart, III, *The Emergency Employment Act: An Interim Assessment*, Committee print, Senate Committee on Labor and Public Welfare, Subcommittee on Employment, Manpower, and Poverty, 92d Cong., 2d Sess., 1972.

[62] National Urban Coalition, *The Public Employment Program: An Evaluation by the National Urban Coalition* (Washington, 1972), pp. 4, 6, 14–19, 49.

[63] *The Budget of the United States, 1974* (Washington: GPO, 1973), pp. 130–31.

[64] *Congressional Record*, April 18, 1973, pp. H2894–H2951.

[65] *Ibid.*, July 24, 1973, pp. S14547–73.

[66] *Ibid.*, July 25, 1973, pp. S14663–79; July 31, 1973, pp. S15164–90.

[67] *Ibid.*, December 18, 1973, H11571–90; December 20, 1973, pp. H11793–807, S23613–26.

[68] *New York Times*, December 18, 1973.

[69] *Congressional Quarterly*, August 31, 1974, p. 2348; September 7, 1974, p. 2420.

part five

CONGRESSIONAL POLICY-MAKING

12
THE BASIC
PATTERNS

Misconceptions about the Policy Process

An Old American Tradition: The Fear of Concentrated Power The normal state of American government is one of internal division and belated response. This is no accident. Our political system was designed by people who saw government as the central threat to liberty, and who developed numerous checks and balances to limit the power of each major institution. The Founding Fathers tried to prevent tyranny by systematically fragmenting authority and building institutional competition into the heart of the governmental process. The solution has usually worked, but often at the price of crippling the ability of the government to deal forcefully and rapidly with the critical needs of an increasingly complex and densely settled society. In spite of these difficulties, however, the system has persisted and its basic premises enjoy wide and deep support. While people complain about inaction on individual problems, there is still a strong fear of excessively active national government. Contemporary public support for fragmentation of governmental power has probably been greatly expanded by President Nixon's resignation in the face of imminent Congressional impeachment.

When there is a commonly perceived sense of urgency and a broad public desire to deal forcefully with a particular problem, the obstacles built into the political system can often be overcome. When the dominant wing of either party wins effective working control of both the White House and Congress, its program can be enacted. The problem for reformers is that this rarely happens. It is made unlikely by the great diversity of the country, by the stability of its political orientations, and by the generalized public suspicion of "big government."

While political scientists, many administrators, a number of commentators, and most reformers complain of the costs of divided, slow-moving, and unresponsive government, Americans generally continue to favor only a limited role for federal programs. In spite of serious deficiencies in some of our state and local governments, there is broad public support for keeping these institutions strong and autonomous. State and local governments dominate most areas of domestic policy and program administration, and these institutions are being strengthened by the transfer of national resources, without strings, through revenue sharing. A survey conducted in the fall of 1973 by the University of Michigan's Institute for Social Research showed, for example, that of fifteen major sets of public and private institutions, the public rated the President and the Administration lowest and the federal government next lowest. State and local governments rated higher, and local public school systems much higher. Several surveys between 1968 and 1972 showed that majorities of between 60 and 77 percent favored turning over money for revenue sharing. Although most Americans give the political system a "fair" or "poor" grade for efficiency,* the costly division of power is seen as preferable to a potentially dangerous concentration of power in the national government.[1]

Congress's Role Obscured   Many students of Congress have erred in two basic ways in describing the role of Congress in our political structure. First, because they have been insensitive to the continuing reality of fragmented power in Washington, they have often overestimated the President's power and obscured the strong continuing role of Congress in shaping do-

---

* Public ratings for the efficiency of the governmental system were as follows: excellent, 5%; good, 33%; fair, 50%; poor, 11%; don't know, 1%.

mestic policies. Secondly, because they overestimated the permanence and inevitability of the political alignments crystallized in the 1930s, they assumed that there was something inherent in the nature of the modern Presidency that made the executive branch more responsive to social problems. Yet in point of fact, so long as the White House and Congress retain independent sources of power, and political coalitions continue to evolve and change across the country, the objectives of the men holding power within each major institution will continue to change, most often gradually, but sometimes with dramatic abruptness. One of those sudden changes in the roles of the national institutions came in 1968, when the Republican Party succeeded in capturing the Presidency by constructing a new and far more conservative coalition than that supporting any recent President. The change in the White House served to illuminate other, more gradual changes—in a liberal direction—within Congress. Congress, at least for a time, was clearly the more progressive institution.

Most serious scholarly studies of Congress and the Presidency have been written during recent decades of widely publicized Presidential leadership. Undeniably, the vast expansion of American government since the 1930s has magnified the power of the Presidency. The growth of the office has been facilitated and publicized by the simultaneous development of national broadcast media that simplify and personalize the news, and that are best adapted to simple communication between a single leader and mass audiences. The enormous expansion of American military power, and of American influence in international affairs, has produced beliefs about Presidential leadership that have often in turn engendered assumptions about Presidential dominance of domestic policy. The result has been an unreal focus of public expectations on the President. This tendency has obscured the simultaneous development of greatly enlarged Congressional power, particularly in domestic affairs.

The longstanding inclination of observers to exaggerate the tendency toward Presidential dominance has been intensified by the Watergate scandal. Evidence of corruption, and of cynical White House efforts to manipulate other governmental institutions, tends to reinforce warnings about "Presidential dictatorship." Clearly, the Watergate scandal has revealed both the corrupting influence of private campaign financing, and the White House attempts to misuse both national security powers and a variety of federal agencies, including the Justice Department and the Internal Revenue Service. But it is extremely important to accurately assess what the scandal has shown about the Presidency.

To assume that misuse of power means that there is too much power, and to destroy that power so as to correct the abuse, is to engage in dangerous oversimplification. This was precisely the mistake made by the reformers in the House of Representatives in 1910, when they fought abuse of leadership not by removing the incumbent, but by destroying much of the power of the Speakership. The result weakened the entire House and gravely diminished its role for generations. The Watergate scandal certainly reveals the need for more Congressional overseeing of national security and the investigatory agencies, and for reform of campaign finances and techniques; yet the probable result of the scandal will be a general weakening of the Presidency, and only a desultory attempt to correct the specific abuses. We will likely respond to the misuse of office by diminishing the possibilities of leadership in office.

The reaction has grown to the point where Arthur Schlesinger, Jr., a major historian who long celebrated Presidential leadership, now condemns the "Imperial Presidency." Schlesinger claims that President Nixon was a "revolutionary" President, intently carrying to their logical extreme all the vast powers of executive dominance that had been accumulating for decades. He "aimed at reducing the power of Congress at every point along the line and moving toward rule by presidential decree." He sums up his case:

> As one examined the impressive range of Nixon's initiatives—from his appropriation of the war-making power to his interpretation of the appointing power, from his unilateral determination of social priorities to his unilateral abolition of statutory programs, from his attack on legislative privilege to his enlargement of executive privilege, from his theory of impoundment to his theory of the pocket veto, from his calculated disparagement of the cabinet and his calculated discrediting of the press to his carefully organized concentration of federal management in the White House—from all this a larger design ineluctably emerged.[2]

This dismal view of our situation under Nixon is extremely misleading; untangling its misstatements about the past is essential to understanding the present shape of the political system. President Nixon did indeed assert many broad powers, but even before Watergate Congress had come up with some impressive answers. Presidential war powers had been limited, both by passage of legislation requiring consultation with Congress before future long-term commitments of American forces, and by Congress's unprecedented action in forcing an end to American bombing of Cambodia by cutting off funds. Congress squarely rejected the President's theory of the appointment process by handing him more defeats than any other twentieth-century President on his Supreme Court nominees. The President's claims of massive powers to impound or abolish programs were rejected both in the courts and in Congress. The very President who asserted the most sweeping version of executive privilege found himself forced by Congress and the courts to sacrifice any privacy on the most personal and degrading materials ever extracted from the White House. The President who acted as if he possessed vast powers found his modest program proposals rejected by Congress with more monotonous regularity than any other recent President.

The only alternative to the misleading global clichés that usually dominate our discussion of our major institutions is an effort to seriously examine their roles in a number of important policy decisions. When the subtleties of the policy process are sorted out and the strands of influence unwoven, it is evident that Congress is a major source of domestic policy, and often the dominant source in government. While the case studies of the earlier chapters document some of Congress's recent contributions to domestic policy, it would of course be a mistake to reach comprehensive conclusions on the basis of such a limited range of evidence. However, the general arguments set forth here are supported by the few serious scholarly efforts to systematically assess legislative contributions to a range of domestic issues.

Lawrence Chamberlain's study of the history of ninety laws from 1890 to 1940 credited Congress with initiating twice as many as the President and with sharing the responsibility for most of the rest.[3] An effort to update this analysis by looking at case studies of bills passed between 1940 and 1967 concluded that "Congress is very capable of conceptual innovation, legislation modification, and energetic oversight. . . . the evidence suggests that Congress continues to be an active innovator and very much in the legislative business. Thus the findings here tend to confirm the findings Chamberlain made a quarter of a century ago."[4] Finally, David Price's careful 1972 study of the role of three major Senate committees in shaping thirteen important recent bills concludes that, even under President Johnson, Congress's role was "more prominent and diverse than is often sup- 257 posed and—what is particularly important in the current period of reduced executive creativity and leadership—that the congressional 'input' can and should become a more substantial and innovative one in the years ahead."[5] These studies of particular pieces of legislation tend to reinforce the conclusions that this book draws from examining legislative activities in certain broad areas.

The following chapters outline the overall conditions that maximize the possibility for Congressional leadership; the constraints on that leadership; and the continuing flaws in the system of Congressional representation. The analysis will draw not only on the cases studied earlier, but also on briefer treatments of a broader range of contemporary issues.

The Conditions for Congressional Innovation

While the case studies in this book have illustrated Congressional activism in the face of a conservative President, a scholar wishing to prove Congressional impotence might prepare apparently contradictory studies on Vietnam or welfare policy. Obviously, the conditions and the limitations of Congressional policy initiatives must be far more clearly specified.

The diffusion of power and the diversity of political viewpoints within Congress make it easy to support a wide range of interpretations of Congressional authority. Within an institution where great influence over the same issue may rest in one house with a reactionary Southern planter, and in the other with a very liberal New York City lawyer, a casual observer can easily become confused about Congress's position. It often is far easier to examine issues apparently supporting the thesis of dominance by a progressive Presidency than it is to sort out the net effect of the ebbs and flows of power within the complex overlapping policy systems that make up Congress. The sorting out of real policy influence is further complicated by the frequent Congressional practice of disguising real changes as "technical" alterations, or accomplishing change through private negotiations between the executive branch and powerful members of Congress.

Most existing interpretations find Presidential initiative and Presidential dominance because they focus on three types of issues: foreign policy crises, military problems, and the President's own domestic agenda. Other analysts reach conclusions about Congressional impotence based on Congress's failure to respond to national crises or critical national needs—but in so doing tend to rely on their own interpretation of national needs, rather than on the perceptions and demands of the public. Often the deadlock caused by Congress actually reflects cross-cutting public concerns and deep uncertainty about the best policy solution.

Congress and International Affairs The President retains a decisive initiative in diplomacy and military policy. He enjoys broad and clear grants of constitutional authority in these fields. Given the need for unity of military command and for speed and secrecy in crisis diplomacy, Congress can often do little more than respond to a White House initiative or *fait accompli*.

Even in foreign and military policy, however, Presidents are constrained by Congress, particularly in the development of long-term policies. Congress, for example, has made sharp and consistent cuts in foreign and military aid programs, denying Presidents an important policy tool. Congress has always played a very important role in shaping trade legislation—a fact underlined by its 1973 refusal to grant trade privileges to the U.S.S.R., a decision significantly impairing the President's basic policy line of détente. Presidents involved in major international negotiations do not forget the destruction of Woodrow Wilson's Administration by the Senate rejection of the Versailles Treaty.

Liberals have frequently concluded that Congress's inability to end the war in Vietnam illustrates legislative impotence. The fact is that Congress did not even try to end the war, because there was no Congressional majority opposed to the war. In the House of Representatives there was a consistent majority, including the leadership of both parties, that supported the general Presidential policy toward Vietnam. Even in the Senate the division was very close. The fact that a majority of Congress may have been wrong does not show that it was impotent, or even that it was unrepresentative. Indeed, polls show deep contradictions in public attitudes toward the war. When a particular Presidential action stirred up strong public and Congressional protests, such as the 1970 invasion of Cambodia, the threat of Congressional restrictions on the White House was sufficiently serious to bring a rapid Presidential retreat.

In the final period of U.S. military involvement in Indochina, Congress was far more responsive to war critics than was the President. The Nixon Administration found it necessary to continually fight hard against Senate attempts to legislate an end to the war. After American troops were withdrawn, it was Congress that forced an end to further U.S. bombing, and Congress that tried to restrain continued massive military aid.

In evaluating Congress's performance on the Vietnam issue, one must recognize that the American role in the war was a direct outgrowth of widely shared basic assumptions about foreign policy, and about the nature of the contest with communism in Asia. During the early phases of the war, Congressional support reflected backing by leading conservatives and liberals alike throughout the country.[6] In retrospect, we tend to blame Congress for "going along" with the war. It is hardly fair to disparage Congress as an institution for a general failure of American liberal ideology.

Although Congress did not end the war, some members and some committees did play a crucial role in reformulating the issues. By the late 1960s Congress had produced the leading figures of the opposition and provided the principal forum for their attacks. From it emerged such preeminent antiwar critics as Eugene McCarthy (D-Minn.), George McGovern (D-S. Dak.), and Paul McCloskey (R-Calif.), while the hearings of the Senate Foreign Relations Committee did more than anything else to touch off the national debate that helped persuade Lyndon Johnson, a very powerful President, to step down. After the Vietnam conflict ended, Congress moved in 1973 to extend its power with measures forcing the President to end the bombing of Cambodia and requiring advance Congressional approval of sustained military action in the future.

The Conditions of Domestic Leadership Although Congressional helplessness in international affairs has been overstated, it is certainly true that Congressional power is vastly greater in most realms of domestic policy. Even here, however, the degree of Congressional authority varies greatly from one issue area to another. Congressional influence and innovation are most likely when the President is either conservative or passive, and when one or more of the following conditions prevails:

(1) The other party controls Congress by a substantial margin.

(2) The issue in question unites the major factions of the other party.

260

(3) The relevant committees are led by, or contain com-

mitted majorities of, supporters of the new program proposal.

(4) The process of innovation has already been set in motion by outside forces such as judicial decisions or administrative interpretations of existing laws, and momentum can be sustained merely by vetoing conservative proposals of the President.

(5) The innovation is not highly controversial, and supporters of change have organized constituency support from various parts of the country.

(6) The policy change can be accomplished through amendments to legislation the President cannot afford to veto.

(7) A national movement, a skillful media campaign by reformers, or a highly visible scandal has produced an insistent public demand for action.

(8) The President's public support has been so seriously eroded that he cannot maintain leadership of his own party.

(9) Legislative tactics permit proponents to present the issue for a rapid decision before existing and potential opponents have an opportunity to mobilize.

The chances of Congressional leadership diminish when one or more of the following conditions holds:

(1) The President is exercising one of his most unambiguous constitutional functions: when he is acting as Commander-in-Chief during active military operations; when he is serving as national spokesman in the conduct of international negotiations or the management of an international crisis; or when he is exercising administrative authority over the executive branch.

(2) The President is prepared to use his veto, and can hold his party's support to sustain it.

(3) Congressional leaders of the President's party are strongly united against the proposed new program.

(4) Majority party leaders and committee chairmen seriously disagree.

(5) The issue is already highly controversial, or the President is ready to make it so through his unrivaled access to the media.

(6) The policy threatens the traditional powers of state or local governments.

(7) The policy is strongly opposed by powerful and well-organized groups or industries that have effective Washington representation, strong local branches, or major roles in providing campaign funds.

(8) Congressional advocates of change lack the technical staff resources necessary to deal with extremely complex issues.

(9) The change would require a visible tax increase.

Progressives in Congress are most successful when their goals can be accomplished by killing a conservative White House initiative, or by creating an additional, relatively noncontroversial program of federal grants or federal regulation. Congressional initiatives are frequently most important when the issues are comparatively new. Committees often develop specialists on such issues long before they appear on the President's agenda or in national political discussions, and long before the task of administering legislation has given the executive branch a reservoir of expertise. At this point—when little is known, positions are unclear, and major interests are not yet mobilized—the opportunity for legislative creativity is large. Congressional activity of this type was seen in the early phase of antipollution legislation, in the development of bilingual education programs, and in the extension of job discrimination protection to women and to state and local employees.

For a number of easily understandable reasons, Congress is far more responsive to the need for new programs than to basic fiscal or social rearrangements. Redressing general social or economic imbalances always means helping some while denying to others a portion of their goods or of their social objectives. The resulting controversy brings political trouble and a greatly increased probability that the policy will be vetoed at one of the many decision points in the Congressional process. Most new grant programs, on the other hand, give additional benefits to some groups while seldom disturbing the others. When a Senator fights for more housing or better health care for old people, or for better education benefits for veterans, he usually gains strength from a segment of his constituency without deeply offending anybody else.

Proposals to redistribute income, close big tax loopholes, break up the existing pattern of urban racial separation, or undertake other forms of basic social or economic change have very different effects. They alienate segments of the local constituency, and other members of Congress as well. By forcing

262

members to make basic choices that are very salient, rather than mutual accommodations that pass unnoticed, they greatly increase the chances for veto. Unless there is strong and unambiguous public pressure for it, such a change is exceedingly difficult to successfully initiate within Congress.

(On the other hand, Congress is frequently important as a place where discussions of new issues can be launched. This is because of the enormous variation among districts and states represented, and the fact that problems almost always become much more acute and obvious in particular localities first. The representatives of these localities can then speak out in favor of real change without facing any personal political risk.) Presidents confront very similar difficulties and generally show similar caution.

The Influence of the Committee System

The Committees' Political Complexion The tendency for reform supporters to concentrate on creating new federal aid programs is reinforced by the way members are often placed on committees. Most activist members see their goal as writing new laws or amendments in response to particular policy problems. They seek assignment to committees specifically responsible for measures dealing with education, housing, jobs, urban programs, and civil rights. Since these committees do not enjoy a great deal of prestige, it is often possible for a member to win assignment to one at the beginning of his Congressional career. As a result, the Democratic majorities on these key domestic policy committees tend to be more liberal ideologically and more activist politically than the party caucus as a whole.

Conservatives, on the other hand, enjoy disproportionate strength in the powerful committees controlling the budget, taxation, health and welfare policy, military policy, and the internal legislative processes of Congress. The seniority system has its most drastic impact on the character of these committees, since considerable seniority is usually required for an appointment, and virtually no one leaves the committees while he remains in Congress.[7] Thus on the most important committee in the House, Ways and Means, the least senior of the Democratic members, as of 1973, had been in the House for nine years, and the average member for sixteen. The GOP minority averaged eleven years of service and contained no representation of the moderate wing of the Republican party.[8] 263

This meant that the typical member had come to Congress in a different era, and also that the membership reflected the conservative views prevalent in the House when the appointments were made. This pattern was strikingly apparent on the powerful House Appropriations Committee, where in 1973 the six senior members of the majority party had an average service of thirty-one years. Five of these men controlling powerful subcommittees came from the South, while the other one, John Rooney, was an elderly conservative from New York.

The time lag before new trends in the parties show up on the most important committees is reinforced by the tendency of more liberal members who do win assignment to these panels to be converted to the views of older committee leaders. The most powerful committees are usually very stable social systems in which new members are judged by their acceptance of a well-established set of committee values and expectations. Members of the Ways and Means and the Appropriations committees gain reputations with their colleagues by their attention to detail, their dedication to cutting the executive-branch budget, and avoidance of "irresponsible" changes in the tax structure. By the time a member has been on a committee long enough to influence legislation strongly, his views often tend to agree with committee expectations.[9]

An Obstacle Course for Programs The fact that the development of each federal program depends on two different sets of committees with very different memberships often deepens public confusion. Before any new program can begin operation, Congress must first pass a new law or amend an old one. This means that, before the final floor votes, the program's supporters must win majorities first in the specific subject matter subcommittees in each house, then in the committees with the appropriate jurisdiction, and finally in the House Rules Committee. These basic laws often set maximum levels of permissible spending for each part of the program, or they may just allow "such funds as necessary." Mass media coverage of the legislative process is usually limited to the climactic stages of shaping these laws.

These basic laws *authorize* the government to provide certain new services and set the fundamental framework for the programs, but they do not provide any money to carry them out. After the authorizations are enacted, then the Appropriations subcommittees and committees must decide how much money to *appropriate* each year.

264

Differences in membership between the program committees and the appropriating and taxing committees contribute to the confusing practice by which Congress authorizes a large new program and then allows the administrators only a fraction of the authorized funds. Democratic liberals, working from power bases on a few key legislative committees, often see their heralded legislative accomplishments eviscerated by Democratic conservatives who work from power bases further along in the legislative process. Progressives by this time have typically committed their energies to new legislative proposals, rather than fighting for resources to implement programs.

Committee differences can, of course, be exaggerated. No committee can deal with policy issues in total isolation from Congress as a whole. Committee action on visible issues where active floor debate may occur is often influenced by a desire to prevent an embarrassing floor defeat for the committee bill. Since committee power is threatened once members learn that a committee bill can be successfully challenged on the floor, committees often try to preserve their power and prestige by making the necessary accommodation to any strong and determined majority. Appropriations policy-makers also generally avoid alienating constituencies of already established programs by permitting unchallenged continuation of programs at the "base" established in previous years. This tends to limit committee power to new programs and to substantial changes in existing ones.

The process of accommodation tends to break down completely only when very sensitive social issues are involved. Thus, for example, the House Appropriations Committee tried to alter a national housing policy meant to break up ghetto concentrations by denying any money at all for enforcement of the 1968 fair-housing law, and by trying to kill a program of federal rent supplements designed to let poor people live in standard new housing. While committee resistance was eventually overcome, both programs started at a fraction of the planned level. In addition, the rent supplement program was hamstrung by an amendment requiring approval of each suburb where the money was to be spent. Thus two major elements of President Johnson's housing policy were crippled at birth. In the area of school desegregation, the Appropriations committees in both houses have similarly attempted to change the law and weaken the administrative enforcement machinery.

While major problems remain, the recent past does show a slowly diminishing role for the Appropriations committees. 265

Both the legislative stalemate created by President Nixon's opposition to new domestic programs, and the activation of strong constituency concern as a result of the drastic Nixon cutbacks in existing programs focused unprecedented attention throughout Congress on spending decisions. Once coalitions of program supporters, such as the education groups fighting for more money, took on the House Appropriations Committee and defeated it on the floor, the committee was inclined to yield in advance rather than face further humiliation.

Meanwhile, within that same committee there were a growing number of liberals gaining seniority and influence on important subcommittees. By 1973, for example, liberals predominated in the Democratic contingents on the subcommittees controlling the budgets of HUD, HEW, the Labor Department, and the Interior Department.[10] By the beginning of the 1973 session, ten of the committee's thirty-three Democratic members had been appointed in the 1970s. The roll call votes that year show the change in the committee. According to the ratings prepared by the liberal Americans for Democratic Action (ADA), the ten newest members voted correctly an average of 57 percent of the time, while the five members with greatest seniority voted wrong 90 percent of the time.[11] The GOP, on the other hand, was continuing to name members from the extreme conservative end of the House political spectrum, so that the impact of the new moderate and liberal Democrats was only beginning to be felt.

Complexity and Confusion The different policy perspectives of the law-writing and financial committees tend to confuse and disillusion many citizens. Few realize that when Congress enacts a billion-dollar program for park land, for example, it is merely setting the *ceiling* figure for future bargaining for appropriations. Few understand the intricate game Congressmen play when they take the pose of supporting a particular constituent group by voting for its authorization, then later quietly oppose its goals by voting for a low appropriation. This way a member can claim to be both a supporter of the policy and a defender of economy in government. Members and Presidents alike often exploit this opportunity to play both sides of the issue.

The fragmentation and internal inconsistency of policy and money decisions within Congress reflect both the lack of a coherent structure of party leadership, and also the ideological deficiencies of both conservatives and liberals. There is no policy

266

and budget coordination, because there has been no working institutional arrangement for establishing priorities and making the decision stick. The Appropriations committees were initially created to make such judgments, but they fragmented their own decisions along agency lines, and the seniority system skewed their membership in the conservative direction, creating a division between the committees and the House leadership.

Congress attempted to address this problem in June 1974 with passage of the Congressional Budget and Impoundment Control Act of 1974, potentially the most important change in Congressional organization in decades. The new law established Budget Committees in each house. The legislation also created a Congressional Budget Office to provide to Congress some of the technical expertise and staff resources available to the President through the Office of Management and Budget. Each year these committees were expected to recommend spending priority targets in the spring and ceilings in the fall. For the first time, both normal appropriations and the huge "backdoor spending" through federal contractual arrangements would come under the purview of single committees.

The legislation provided the framework for Congress to debate the relative importance of various national objectives and the general fiscal policy of the country more clearly than ever before. The Senate named a progressive committee chaired by Senator Muskee (D-Me.), while the House Democratic caucus rejected the Speaker's liberal nominee and chose instead Ways and Means Committee moderate Representative Ullman (D-Ore.).[12] Although the legislation seems likely to increase Congress's influence in the shaping of the national budget, the political consequences remain unclear.

The discontinuities of policy-making reflect blind spots in the American liberal and conservative outlooks toward the political system. Liberalism has no coherent institutional focus or set of priorities, and tends to place tremendous emphasis on the creation of new programs, leaving little time for monitoring administrative decision-making or fighting for program resources. If an old program, poorly financed and denied administrative resources, fails to solve a problem, the assumption is that creating a new program will correct the problem. Conservatism, on the other hand, is rather strongly reflected in Congress, especially among House Republicans, but has very few substantive programs. Its basic assumption is that the federal government is too big; that state or local or private business decisions are normally preferable to national public policy; that money for 267 program administration is money wasted on bureaucrats; and that the government should not interfere with social arrangements. It frequently represents less a program to conserve certain valued aspects of the society than an uncritical hostility to the federal government itself—an attitude with deep roots in American history. The net result is often a series of sporadic, narrowly focused reform movements on the liberal side of Congress that confront a general opposition to the growth of government, and a strong resistance to new social programs from the conservative side. Similar inconsistencies frequently afflict the executive branch as well.

The ideological muddle in Congress reflects the persisting and deeply held beliefs of most Americans. Public opinion polls normally show strong support for many of the specific existing or proposed domestic programs of the federal government, but also keen opposition to "big government" or higher taxes. Gallup polls conducted in late 1972 and early 1973 revealed, for instance, that 65 percent of the public thought their income taxes were too high, and that 60 percent said a balanced budget was "very important." At the same time only 38 percent supported the President's impoundment of domestic program funds "as a way of controlling the federal budget." On yet another question, 54 percent expressed support for the President's battle to "hold down government spending and taxes," and opposed Congressional attempts to "pass social programs that would give more money to the poor, the aged and to schools and the like."[13] Had the survey asked about increasing funds for particular popular programs, the confusion would doubtless have been even greater.

Each of these inconsistent positions of the public is strongly represented in the policy-making process, although the multiple vetoes built into the system produce a normal bias toward inaction. The conflict is particularly clear when Congress is controlled by one party and the Presidency by the other. Perhaps recent polls showing an actual public preference for such divided government reflect satisfaction with this clash of values, even at the price of governmental deadlock.

The Special World of Regulatory Policy

While most social program legislation is caught in the constant tension between the policy and money committees, two major kinds of social policy measures are shaped in very different environments. Policy on race, Constitutional rights, and discrimination is largely initiated in the two Judiciary committees, while another set of extremely powerful committees allocate tax benefits and liabilities, rights to retirement income and medical care, and welfare program policies.

The Judiciary Committees Policies forbidding discrimination, or providing a legal definition or administrative support for the assertion and protection of the rights of a particular group, generally are considered by the House and Senate Judiciary committees. These policies sometimes impose sanctions on certain forms of behavior defined as illegal, and sometimes create administrative machinery to enforce the new rights, but they seldom require large expenditures. Enforcement of the sanctions requires some resources, but often depends primarily on the political judgments of the executive branch.

Civil rights legislation has been the most prominent example of massive social change through regulation. During the period between 1957 and 1972 Congress enacted six major pieces of legislation and one Constitutional amendment fundamentally affecting American race relations. In addition, there were innumerable Congressional battles in response to vigorous action for racial change by the federal courts and by the executive branch during Lyndon Johnson's Presidency. Apart from the historic struggle over civil rights, the Congress has also enacted policies against sex discrimination and granted voting rights to eighteen-year-olds.

Until recently, the House and Senate Judiciary committees reflected the polar extremes of the Democratic Party. The House committee, led for many years by New York Congressman Emanuel Celler, was a bastion of liberalism. The Senate committee, under James Eastland (D-Miss.), was the burying ground for even the most modest civil rights proposals. However, once civil rights became a constant focus for Congressional struggle in the late 1950s, the Senate Democratic leadership named a number of strong liberals to the committee, while the GOP leadership allocated some seats to the party's moderate wing. By the early 1970s the Senate committee was evenly divided, with liberals such as Philip Hart (D-Mich.), Birch Bayh (D-Ind.), and Edward Kennedy (D-Mass.) using it as an important forum for raising civil rights issues. Even so, throughout the struggle the principal point for initiating civil rights laws, and the only place for serious and systematic ex- 269 amination of proposed legislation, has been the Judiciary Committee of the House. In the Senate the two most important bills were enacted, in 1964 and 1965, by bypassing the committee through direct negotiations between the Democratic and Republican Senate leadership. A third measure, the 1968 fair-housing law, began as a floor amendment to a minor bill, while in 1972 the extension of the enforcement powers and jurisdiction of the Equal Employment Opportunity Commission came through the Senate Labor and Public Welfare Committee. Thus it has been the political circumstance of liberal Democratic seniority on the House committee that has made possible a Congressional response to the movement for civil rights.

Short-circuiting Committee Power: The Role of Tactics Two of the other major changes extending important rights to large categories of citizens came about largely independent of committee action. The extension of the suffrage to eighteen-year-olds happened suddenly in 1970, after decades of futile student demands. There was in fact little visible public demand for the change, the idea had been defeated in several state elections, and the necessary legislation had never been reported out of the Senate Judiciary Committee. Even so, Senator Edward Kennedy forced a vote on the issue through a parliamentary stratagem. When the 1970 Voting Rights bill was on the floor and the Senate was debating extending protection for the voting rights of Southern blacks for five more years, Kennedy suddenly moved to amend the bill with the unrelated measure allowing eighteen-year-olds to vote. Senate rules permit such extraneous amendments and Kennedy received the powerful support of Majority Leader Mike Mansfield. Confronted with the necessity of a public vote on the issue at a time when eighteen-year-olds were being killed in an unpopular war in Vietnam, and when the campuses were in an uproar over the invasion of Cambodia and the Kent State University shootings, a majority supported the amendment.

The Senate amendment asserted federal power to change voting-age requirements by a simple statute rather than a Constitutional amendment. This was a highly controversial theory of law, since the Constitution grants the states broad powers to regulate suffrage standards. Some liberals, including the chairman of the House Judiciary Committee, had deep reservations about the constitutionality of the measure. Since the Voting Rights Act was so terribly important to protect the political rights of Southern blacks, a reluctant House conference committee delegation accepted the eighteen-year-old amendment and sent the issue on to the courts. President Nixon was then confronted with the choice of signing the bill or vetoing a civil rights measure with broad public support. He decided to sign, but in signing, expressed his basic doubts about the constitutionality of the voting-age provision.

The issue came quickly to the Supreme Court. In a divided and confusing decision, the Court held that Congress had authority to lower the voting age for federal elections for President and Congress, but not for state and local elections. The decision threatened to produce electoral chaos. The unmanageable problems of maintaining two separate electorates led to rapid Congressional and state legislative approval of a Constitutional amendment lowering the voting age for all elections. Skillful use of legislative leverage had precipitated the extension of voting power to millions of young Americans, even before substantial public pressure had built up behind the reform movement.

Committees were almost equally unimportant in decisions to extend rights to women. The chairman of the House committee, in fact, was a leading opponent of the most important change, the Equal Rights Amendment. The key move was a discharge petition, which forced the issue to the House floor without any committee action.

In major cases of social regulatory policy, then, change has frequently come through parliamentary tactics forcing the issue to a floor vote. While opponents often pay little political price for quietly bottling up a bill in committee, the calculations change once a visible issue with a substantial local constituency comes up for a public vote on the floor. Members do not relish alienating major groups like young voters, the female majority, or the black, labor, and church groups that formed the backbone of the civil rights coalition.

Social change issues also are relatively more insulated from technical control by committee experts. While it may be a staggeringly complex job for the average Congressman to really comprehend the issues involved in a major bill amending the tax code, it requires little technical competence to reach a decision about whether the rights of blacks or students or women need more protection. For the same reason, the decisions are much more visible to the concerned public, and this puts members even more on the spot politically when a popular issue is forced to the floor. There it is far more difficult to sabotage reform legislation by making apparently "technical" changes or

271

sending it back to committee than it would be in the case of complicated tax, appropriations, or welfare bills.

The drive for social reform legislation in the 1960s and 1970s was aided not only by success in bringing issues directly to the floor, but also by the existence of some committees that actively supported significant reforms. This was particularly true in the House, where the Judiciary Committee consistently endorsed civil rights bills.

As progressives succeeded in enacting much of the existing agenda in the 1960s, they soon discovered that another, more difficult, set of issues lay behind the regulatory changes. When the civil rights leaders came up against the hard fact that regulatory legislation could limit some forms of discrimination but still leave vast inequalities, they had to face the more arduous task of changing economic and welfare policies. This required them to shift their struggle from relatively responsive Congressional arenas to bastions of conservative power. The results were deeply discouraging.

Committee Autocracy: Taxes and the Ways and Means Committee In sharp contrast to the committees controlling civil rights legislation, those which allocate the tax burden operate under little effective Congressional or public scrutiny, specialize in highly technical decision-making, and exhibit continuing hostility to serious reform. Although Congress has always jealously guarded its control of the power to tax, a very strong and ancient source of legislative influence, taxation decisions are very largely isolated from effective control by Congressional majorities. While virtually no Congressional actions have so immediate an impact on so many citizens as those setting tax rates and allocating retirement, medical, and welfare benefits, the social policies are obscured by incredibly complex bills amending voluminous and arcane codes understood by only a handful of specialists either inside or outside Congress.

Complexity is conducive to committee power, as is the House tradition of sending tax bills to the floor under closed rules permitting no amendment—rules intended to forestall massive efforts to write into the tax code special tax privileges for a great many local interests. The House Ways and Means Committee tends to dominate tax policy by virtue of the Constitutional requirement that the House initiate tax measures; by virtue of the greater technical mastery of House committee members; by its authority to bring bills to the floor under closed rules; and through the power it derives from its function of allocating committee assignments for the majority party. The House committee's power is further enhanced by the often bipartisan nature of its decisions, and the unusual respect enjoyed by its longtime chairman, Wilbur Mills (D-Ark.).

Ways and Means is the most prestigious committee in the House, and perhaps the most important single committee in the shaping of social policy. It is also, however, perhaps the clearest illustration of the remaining deficiencies of the Congressional process. Since no one leaves the committee once appointed, and since seniority is generally required to win a seat, the time lag before changes in the political parties are reflected on the committee is probably the greatest in Congress. Thus, for example, some of the present members were appointed by former House leaders who were concerned not about contemporary issues of national health insurance, tax reform, or welfare policy, but about the older ones of free trade and the oil depletion allowance. At a time when House Democrats were primarily Southern, committee membership was influenced by a traditional twofold commitment of the agrarian South: to low tariffs designed to hold down the costs of manufactured goods and support a free international trade for the regional farm exports; and to the special tax privileges of the powerful oil barons of Texas and Louisiana. The Democratic Party's continuing practice of allocating seats on the committee to certain states or regions further increases the obstacles to control of the committee by the party's leadership.

Until recently, Southern Democrats were vastly overrepresented on the committee, usually claiming six or seven of the fifteen majority-party seats. The panel's conservative bias was intensified by the GOP practice of naming only rock-ribbed conservatives to the ten minority seats. The committee's conservative coalition was evident, for example, when it rejected a popular 1960 medical care bill 17-8, with almost half the Democrats joining all the Republicans to destroy the chance of enacting a basic part of the party's platform during a Presidential election year. Not until 1965 did new appointments produce a slim one-vote margin for Medicare—almost two decades after President Harry Truman had made national medical insurance a part of the Democratic Party's goals.[14]

The committee's continuing role in defusing progressive efforts was very clear in the tax reform drive of the late 1960s and early 1970s. Congress was crucial in initiating this drive, but the Ways and Means Committee and the Senate Finance Committee protected the status quo. Congress helped bring the 273 issue to public attention, directing the Johnson Administration to prepare a reform proposal and then providing the forum for the outgoing Treasury Secretary to denounce the scandalous level of tax privileges for the rich in early 1969. Under pressure, the new Nixon Administration responded with a major tax bill repealing the existing wartime 10-percent income tax surcharge, ending the business investment tax credit, and removing from the tax rolls about two million very low-income families then paying small amounts of tax. The bill included only one modest reform proposal that narrowed the use of tax shelters, and left the basic structure of tax loopholes intact.[15]

In 1969 strong public interest in reform and active pressure on the committees by unusually concerned members of the House and Senate produced some changes in a muddled bill intended to please virtually everyone. The price of this confusing compromise and the largely symbolic reforms was a permanent cut in the revenue-raising capacity of the federal government.

Congress altered the President's bill, shifting some tax relief from industry to individuals and narrowing some loopholes. The final bill, enacted in the face of a threatened Presidential veto, ended taxation of most people below the official poverty level, and also raised personal exemptions for all taxpayers—this last a popular change, but one that saved the most dollars for taxpayers in the highest brackets. The bill went beyond the President's recommendations in lowering the previously sacrosanct oil depletion allowance, restricting some forms of real estate tax shelters, and closing a total of $6.6 billion in loopholes. The final bill also incorporated a large increase in Social Security benefits—one 50 percent greater than the President had asked.[16]

The Congressional change in the social impact of the White House bill was heavily influenced by pressure from outside the tax-writing committees. In the House, liberals attacked the Ways and Means Committee's draft bill shortly before it was to go to the floor; this produced additional cuts for the five lowest tax brackets, and significant relief for working families earning between $7,500 and $13,000 a year. The result was a bill that tripled the low-income exemptions proposed by the President, and provided another $2.4 billion in cuts for average wage earners. In the Senate the fight for raising the personal exemption was conducted by Senator Albert Gore (D-Tenn.).

The liberalizing amendments, however, carried a cost. The price for offering some relief to all taxpayers earning less than 274 $100,000 and for reducing the tax rates for the highest incomes without cutting deeply into loopholes was the transformation of a tax reform bill into a large tax reduction bill. The measure sacrificed $2.5 billion in federal revenue the first year and more in succeeding years. The revenue loss limited options for new social programs. The President pointed out the problem in reluctantly signing the popular measure.[17]

President Kennedy had pioneered the idea of federal tax cuts to stimulate the economy in 1962, when the proposal was seen by economists as a strategy for putting money into the economy without confronting the Congressional deadlock over domestic programs. Congress and the President carried the approach into the Nixon period, in spite of the fact that the deadlock had been decisively broken. Tax cuts in 1969 and 1971, combined with Administration-supported cuts in corporate and excise taxes, had reduced government revenues in a full-employment economy by the staggering sum of $45 billion a year by 1972.[18]

In effect, Administration conservatives and the conservatives on the tax-writing committees had eliminated the increment of federal resources necessary to finance many of the national policy commitments made in the major Great Society bills. Since the beginning of the Johnson Administration, Congress had been financing the growth of domestic programs with annual budget increases of more than 9 percent a year—a sharp break with the pattern of the previous decade. By 1972, Great Society programs accounted for about $38 billion in federal spending, with another $32 billion added for Social Security and Medicare since the Johnson Presidency began.[19]

The Johnson programs were planned around the expectation of steadily growing federal resources. Some were still in the planning phase when Nixon took office, and there was mounting constituency and Congressional support for implementation funds. In addition, there was strong support for a range of new programs, including revenue sharing. The tax cuts and the costs of maintaining existing programs in a time of rapid inflation left very little money either for fulfillment of old commitments or for starting new ones. Few in either the White House or the Capitol weighed the long-term impact.

While a series of incremental decisions were cutting back the nation's ability to finance social programs, another series of decisions was increasing the regressive impact of the payroll tax on working-class and middle-class people. Since the tax allowed no deductions, and exempted all income above a fixed figure and all nonwage income as well, increases were a disproportionately heavy burden on lower-income families. Between

275

1963 and 1973, payroll tax receipts quadrupled, reaching one dollar in every twenty-five in the economy. For millions of lower-income families the net effect of cuts in income taxes, combined with the huge increase in payroll taxation, was an increase in their share of the tax burden.[20] A highly sophisticated 1974 study of the total federal, state, and local taxes paid by Americans found that the net effect of the nation's tax system was to tax almost all income groups at the same level. Families earning between $3,000 and more than $100,000 paid about the same percentage of their incomes in taxes. The very rich paid only a moderately higher level of taxes. Amazingly enough, those earning below $3,000 actually paid a significantly higher level of taxes than a great many far more affluent families.[21] The rapidly growing dependence of the federal government on Social Security payroll taxes was increasing the tax burden on millions of lower-income working families.

The payroll tax increases had been routinely passed without serious discussion. For decades most Congressmen and Senators had accepted the argument that the Social Security system was an insurance system, even though its actual functions and financing were always very different. (In actual practice, the benefits greatly outstrip typical contributions, and the size of the payment is only very imperfectly related to the amount of contributions.) When a challenge to this assumption was made in the House in 1973, the conservative role of the Ways and Means Committee in perpetuating this regressive system became very apparent.

The House Democratic leadership, working in cooperation with the Rules Committee, bypassed the Ways and Means Committee in October 1973, authorizing liberals to try to amend a bill raising the federal debt ceiling. This tactic was intended to put the reform in a measure President Nixon couldn't afford to veto, since the government would otherwise lack authority to pay its bills. The amendment added a 7-percent boost in Social Security benefits, and obtained the necessary revenue by increasing the minimum tax on tax-sheltered earnings of companies and the rich. "It's an opportunity," said House Majority Leader Thomas O'Neill, Jr. (D-Mass.), "to raise $3 billion from people who can afford it and give some of it to senior citizens who need it." In response to the leadership initiative, however, the Ways and Means Committee rapidly cut off the reform drive by reporting out a long-stalled Social Security benefit increase financed by more payroll taxes.[22]

In spite of some stirrings of reform, and occasional grudging concessions from the tax committees, the committees retain vast power and autonomy. This power was often used to protect special interests. A study of the 1969 tax reform bill concludes:

> . . . the worst tax loopholes still remain. Percentage depletion and write-offs for intangible drilling expense for the oil and gas industry emerged from the battle virtually unscathed. A strong challenge to the tax-exempt status of state and local government bonds was successfully beaten back. . . . Proposals to eliminate entirely the preferred tax treatment of capital gains . . . were substantially softened. Many other major escape hatches . . . still remain to be dealt with.[23]

The committees have retained control for several reasons. Until recently neither committee allowed subcommittees or permitted staff aides of various members to sit in on sessions. Thus members other than the chairman could not develop expertise through running hearings, and did not have any real working access to staff experts. This put an almost impossible burden on most members:

> A final element that freezes out the average Congressman or Senator and tightens the grip of the Tax Establishment is the hideous complexity of the tax laws and the virtual unintelligibility of most of their provisions. How is the average member of Congress . . . to deal with provisions such as this one (taken at random from the Internal Revenue Code):
> ". . . For purposes of paragraph (3), an organization described in paragraph (2) shall be deemed to include an organization described in Section 501 (c) (4), (5) or (6) which would be described in paragraph (2) if it were an organization described in Section 501 (c) (3).[24]

The complexity, says reformer Philip Stern, "endows the experts and the 'insiders' with unusual powers, and robs even the most vigilant Congressman or newsman of his normal powers of scrutiny. What casual observer, for example, would be able to spot a provision in a 585-page tax bill innocuously headed 'Certain New Design Products' and know that it was tailor-made to confer more than $20,000,000 in tax saving upon the Lockheed and McDonnell Douglas companies?"[25]

The power, the isolation, and the unrepresentative character of the tax-writing committees distort social policy in a conservative direction. Since it is so firmly rooted in the seniority system and the decentralized system of committee power, this distortion is difficult to rectify. Only a long series of appoint- 277 ments by leaders sympathetic to a contemporary party majority could turn the committee around.

While this is not likely to happen soon, there is some evidence that the committees are coming under more pressure from Congress as a whole. While the tax reform bill of 1969 was weak, it did begin the long-resisted effort to whittle down some of the least defensible deductions. Outside pressure pushed Social Security payments up far more rapidly than the committees desired in the late 1960s and early 1970s. There were efforts to challenge the committee directly on the House floor, and the House Rules Committee no longer showed a determination to forbid amendments to the major bills from the Ways and Means Committee.

Congressional Inconsistency: A Spectacularly Visible Phenomenon

The committee system, with its different political and institutional biases in various committees with overlapping responsibilities, frequently produces the appearance, and sometimes the reality, of wildly inconsistent policy decisions. The Judiciary committees may forge legislation protecting the rights of black Americans, even as the Appropriations committees starve the programs that are intended to make those rights real. The House Education and Labor Committee can shape creative new public employment programs, even as the House Ways and Means Committee forces welfare mothers to work at terrible jobs for poverty-level pay without adequate child care.

The committees distort policy development in different ways, but most of their positive decisions are at least subject to correction by the majority on the House or Senate floor. The most drastic distortions come through negative action, through refusal to take action on legislation at all, or through votes not to report measures to the floor. When the Senate Finance Committee refuses to act on tax reform at a time of great public interest, or the House Judiciary Committee stalls popular antibusing legislation, the ability of Congress to respond to strong majority wishes may be severely undermined.

The fact that Congressional policies affecting the same group often go in two different directions at the same time does not mean that Congress is either hopelessly confused, or that it is the most conservative element of the policy-making process. In fact, the internal divisions and contradictions in Congress

278

are paralleled by less visible but very important divisions within the other branches of government. Because the executive branch is legally subject to Presidential direction, and the President approves a general set of legislative and budget priorities, there is a strong incentive to compromise disagreements into a semblance of unity. Often, however, basic differences persist. Thus, to cite one Nixon Administration example, education officials can persuade the President to announce a massive Right to Read program, only to have budget officials convince him to actually cut back on the federal share of school costs. The inconsistencies are even clearer in the simultaneous pursuit of contradictory policies toward the same clientele by a variety of executive agencies. The Public Health Service, for example, struggles against cigarette smoking, while the Agriculture Department promotes tobacco growing and exports.

Even on the Supreme Court the majority opinion is often a compromise that is unclear or even internally contradictory. To maintain unity on the landmark 1954 and 1955 school cases, for example, the Court declared that black children had an unambiguous right to a desegregated education, but then refused to give any significant enforcement to the right.

The divisions and inconsistencies in the other branches of government are generally kept private. The media usually treat the compromise statements and decisions as if they were relatively clear and rational policies, giving the President and the Court the benefit of a doubt. It is Congress's misfortune that its disunity is so painfully public and so easily publicized.

The other branches, however, at least have a recognized structure of legitimate centralized decision-making, and provide strong incentives toward quiet internal working out of conflicts. In Congress this problem is magnified by the lack of strong party leaders in recent decades. There is usually no legitimate focus for policy-making on the large divisive issues, except the total membership voting on the floor. Naturally, observers of Congress focus more on the interesting and highly visible conflicts than on the direction and significance of the legislation that eventually emerges. With so many of these conflicts to report, they pay little attention to the skillful building of consensus within committees that often precedes major legislation. And if an analyst does attempt to assess the outputs, he must weigh a complex body of laws, appropriations measures, and committee decisions to pigeonhole bills, as well as the reports and floor debates, to discern the "intent of Congress."

279

Congressional policy-making is often characterized by inconsistent or even contradictory policy directions. While this may well be the character of governmental decision-making in general, it is spectacularly visible in Congress. Assessment of the actual net impact of the array of Congressional policy decisions is an extremely complex undertaking, but it is essential to evaluating the real policy impact of the legislative branch. When this effort is made, the importance of Congressional policy innovation becomes far clearer. It also soon becomes evident that any effort to stereotype Congress as inherently passive or conservative is doomed to failure. Any serious attempt to describe the policy impact of Congress must obviously describe the time period, the policy areas under consideration, and the existing division of power within Congress during that period.

NOTES

[1] *Washington Post*, May 9, 1974; William Watts and Lloyd A. Free, eds., *State of the Nation* (New York: Universe Books, 1973), p. 243, 246.

[2] Arthur M. Schlesinger, Jr., *The Imperial Presidency* (Boston: Houghton Mifflin, 1973), pp. 246–52.

[3] Lawrence Henry Chamberlain, *The President, Congress and Legislation* (New York: Columbia University Press, 1946).

[4] Ronald C. Moe and Steven C. Teel, "Congress as Policy-Maker: A Necessary Reappraisal," in Ronald C. Moe, ed., *Congress and the President* (Pacific Palisades, Calif.: Goodyear, 1971), p. 50.

[5] David Price, *Who Makes the Laws: Creativity and Power in Senate Committees* (New York: Schenkman Publishing, 1972), pp. 331–32.

[6] See David Halberstam, *The Best and the Brightest* (New York: Random House, 1972), for a good description of the relationship between the prevailing liberal ideology and U.S. involvement in Vietnam.

[7] Charles S. Bullock, III, "Committee Transfers in the United States House of Representatives," *Journal of Politics*, February 1973, p. 94.

[8] *Congressional Quarterly*, April 28, 1973, pp. 989, 1001–03; *Congressional Directory*, 93rd Cong., 1st Sess., 1973.

[9] Richard Fenno's *The Power of the Purse* (Boston: Little, Brown, 1966) is particularly good in explaining how this process works on the House Appropriations Committee.

[10] *Congressional Quarterly*, April 28, 1973, p. 974.

[11] *Congressional Quarterly*, March 30, 1974, pp. 816–17, contains ratings of 1973 roll calls by four organizations. Committee membership is taken from appropriate volumes of the *Congressional Directory*.

[12] *Congressional Quarterly*, August 10, 1974, p. 2163.

[13] *Gallup Opinion Index*, March 1973, pp. 4–6.

[14] John F. Manley, *The Politics of Finance: The House Committee on Ways and Means* (Boston: Little, Brown, 1970), pp. 27–29, 36–38.

[15] *Congressional Quarterly Almanac*, 1969, pp. 589, 602–03.

[16] *Ibid.*, p. 605.

[17] *Ibid.*, p. 1649.

[18] Charles L. Schultze, Edward R. Fried, Alice M. Rivlin, and Nancy H. Teeters, *Setting National Priorities: The 1973 Budget* (Washington: Brookings Institution, 1972), p. 75.

[19] *Ibid.*, pp. 398–400.

[20] Joseph A. Pechman, *Federal Tax Policy* (Washington: Brookings Institution, 1971), pp. 173–74; *Setting National Priorities: The 1973 Budget*, pp. 428–29.

[21] Joseph A. Pechman and Benjamin A. Okner, *Who Bears the Tax Burden?* (Washington: Brookings Institution, 1974), pp. 4–10.

[22] *Washington Post*, October 31 and November 2, 1973.

[23] Joseph A. Ruskay and Richard A. Osserman, *Halfway to Tax Reform* (Bloomington: Indiana University Press, 1970), p. 217.

[24] Philip M. Stern, *The Rape of the Taxpayer* (New York: Random House, 1973), pp. 393–94.

[25] *Ibid.*, pp. 394–95.

13

CONGRESSIONAL POWER, PRESIDENTIAL DEADLOCK, CONTINUING PROBLEMS

Congress's Cumulative Impact on National Priorities

A Reversal of Attitudes toward the Budget Many experts look at the annual budget as perhaps the most important and reliable summary of changes in national policy. They frequently tend to make judgments on the basis of what the President proposes, rather than in terms of the changes that Congress insists on before the money can actually be spent. The tendency is to accept the generalization that the President sets the basic structure of the budget, and Congress merely elaborates it with a series of incremental changes. The old stereotypes portray Congress blindly voting whatever the military wants, while the President tries to wheedle some money for neglected domestic programs from the powerful Congressional stand-patters. In recent years, however, Congress has made a significant impact on the development of altered national priorities, and that impact has been in a direction precisely opposite to that prescribed by the old stereotype.

Since the mid-1960s there has been increasingly severe pressure on the federal budget, and a major reversal of the roles of the White House and Congress in the budget process. In many cases the President has assumed the position, once occupied by the House Appropriations Committee, of chief naysayer to the expansion of domestic programs. Growing deficits, massive tax cuts, severe inflation, and the built-in growth of well-established programs have sharply constrained budget options for both the President and Congress, creating strong pressure against new programs. Since the late 1960s the President has often responded most vigorously to these fiscal problems, but Congress has tended to become increasingly responsive to the new program constituencies created by the Great Society legislation.

While it is unsurprising that conservative Presidents try to restrain domestic expenditures, it was indeed a major development when President Lyndon Johnson found it necessary, in the late 1960s, to hold back Congress from expanding his own programs. Equally significant in the early 1970s was the weakening of a long Congressional consensus for military spending that had repeatedly resulted in the financing of weapons systems the President said were unnecessary. Under President Nixon the once routine, virtually unanimous passage of the military finance bills gave way to a series of fierce fights. Even intensive White House intervention did not forestall some military cutbacks.

The new budget patterns became a central feature of the Nixon Administration. Coming to office when the costs of the Great Society programs were mounting rapidly, President Nixon, being committed to lowering taxes, responded to the budget crunch by abolishing a number of domestic programs, by vetoing a series of major Congressional initiatives in domestic policy, and by refusing to spend billions of dollars appropriated by Congress. The President's strongest legislative efforts, on the other hand, often focused either on winning a grudging Congressional approval for new defense-related projects, or on resisting Congressional efforts to use the power of the purse to end the Vietnam War and limit future military involvements.

The Nixon period saw Congress push up domestic spending at a rapid rate and bring down military costs, marginally, altering the President's priorities. Congress succeeded in preserving some major domestic programs the President wished to eliminate or drastically cut back. Congressional pressure was so strong that the President not only frequently employed his veto, but also found it necessary to resort to the unusual 283 weapons of impounding funds (refusing to spend appropriated money), abolishing agencies, declaring mass freezes, ending programs by unilateral declaration, and asserting authority for an absolute pocket veto that could not be overridden by Congress. The intense conflict eventually produced a rare Constitutional confrontation over the limits of the President's budget powers. The courts usually held against the President.

When he chose to deal with the budget problem by sharp cuts in domestic programs, President Nixon might have expected aid from the House Appropriations Committee, traditionally the toughest obstacle to domestic spending programs. The President's strong conservative initiative, however, soon revealed that changes in Congress had weakened the commanding authority and dogmatic conservatism of the House committee, and left the White House as the bastion of fiscal austerity.

The House Committee enjoyed vast power partly because it could almost never be defeated on the House floor. Few politicians desire to take on a very powerful foe when victory is impossible. During a fifteen-year period studied by Richard Fenno, the committee had rarely been challenged, and had defeated 90 percent of the amendments offered.[1]

As major domestic programs were threatened by the President's budget, the House committee came under effective attack. At first the House panel was a natural ally for the White House strategy of cutting back Great Society programs, or at least holding them to constant dollar levels and thus letting inflation reduce their scope each year. Within the House as a whole, however, supporters of the more popular new programs succeeded in forming coalitions that were able to defeat the barons of the appropriations process in several key tests. Once this happened in such fields as education, health, and pollution control, the mystique that constituted the basis of much of the committee's power was gravely threatened. Faced with the unhappy choice between further defeats and adapting to majority demands, the committee chose to adapt. With the committee forsaking its traditional role in some areas, the White House was forced to deploy its full energy to fight Congressional increases. It was a striking change from the struggles of the 1960s, when the committee had frequently been the principal obstacle to program expansions supported by the President.

The committee itself was undergoing internal changes. HEW's health and education budgets had been considered by a reasonably responsive subcommittee most of the time since

1949. After the 1970 election the subcommittee on housing and urban programs came under the leadership of a Massachusetts liberal, Edward Boland, who replaced a small-town Tennessee conservative. Some modest centers of moderate and liberal influence were taking shape within the conservative committee.

Cutbacks in Military and Foreign Aid Spending Adding some funds to domestic programs without either raising taxes or increasing the deficit was made possible by a significant break with the pattern of uncritical Congressional support of military spending. As participation of American troops in the Vietnam War finally ended, the central budget policy question was whether or not the Defense Department would capture the money saved by troop withdrawals as part of its permanent budgetary base. Defense officials said it was needed to pay for programs deferred during the war. Liberals, on the other hand, called for transferring the "fiscal dividend" to domestic programs. The President advocated small initial reductions, but called for commitment to major new weapons systems. He eventually advocated substantial growth in the Pentagon budget. President Ford early endorsed this approach.

During President Nixon's first three years in office, Congress cut a total of more than $10 billion from the military budgets. The cumulative effect was surely greater, since one year's spending level becomes the base point for calculating the next year's increase. In the fourth year the President asked for an increase of $5.6 billion, which Congress cut by $5.2 billion.[2] While Vietnam expenditures had dropped almost $21 billion a year between the last fiscal year of the Johnson Administration and the 1973 budget, the President was requesting a virtually identical level of overall Defense spending, clearly enlarging the Department's peacetime base even after discounting inflation.[3] Congress fought this trend.

At the same time, Congress was cutting back drastically on another major tool used by the President in international relations: foreign aid, especially military aid. Even before Nixon took office Congress had drastically curtailed both the annual appropriations and the authority to send American arms aid abroad. During President Johnson's last year an alliance of conservatives and liberals, suspicious of military entanglements, sliced a small budget request by 40 percent and almost eliminated the program.[4]

The attacks intensified under President Nixon, with the bat- **285** tle focusing on efforts to control Indochina war policies. Small Administration bills were cut $1.1 billion in 1969, $340 million in 1970, and $1.2 billion in 1971. The next year the program barely survived after the Senate defeated the entire bill amid a stormy struggle to force the President to end the war. Months passed before a compromise was worked out.[5] The ultimate use of Congressional leverage came in 1973, when Congress wrote into the bill a proviso ending American bombing of Indochina by August 15. The Congressional action, affecting several important pieces of legislation, forced the President to negotiate a compromise ending American military action in Cambodia. It represented the most important assertion of Congressional war powers in recent history.

While cutting back on military funds and restricting their use, Congress was at the same time providing substantial spending increases in a few major areas of social policy. During President Nixon's first year, Congress raised domestic spending over $2 billion, with most of the money going to education, environment programs, food stamps, and housing and urban programs. During the second year the President responded to Congressional increases by vetoing the appropriations bills for both of the two central domestic departments, HEW and HUD. He also vetoed a large new public employment program. Congress overrode the education veto. In the third year hundreds of millions were added to the education, water and sewer, urban, and health programs. These increases were made not by increasing the budget but by reallocating funds. Each session the total appropriations were substantially below the President's budget.[6]

The Presidential Counterattack

The Massive Use of the Veto Only extensive use of the Presidential veto power forestalled more drastic reorientation of budget priorities. Three times during his first term, for example, the President vetoed school appropriations bills. In spite of increased unemployment, he vetoed both the 1970 manpower bill and the 1971 accelerated public works measures. In 1971 Mr. Nixon killed a day-care program that would have cost billions a year, as well as several health measures and a massive antipollution program. The use of the veto became a central tool of the Presidency in 1972, when the President vetoed sixteen bills, including two versions of HEW appropriations. Other major programs affected included a huge $25-billion antipollution measure, a public works and economic development bill, a substantial vocational rehabilitation program, and two major bills extending services for the aging. Most of the 1972 vetoes were pocket vetoes, made after Congress recessed, and described by the President as action against "spending far in excess of my no-new-taxes budget."[7]

During 1972 President Nixon made Congressional spending a major campaign target and appealed unsuccessfully for authority to make discretionary cuts holding the budget to $250 billion. Although Congress had imposed spending ceilings on President Johnson in 1967 and 1968, it now rejected Nixon's request for similar authority. In the face of strong election-year pressure to vote against "big spending" and inflation, Senator Humphrey led a successful battle against the measure, claiming it would severely undermine legislative prerogatives. In four years' time, Congress had moved from a position of insisting that the President exercise restraint in domestic programs to denying the President the opportunity to make cutbacks.

Although Presidential vetoes directly eliminated billions of dollars for new and enlarged social programs, their indirect effect in restraining Congressional efforts to change priorities was much greater. Once it becomes evident that the President is determined to veto, and that he can hold the members of his own party to sustain the veto, program supporters have an incentive to set spending levels at the maximum they think the President might be persuaded to accept, rather than at the level they think necessary. Although it is possible to try to create an issue or to demonstrate commitment to concerned constituencies by passing a bill that is surely doomed, it doesn't put any program in operation. Members primarily concerned about getting some program functioning must anticipate the reaction of the President in drafting the bill.

Vetoes also have a cumulative effect. Since the development of a budget for any program usually starts with the current year's spending as a base, a cut one year means the program's advocates start behind in subsequent years' bargaining as well. Legislators facing apparently inevitable vetoes hesitate to make the enormous effort necessary to win passage of a major bill. Vetoed programs, of course, are unable to develop the constituencies that play such an important role in expanding funding in future years. Members of Congress forced to choose between a veto and a severely limited program often conclude that any-

287

thing is better than nothing. While it is impossible to estimate the full impact of Mr. Nixon's vetoes on restraining Congressional desires, it must amount to at least several billion dollars of domestic programs a year.

The veto emerged as a particularly crucial instrument of Presidential power in 1973, after President Nixon's landslide reelection in the previous year. The President's response to his mandate, and to his failure to carry either house of Congress, was to become increasingly insistent about imposing his budget priorities through use of the veto. The President submitted a budget cutting deeply into a number of programs, and threatened to veto any domestic bill exceeding that budget, or any Defense bill reducing the President's proposal. The White House launched a major Administration-wide publicity drive against "budget-busting" bills. The President intended to impose his priorities on the country through vigorous use of the veto, with the support of the GOP minority—particularly the very conservative Republican group in the House.

The contest began early and the President enjoyed striking success with his strategy of "one-third plus one" control of the budget. Only the immense crisis created by the revelation of the Watergate scandal moved the President toward compromise with Congress. His strategy clearly demonstrated the impressive power that a conservative President, who wanted little in the way of positive legislation and had no more elections to face, could exercise over program development.

Congress returned in 1973 with the Democratic leadership determined to reinstate some of the programs pocket-vetoed by the President after the conclusion of the last session. They also returned to confront the problems created by the President's cancellation, between the election and the convening of the new Congress, of some popular agriculture measures and the vast bulk of housing and urban programs.

The President's budget rested squarely on the principle of cutting back government involvement in social problems. In his inaugural address the President had sounded the theme of his second term when he said, "Ask not what government can do for you but what you can do for yourself." In his State of the Union budget message the President attacked the "impatient idealism" of the Great Society programs that had led to "sweeping, sometimes almost utopian, commitments in one area of social concern after another."

He promised to jettison bad programs and to proceed with a "healthy skepticism about Federal Government omniscience and omnicompetence, and . . . a strong reaffirmation of the right and capacity of individuals to chart their own lives and solve their own problems through State and local government and private endeavor."[8] The budget represented a cut of approximately $10 billion in projected social expenditures, according to Budget Director Casper Weinberger.[9] Summarizing the philosophy of the budget in a radio address the night before the document was sent to Congress, President Nixon told the public, "It is time to get big government off your back and out of your pocket."[10]

The strident tone of the battle was apparent in the White House guidebook "The Battle of the Budget, 1973," which informed officials throughout the executive branch how to attack Congressional appropriations decisions. Officials were told to describe the legislative branch as "the buck-passing Congress" or "the credit-card Congress," and to threaten a 15-percent tax increase unless the President's budget cuts were sustained. "One-liners" to be inserted into speeches included:

Does the Congress really want programs of compassion for the poor, or does it just want to indulge its passion for poor programs?

When one man helps himself to another man's bank account, that's called embezzlement. But when a big-spending Congressman helps himself to the taxpayer's income with higher prices and taxes, then it's called "compassion."

The material was soon incorporated in speeches of cabinet members and other Administration spokesmen.[11]

The most extensive scholarly analysis of the new budget, by a team of Brookings Institution economists, concluded that "the President is proposing cuts in some existing programs and consolidation of others, on a scale far beyond anything presidents have recommended in the past." Their analysis showed a cut of $12.2 billion in previously planned expenditures for the fiscal year starting in mid-1973, and $15.2 billion for the following year. About $10 billion was to come from domestic programs, mainly health, manpower, welfare, education, and pollution control. It was a budget attempting to drastically revise the "scope and role of the federal government in society." Even the programs that remained were to be altered by combining numbers of federal programs aimed at particular objectives into a few broad sets of grants allowing wide state and local discretion.[12]

The budget produced a chorus of bitter attacks. Senator   289

Walter Mondale (D-Minn.), designated as Democratic spokesman by the party's Congressional leadership, assailed the new priorities:

> The President's budget calls for severe cutbacks in our existing investments in decent housing . . . employment . . . education . . . health . . . the poor and the aged . . . the family farmer.
> This budget would, among other things, eliminate 180,000 desperately needed jobs . . . end the federal aid for low and moderate income housing . . . slash health research, aid to education, medicare benefits for the aged . . . and abolish practically every effort to strengthen rural America.
> While nearly 100 programs to help people would be destroyed, the defense and foreign aid budgets would rise dramatically and not a single tax loophole for the rich would be closed.[13]

As usual, the public response to the budget battle was ambiguous. White House aides happily cited Gallup Poll surveys showing the public agreed that taxes should be lowered, the budget balanced, and spending reduced. On the other hand, a Harris Survey asking about specific programs found the public supporting increased federal school aid, maintenance of the poverty program, and continuation of existing job training, medicare, rural assistance, and preschool programs—all by large margins.[14] There was pressure to hold down spending, but no sign of agreement about the President's priorities.

The veto battle rapidly began. Congress set to work reenacting a series of bills vetoed by the President at the end of the 1972 session. The Democratic leadership decided to bring the issue to a head first over a popular and noncontroversial bill to expand vocational rehabilitation programs. This measure, which would have authorized help for new categories of disabled people, passed the Senate 86-2 and the House 318-57. After the President vetoed the bill, however, the GOP leadership in the Senate succeeded in changing enough votes to sustain the veto. Thirty-one Republicans joined five Southern Democrats in frustrating the sixty Senators attempting to override the veto.[15]

The Senate vote was a smashing victory for the President. If he could obtain the necessary support for his veto of an extremely popular bill in the Senate, there would be little trouble defeating less popular measures. Two months later the Senate Watergate hearings began to unravel White House influence. "The President," said Senate Democratic Leader Mansfield, "is in the driver's seat, at least for now."[16]

290

The veto was the beginning of a year of Presidential cutbacks and policy stalemate. With more than the necessary one-third of the Senate prepared to support the White House on popular, noncontroversial measures, there was little hope for enactment of significant new departures. The President went on to win support for a series of vetoes. Among the measures the President struck down were increased minimum wages, rural environmental assistance, restrictions on Presidential impoundments of appropriated funds, and medical services. By November 1973 the President had won eight successive veto contests. Sustained by Congress, he had killed more legislation in part of one year than either Kennedy or Johnson had vetoed in their entire term of service.[17]

Even the mounting disaster of the Watergate scandal and the dramatic decline in the President's public opinion poll ratings did not shake the GOP support necessary to sustain vetoes. When the President was finally overridden, the issue was not domestic priorities but Congressional war powers. On November 7, 1973, the House followed the Senate in writing into law a requirement that Congressional approval be required before there was any prolonged commitment of American forces to military action. This measure enjoyed support across much of the political spectrum, and many viewed it more as a question of the institutional authority of Congress than as a liberal objective.[18]

The veto threat cast a general pall over most of the domestic legislative process. The rock-hard GOP support, particularly in the House, gave the President virtually an absolute veto over domestic programs, unless they were combined with one of the few bills the Administration had to have. The gloom about new legislation was intensified by the political isolation of the White House, and its refusal to strike compromises with Congress, agencies, and interest groups in the traditional manner. For example, after the President simply ended the major national housing subsidy programs in January 1973 by freezing new commitments, the White House rejected compromise out of hand. Carl Coan, Jr., chief lobbyist for the powerful National Association of Home Builders, commented on the unique political situation where the White House refused to "work something out" or to "deal with any other viewpoint." "That's a very powerful thing," he said, "especially when you have a President willing to use the veto." Representative Wright Patman (D-Tex.), chairman of the House Banking and Currency Committee, agreed that major housing legislation was 291 unlikely since the President was "stuck on a no compromise attitude."[19] Nixon tried to ignore Congress.

Similar paralysis was afflicting one area of policy-making after another. The President had not captured the power of domestic initiative from Congress; rather he had chosen to spend his political power to try to freeze the status quo. The result was a massive deadlock on domestic policy.

During President Nixon's first term, program supporters had fought a hard and persistent battle to protect programs and sustain them. Now the President was moving from a position of insistent confrontation with Congress to one of total intransigence. He in effect declared that he would accomplish his main purposes of holding down domestic spending and decentralizing power in federal aid programs whether Congress approved or not, through use of broadly defined executive power. As a minority President who wished to broaden his support for reelection, during his first term he had had some incentive to bargain. Now, as a lame-duck President with a massive mandate and very little positive legislation that he wanted from Congress, he was in a strong position to make his will stick.

The disturbing thing about the beginning of the second term was the almost total absence of a sense of comity, of shared power and mutual respect, which is so important to keep the complex Constitutional machinery functioning. Although the Democratic Congress also had a strong electoral mandate, the President and his principal advisors were determined to nullify its actions rather than reach an accommodation. This meant Constitutional crises that would be forced into the courts when the President tried to expand executive power to new limits, and a political crisis that would lead to a strong Democratic drive for the election of a veto-proof Congress in 1974.

It is interesting and perhaps revealing that the White House advisors most involved in fostering this Presidential strategy, Haldeman and Ehrlichman, were also at the heart of the abuses of executive power in the Watergate scandal, of which they were early casualties. After Ehrlichman was replaced by former Congressman Melvin Laird as chief domestic advisor, the policy was rapidly softened.

A Subtler Weapon: Impoundment While the veto often proved an effective weapon in preventing new departures in domestic policy, it was not always successful. Nor did the

President always wish to veto an entire bill to get at a single objectionable program or expenditure. While the veto was a formidable weapon, it tended to be more a meat ax than a scalpel. Then there was the problem of what to do after Congress overrode a veto, as it had five times in Mr. Nixon's first twenty-two regular vetoes. Obviously, the President needed a more delicate weapon, more isolated from Congressional power, if his program was to be maintained in the face of legislative opposition.

Mr. Nixon attempted to impose his priorities on federal programs through assertion of a very broad authority to unilaterally cut spending levels, after Congressional action, without being subject to Congressional review. Earlier Presidents had impounded program funds, usually over questions of efficient administration, or the military necessity of certain weapons systems, or the economic impact of spending large sums at a particular time. Often these earlier decisions led to negotiations and eventual release of the impounded money. Congress had recognized, in bills passed in 1905 and 1950, Presidential authority to prevent overspending by agencies, to create reserves, or to realize savings made possible by new developments. With the possible exception of certain military expenditures, however, earlier Presidents had not claimed any broad authority to override Congressional judgments.

The impoundment question posed one of those boundary problems between legitimate executive and legislative authority that are usually solved by compromise and negotiation rather than by confrontation. Obviously, Congress has the basic Constitutional authority to establish programs and appropriate funds. The President's power as the Chief Executive, on the other hand, necessarily implies some discretion. Discretion is necessary if the executive branch finds that unforeseen circumstances or administrative difficulties make it impossible or counterproductive to implement legislative directives. It is likewise necessary if administrators find that the end desired by Congress can be accomplished for less money than Congress appropriated, or if they find that orderly administration requires the establishment of a financial reserve fund for unforeseen contingencies. These things are only good sense, and there is little objection to them so long as a reasonable level of good faith and mutual trust are maintained.

Controversy arises when the President impounds funds, not for technical reasons, but to intentionally reverse policy declared by Congress. Presidents Truman, Eisenhower, and Kennedy all refused to spend some of the money appropriated for military hardware. Truman refused to spend $735 million for ten more Air Force groups, Eisenhower held back $137 million for an early antimissile system, and Kennedy refused to spend an extra $180 million for more work on the development of a manned bomber. In each case, however, there was an explanation. The Senate had reluctantly approved the Air Force money, with the clearly stated supposition that the President might choose not to spend it. In Eisenhower's case, he said it would be a mistake to purchase the weapons until their tests were completed. As for Kennedy, his Secretary of Defense decided that more funds were not necessary at the time, and Congress gave a sort of backhanded ratification of the decision by defeating a move the next year to "direct" the President to spend the money.

President Johnson opened a new chapter in the struggle with a 1966 decision holding up $5.3 billion in highway, urban, and a variety of other funds, so as to lessen the inflationary impact of Vietnam spending. The decision produced widespread local and state protests. Before it reached the stage of confrontation, the Administration backed off and released much of the money within four months.[20]

President Nixon developed a much more sweeping concept of the impoundment power. Eventually he asserted the right to eliminate entire programs, to substantially alter the domestic budget approved by Congress, and even to nullify Congressional action overriding his veto. As early as the first months of 1971, the White House was holding up about $1.5 billion in urban programs, and was ready to announce the cancellation of the large Model Cities effort. Only strong local protests temporarily spared the program.[21] The withholding led to Congressional hearings and the beginning of a Congressional attack on impoundment. Senator John Sparkman (D-Ala.) pointed out that the President was holding back most of the money appropriated for public housing and water and sewer projects, two-thirds of the Model Cities money, and portions of urban renewal and mass transit funds. Senator Sam Ervin (D-N.C.) questioned the constitutionality of actions that "avoid or nullify congressional intent."[22] By late February 1971, withheld funds totalled $11.1 billion. In the House, both the Speaker and Appropriations Committee leaders challenged the legality of these drastic Presidential actions.[23]

During the 1972 election campaign, Mr. Nixon made Congressional spending a major campaign issue, and challenged

Congress to adopt a rigid $250-billion spending ceiling while giving the President unrestricted authority to make any necessary reductions to reach that figure. Essentially he was asking for clear statutory authority to do what he had been accomplishing through massive impoundments. When the key test vote came in the Senate, Senator Humphrey (D-Minn.) described the bill as an "item veto," altering the Constitution and "willfully, voluntarily, and freely giving away the most important authority, power, and responsibility we have."[24] Senator Gaylord Nelson (D-Wis.) asserted the President wanted "dictatorial control over the appropriations and spending process."[25]

After the Senate defeated the ceiling, the President announced that he would enforce the policy anyway, through impoundment. Secretary of the Treasury George Schultz said the President had authority to impound any amount of money.

The dispute deepened when Congress rejected the President's recommendation and passed a bill calling for a massive $12-billion antipollution program. The President replied that he would impound $6 billion to reduce the program to his original budget. Thus, he claimed, Congress's action overriding his veto of the bill was essentially meaningless.[26]

The impoundment strategy reached new heights after President Nixon's massive 1972 election victory. The Administration began to impound the great bulk of major Congressional budget increases. It justified this action with arguments from the President's Office of Management and Budget, claiming the new programs were objectively inferior to the President's proposals, which had been largely shaped within that office. When urban funds and manpower funds were withheld, for example, Congress was offered the bland explanation that the programs were "scheduled for termination," and that administrators would spend no more money even though the laws establishing the programs were still on the books. In January 1973 the head of the White House Domestic Council informed the Senate that no more money would be spent for the water and sewer, open space, and public facilities programs, until Congress accepted the President's recommendation to collapse these programs into a broad community development revenue-sharing measure.[27] Similar pressure was brought to bear on Congress in the manpower field by a Labor Department threat to implement revenue sharing by administrative fiat, if Congress failed to act.[28]

The President's attempt to expand executive authority to include life and death power over the whole range of established

295

domestic programs led to a confrontation with both the legislative and judicial branches. Some twenty-six federal court cases had been decided on the President's impoundment powers by late summer of 1973, and only one decision upheld the President's claim of authority to withhold money for policy rather than to administrative reasons. In Congress, meanwhile, both houses had passed legislation strongly restraining impoundment authority.[29]

By 1973, three years of expansive use of the President's impoundment procedure had very significantly damaged several Great Society programs and newer Congressional initiatives, but only at the price of a serious Constitutional confrontation with Congress and the courts over the limits of executive authority. Ironically, the ultimate consequence of a sustained effort to limit legislative prerogatives would probably be a constriction of the Presidency. By refusing to respect Congressional power and work out an accommodation on a reasonable definition of impoundment authority, the President forced a showdown on the issue. The question went to the courts and Congress in the form least likely to permit preservation of a useful administrative power: blanket assertions about the right of the President to reverse choices concerning national policy duly incorporated in laws signed by the President or passed over his veto. The court decisions strongly suggested that the assertion of a grandiose impoundment power would end with the White House possessing less authority than it had traditionally exercised. In June of 1974 Congress enacted legislation that flatly denied the President the right to rescind programs without a vote of Congress, and that allowed either house to overturn a White House effort to defer spending. Confrontation with Congress would end by weakening the Presidency.

Who's to Blame for the Deadlock? Critics of Congress's role in the development of national policy frequently point to the recurrence of deadlock on major issues of urgent national need, placing the blame squarely on an obstructive legislative branch. By 1973 a classic deadlock had developed between President Nixon and Congress, enmeshing legislation on education, housing, job training, health care, taxation reform, and a number of other central areas of domestic policy. The deadlock was exacerbated both by the President's refusal to compromise and by the Congressional investigation of White House involvement in the Watergate scandal. For the first time since *Congressional Quarterly* began systematically recording

Congressional treatment of Presidential proposals in 1953, Congress rejected significantly more than half the President's requests. The only time a President had even come close to this record was in 1959, when Eisenhower confronted the overwhelmingly Democratic Congress produced by the 1958 recession.[30] Now, in spite of the continuing power of the conservatives in the House and his own massive 1972 victory, the President was confronting tremendous opposition in enacting a modest legislative program.

This deadlock was very largely due to the uncompromising position of a rigidly conservative White House. There was policy deadlock in most major areas of reform, because the President was opposed to significant expansion in federal responsibilities. In fact, the situation was often worse than a deadlock. In one area after another in domestic policy, the President was urging that less be done, either through outright termination of existing commitments or through year-by-year scaling down of programs. This objective was so crucially important to President Nixon that he was willing to draw on all possible resources of executive power and even risk very serious confrontations with both Congress and the courts to accomplish it.

Even the President's limited initiatives in domestic affairs were ambiguous in character. Most of the Administration's proposed reforms were structural in character, involving the transfer of resources from the federal to state and local governments, with few restrictions on their use. Reformers in many fields saw these as attempts to transfer resources from relatively sympathetic agencies to institutions with little record of positive response to social needs. At any rate, these were basically proposals for governmental reorganization, not social change.

The one exception during the Nixon period was the welfare reform proposal, which was temporarily put forward by the President as a major priority, but later withdrawn. This proposal widely expanded the number of poor families eligible for assistance, instituted rigid work requirements, and, conceivably, lowered payment levels in the large Northern states. It was designed to appeal to both liberal and conservative critics of the existing system. Ultimately it was defeated because it satisfied neither group, and the Nixon Administration was unwilling to work out a compromise with the opponents. This dispute can be interpreted from a variety of perspectives, but even if it is seen as a truly progressive Presidential move, it stands out as a virtually unique and temporary exception.[31]

Many earlier descriptions of policy deadlock have assumed both that deadlock distorts policy in a conservative direction and that Congress is to blame. With the experience of a conservative Administration now in view, it is clear that neither of these generalizations is adequate or accurate. During the Nixon Administration, deadlock frequently was used to frustrate moves away from a progressive status quo reflected in Great Society legislation. On the other hand, the Presidential policy initiatives frequently aimed squarely at the cutback of federal domestic programs. The central instruments for deadlocking progressive bills were no longer the House Rules and Appropriations committees, but the Presidential budget, the impoundment process, and the veto.

Innovation amid Deadlock: The Case of Women's Rights

As the national political system settled into the Presidential-Congressional stalemate of the early 1970s, the emergence of a major social movement to redefine the status of women in American society provided a good test of the responsiveness of the major political institutions. The movement raised a series of new issues and grew in a policy vacuum where there were few firmly established political positions. It enjoyed the unusual advantages of high social status and immediate access to policy-makers that are seldom available to advocates of fundamental social change. When the demands were raised, Congress proved far more responsive than the executive branch.

To be sure, Congressional responsiveness did not show unusually strong sympathy for the plight of women. It did, however, illustrate several features of the Congressional process that lead to certain kinds of new policies. It showed the sensitivity of Congressmen to groups not yet nationally organized, but that constituted potential political threats to members' local coalitions. (Angry local women's groups could easily become a significant influence in the relatively small campaigns waged in most Congressional districts.) The issue also illustrated the ability of a small number of determined members of either house to force a potentially embarrassing issue to a public floor decision. In striking contrast to the ponderous, elaborately staffed policy debates that often precede executive-branch proposals, new ideas can sometimes be brought quite suddenly to center stage in Congress. Thus, although Congress is often justly condemned as a graveyard for reform movements, it also may produce a legislative victory for a movement that hasn't yet gained much political power.

Two of the three most important Congressional actions affecting women's rights in the recent past have been forced to sudden decision on the floor without committee action, while the third was a major Congressional initiative formulated with very little executive encouragement. In one only of these cases was Congress responding to a massive and powerful political drive.

An Accidental Breakthrough: The Ban on Sex Discrimination The issue of sex discrimination in employment was sprung on the House by surprise in 1964 and enacted by accident. Bitter opponents of the job discrimination title in the civil rights bill before Congress decided to try to load up the bill with objectionable features that might split the coalition supporting it. The amendment prohibiting sex discrimination was moved by the South's leading strategist, Rules Committee Chairman Howard "Judge" Smith (D-Va.). Judge Smith called it a move to protect "a very essential minority group, in the absence of which the majority group would not be here today." He joked about the "real grievances" of women and humorously suggested that maybe Congress should pass legislation ending spinsterhood.[32]

The amendment was opposed by most liberal spokesmen. Judiciary Committee Chairman Celler, floor leader for the bill, called it "illogical, ill timed, ill placed and improper."[33] The bill was opposed by the Women's Bureau of the Labor Department and by the American Association of University Women, who saw it as a ploy to weaken chances of passing the civil rights law. Congresswoman Edith Green (D-Ore.) pointed out that the amendment's supporters had only recently led the opposition to a bill requiring equal pay for equal work. She said that discrimination against blacks was more severe and that there hadn't been "one word of testimony" on the amendment. "It will clutter up the bill, and it may later—very well— be used to help destroy this section of the bill."[34]

President Kennedy hadn't asked for any provision against job discrimination at all. The House supporters were afraid that further complicating the issue would increase the already serious obstacles to enactment. This was the Southern plan.

The only strong liberal spokesman supporting the bill was a 299 woman, Representative Martha Griffiths (D-Mich.). Representative Griffiths, who would later play a critical role in passage of the Equal Rights Amendment, argued strongly that women faced job discrimination problems of a kind and severity that paralleled those of blacks, and urgently required a legislative remedy. Otherwise, she said, women applicants would go to the bottom of the list once race discrimination became illegal. The other major speakers for the amendment included an array of the most reactionary Southern members. The amendment was adopted on an unrecorded teller vote 168-133.[35]

When John F. Kennedy's assassination and Lyndon Johnson's strong leadership brought a powerful drive to enact the civil rights bill without change, the amendment went through the Senate with little attention. President Johnson insisted that the House bill be accepted with virtually no Senate changes, so that it could not be sabotaged by conservatives on a conference committee or subjected to a second round of filibustering in the Senate. Thus the prohibition became law as written.

The new amendment had a striking impact. Even in the first year of the new Equal Employment Opportunity Commission, "well over a third of the complaints received . . . alleged discrimination based on sex, and many of the most difficult cases before the Commission (for example, the long unresolved airlines stewardess cases) involve sex discrimination."[36] EEOC action, Justice Department litigation, and very extensive private litigation by individuals and groups in the burgeoning women's rights movement brought an end to sex-role stereotypes in many job classifications, opening up new kinds of careers to both men and women. Some cases, like the mammoth action against the American Telephone and Telegraph Company, have produced plans to make "male" or "female" jobs available to the opposite sex, and agreements to make cash settlements for the unequal pay schedules of the past. Today's male airline stewards and female telephone linemen and steelworkers owe their jobs directly to this amendment, the accidental result of the tactical maneuverings of a policy battle in Congress.

The Equal Rights Amendment The next decisive stage of Congressional action on women's rights was not an accident but an impressive political victory: passage of the Equal Rights Amendment to the Constitution. This victory too, however, depended on the possibility of employing legislative tactics to force a vote on a matter enjoying little enthusiastic support from Congressional males.

300

The equal rights proposal had been submitted to Congress time after time for almost a half century before Congress suddenly acted in 1970 and 1971. Ever since it had first been introduced in 1923, the amendment's sweeping prohibition on any governmental action abridging equality of rights "on account of sex" had frequently been condemned by Constitutional scholars, who feared its uncertain impact on a vast range of laws regulating domestic relations, military service, safety standards, retirement ages, and a variety of other issues. When the Senate passed the amendment in 1950 and 1953, it added language providing that it not "be construed to impair the rights, benefits, or exemptions conferred by law upon persons of the female sex."[37] Although the altered amendment undermined many goals of the feminist movement, even the weakened version was blocked in the House by the implacable opposition of Judiciary Committee Chairman Celler. Each session thereafter, many members of the House routinely introduced the amendment and Celler routinely pigeon-holed it.

With the emergence of a widely publicized women's movement in 1970, however, the number of members making the symbolic gesture of introducing the measure reached a majority. Encouraged, Representative Martha Griffiths took the rare step of challenging one of the most powerful committee chairmen by filing a discharge petition to force the issue out of Celler's committee.

Discharge petitions, which directly challenge the committee system in a legislative body dominated by committee work, almost always fail. When Mrs. Griffiths acted, the House had approved only twenty-four of the 835 petitions filed since the procedure was created in 1909.[38] Representative Griffiths, however, got her majority of signatures in less than six weeks.

Once on the floor, the amendment swept to passage without any serious debate. Confronted with the necessity of publicly voting for or against equal rights for women, Congressmen, in a period of growing feminist militancy, could not risk opposition. With no committee hearings and very little discussion of the issues, the amendment passed 352-15.[39] When conservatives led by Senator Sam Ervin (D-N.C.) succeeded in preventing Senate action that year, the House leadership coalesced behind a modified version exempting women from the draft and authorizing laws prescribing special work conditions for them. When this version came out of the House Judiciary Committee, it was bitterly protested by feminist groups. Members responded by ignoring the advice of party leaders and reinstating the amendment's original language by a three-to-one margin.[40] With delaying tactics exhausted, the Senate added its assent.

Congressional action, triggered by a Congresswoman who forced the issue to the floor, had initiated a change in the nation's fundamental law and carried the idea of sexual equality to the heart of the Constitution. If ratified by the states, the amendment seemed certain to speed the change in sex roles in American society.

In approving the amendment, Congress was not responding to a tidal wave of public pressure. In fact, some opinion polls indicated that American women were generally content with their position in society and opposed to such changes as draft eligibility or basic restructuring of the law of alimony.[41] In this case, therefore, Congress was actually anticipating social change by responding to the potential political power represented by the vanguard of feminists, who were already organized and already articulating demands.

The Fight for Day Care   Perhaps the most severe difficulty confronting young women responding to the growing movement away from the home and into the job market was how to provide some kind of decent care for their children. In 1971 Congress dramatically responded to this problem by enacting a large federal commitment to the establishment of quality day-care centers. The President replied with a veto, accompanied by a harsh ideological condemnation of the whole idea of the federal government underwriting the change in family relationships.

A trend toward smaller families, the change in women's values, and a rapidly climbing rate of divorce and illegitimate births had combined to bring a growing number of mothers with young children into the labor market. The number of employed mothers with children under six climbed from 12 percent in 1950 to 28 percent in 1969.[42] Although the little-publicized White House Conference on Children in 1970 had assigned top priority to providing "comprehensive, family-oriented child-development programs including health services, day care, and early childhood education," the issue had not yet crossed the threshold of public attention. Only a scattering of small and uncoordinated federal programs was available, and they served only about 5 percent of the children needing care.[43]

302   Not much was done on Capitol Hill until 1971, when Sen-

Figure 13-1

Percentage of Married Women (Not Separated, Widowed, or
Divorced) in Labor Force, 1947–73

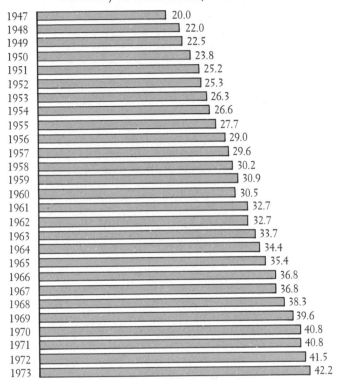

Year	Percentage
1947	20.0
1948	22.0
1949	22.5
1950	23.8
1951	25.2
1952	25.3
1953	26.3
1954	26.6
1955	27.7
1956	29.0
1957	29.6
1958	30.2
1959	30.9
1960	30.5
1961	32.7
1962	32.7
1963	33.7
1964	34.4
1965	35.4
1966	36.8
1967	36.8
1968	38.3
1969	39.6
1970	40.8
1971	40.8
1972	41.5
1973	42.2

SOURCE Manpower Report of the President (*Washington: GPO, 1974*),
p. 289.

ator Walter Mondale became chairman of the Subcommittee
on Children and Youth. After consulting with leading education, women's, labor, and civil rights organizations, Mondale
worked out a bill. The draft was sufficiently noncontroversial
to win cosponsorship from thirty-two other Senators with a
broad diversity of ideological perspectives. Hearings revealed
the wide array of group support, and testimony demonstrated
the chronic shortages of decent child care.

The only serious opposition came from the Administration.
After long debates among themselves, its spokesmen testified
on the final days of the hearings, calling for consolidation of
existing federal programs while strongly arguing that day care 303

Table 13-1

Percentage of Labor Force Participation for Married Women
with Husband Present and Children from 6 to 17 Years Old

1950	12.6
1955	17.3
1960	18.9
1965	22.8
1970	30.5
1973	30.9

SOURCE   Manpower Report of the President (*Washington: GPO, 1974*),
p. 291.

be left to state and local governments. The Administration
planned to expand day care only for welfare mothers, who
would be forced to work by the President's welfare reform
proposal. (In this case, apparently, belief in the redeeming value
of work for the poor was deep enough to override the fear
of government tampering with family life.) The Administration planned to take care of about a tenth of the eligible welfare children, at a cost far below estimated costs of adequate
services for young children.[44]

Both houses ignored the Administration and easily passed
bipartisan bills. The Senate bill called for services to a broad
economic spectrum of families, while the House version was
more geared to the problems of lower-income families.

While House and Senate conferees tried for weeks to work
out their differences, there was a total vacuum of White House
leadership. Eventually, Mondale and Representative Al Quie
worked out a compromise covering 18 million children, a
third of them preschoolers. The comprehensive services would
be offered with diminishing subsidies for families with incomes
ranging up to $15,000.[45] When the White House assailed the
compromise, the conferees attempted to forestall a veto by
cutting the program back. A new agreement limited free services to poor families, though those earning up to $7,000 would
be asked to make only small payments.[46]

President Nixon vetoed the bill anyway, attacking it as an
assault on the family. Although the measure was designed
primarily to give women already in the labor force decent care
for their children, he said it would "commit the vast moral
authority of the national government to the side of communal

approaches to child rearing over [and] against the family-centered approach."[47]

The veto destroyed the coalition and killed the bill. The next year, however, the Senate attempted to answer the President's objections in a new bipartisan measure, which passed 73-12.[48] The new bill lowered the cost 40 percent, underlined the voluntary character of the services, and denied help to any woman who was neither working nor in full-time training. The income ceiling was lowered, and state and local officials were given more authority in running the programs. The bill was opposed only by a small minority of ten very conservative Republicans and two Southern Democrats.[49]

The child-care program was part of the poverty bill. The President vetoed the entire bill and the veto was sustained. The poverty program went through the entire year under a continuing resolution, which permitted the existing programs to maintain operation, but only at the level prescribed by the previous year's budget. This meant no new programs.

The same year the other major source of federal funds for day care was restricted. A little noticed provision of the Social Security Act, Title IVa, authorized states to set up social service programs to support federal welfare programs, and said the federal government would pick up 75 percent of the bill. This program was expected to cost $4.6 billion in the 1973 fiscal year, and a significant fraction of the money was to go for day-care programs. The Administration, however, convinced Congress to accept a $2.5-billion ceiling on the program as part of the bargain in obtaining revenue sharing. Many day-care programs were eliminated.[50]

Congress had responded most rapidly to the women's movement. It was Congressional action that brought the power of law to bear against sex discrimination and attempted to provide a crucial set of child-care institutions for the rapidly growing proportion of working women. It was the President who tried to defend an eroding pattern of sexual relationships by vetoing one of the most important pieces of social legislation in recent decades.

The record of response to the women's issues underlines some of the strengths of the Congressional process. New issues that are not highly controversial can sometimes be forced to the floor, where it is difficult for a member to ignore demands of important newly mobilizing groups of constituents, particularly if their demands can be granted without seriously offending other constituents. Individual members of Congress who

305

specialize in a subject, develop good working relationships with concerned groups, and put together a legislative coalition don't have to engage in the ponderous institutional wrangles and fiscal debates that often paralyze the great executive agencies. Each of these "strengths," of course, can also lead to mistaken or shortsighted action. The fact remains that the Congressional process may be a good deal more responsive to certain kinds of social change than the executive branch.

The Flaws in Representation

While this book hopes to dispel many popular stereotypes about Congress, it certainly does not intend to argue that everything is fine on Capitol Hill. Although Congressional institutions and procedures do not have an inevitably negative or conservative impact on social policy, they do limit the contributions of many extremely talented younger members, particularly in the House. Far more serious than deficiencies within Congress, however, are some glaring defects in the process of getting into Congress. Since this book argues that the rules and procedures are less important than had been thought, and that real change depends upon a change in the membership, this is an extremely serious problem.

Perhaps the gravest distortions in Congressional representation come from the extraordinary difficulty of defeating incumbents, and the great dependence of Congressional campaigns on large contributions from interests with very specific legislative objectives. The slow turnover of members causes Congress to be always dominated by members with a vested interest in the organizational status quo. Sometimes it also isolates the legislative branch from changes in public attitudes. The members' dependency on business, unions, and the more affluent professions greatly increases the difficulty of enacting legislation to reform these institutions.

Frozen Incumbencies Incumbent Senators and Representatives enter campaigns with so many advantages that few are defeated even in periods of major political change. The problem is particularly severe in the House. During the 1950s and 1960s—while the country confronted a social revolution, two divisive wars, three changes in party control of the White House, dramatic economic swings, and numerous technological

Table 13-2

Percentage of Members of the House Who Have Been Elected
for Ten or More Two-Year Terms, 1911–71

1911	2.8%
1921	5.7%
1931	7.8%
1941	9.0%
1951	9.2%
1961	17.4%
1971	20.0%

SOURCE *Charles S. Bullock, "House Careerists: Changing Patterns of Longevity and Attrition," American Political Science Review LXVI (December 1972), p. 1296.*

and cultural changes—there was rarely an election when even a tenth of the House incumbents were defeated.

Even as the pace of social change has accelerated in the twentieth century, the rigid hold of incumbents has intensified. When Woodrow Wilson became President in 1913, he faced a Congress where only one Representative in forty had won election ten or more times. By 1971 a fifth of the members had accumulated this vast seniority, doubling the level of the early 1950s.

With so many old veterans in the House, the operation of the seniority system virtually guaranteed that the chairman of any important committee was the product of an earlier political era. One effect was to overstate the power of the South. During the 1960s the number of Southern Democrats was in fact gradually declining and the number of Northern Democrats growing. At any one time, however, almost a third of the Southerners were twenty-year veterans. As a result, while Northerners accounted for about two-thirds of the House Democratic caucus, they had only half the committee chairmanships and fewer yet of the most powerful chairmanships.[51]

Usually more House seats change hands through retirement or death of incumbents than through election defeats. Redrawing of district lines to comply with the Supreme Court's reapportionment decisions was apparently the largest single factor in the defeats that did take place during the 1960s.[52] Reapportionment sometimes left two incumbents in a single district and often substantially changed a district's political

307

complexion. The surprising fact is that the overwhelming majority of incumbents survived these changes.

What turnover exists in the House is generally limited to the small minority of districts with real two-party competition. During the past several decades, 80 to 90 percent of the districts have been filled by the same party throughout each ten-year period. The fact that most Congressmen face no real electoral threat, one scholar suggests, may account for the failure of House members to represent local beliefs on some issues, and their deferring instead to the position of the party leadership.[53] Such intense political insulation may produce serious representational failure.

Some political scientists thought that reapportionment would increase competition for seats by eliminating many small, static rural districts. The one-man, one-vote decisions required that each Congressional district in any state contain about the same number of people. The decisions, however, placed no restrictions on gerrymandering, the practice of creating bizarrely shaped districts that minimize competition by designing as many safe seats as possible. In many states Congressmen worked together with state legislators to draw a political map protecting incumbents. Incumbents, of course, usually value their security in one-party districts more than the possibility of their party winning additional seats in a more competitive set of districts.

Incumbents enjoy an array of additional advantages. They have existing personal organizations and can use the perquisites of office to maintain them. By devoting much of their staff resources to handling constituents' problems with federal agencies, they create a feeling of loyalty among those constituents. They can generate continuing publicity, both in the mass media and in the newsletters of organizations they assist. Local newspapers will frequently print their columns free, and they can mail newsletters to constituents at public expense. They can use Congress's radio and television studios for production of low-cost reports that will then frequently be carried free in the district. Finally, the public pays for much of the active work in organizing and managing their campaigns done by their home-district and Washington staff members during an election year. A 1970 study made a "very low" estimate that the incumbent starts out with at least a $16,000 campaign advantage through the use of his official privileges.

The Soaring Costs of Campaigning Incumbents, of course, also find it much easier than challengers to raise

Figure 13-2

Advantage of Incumbent Senators in Fund Raising in States
Where an Incumbent Ran for Reelection in 1972

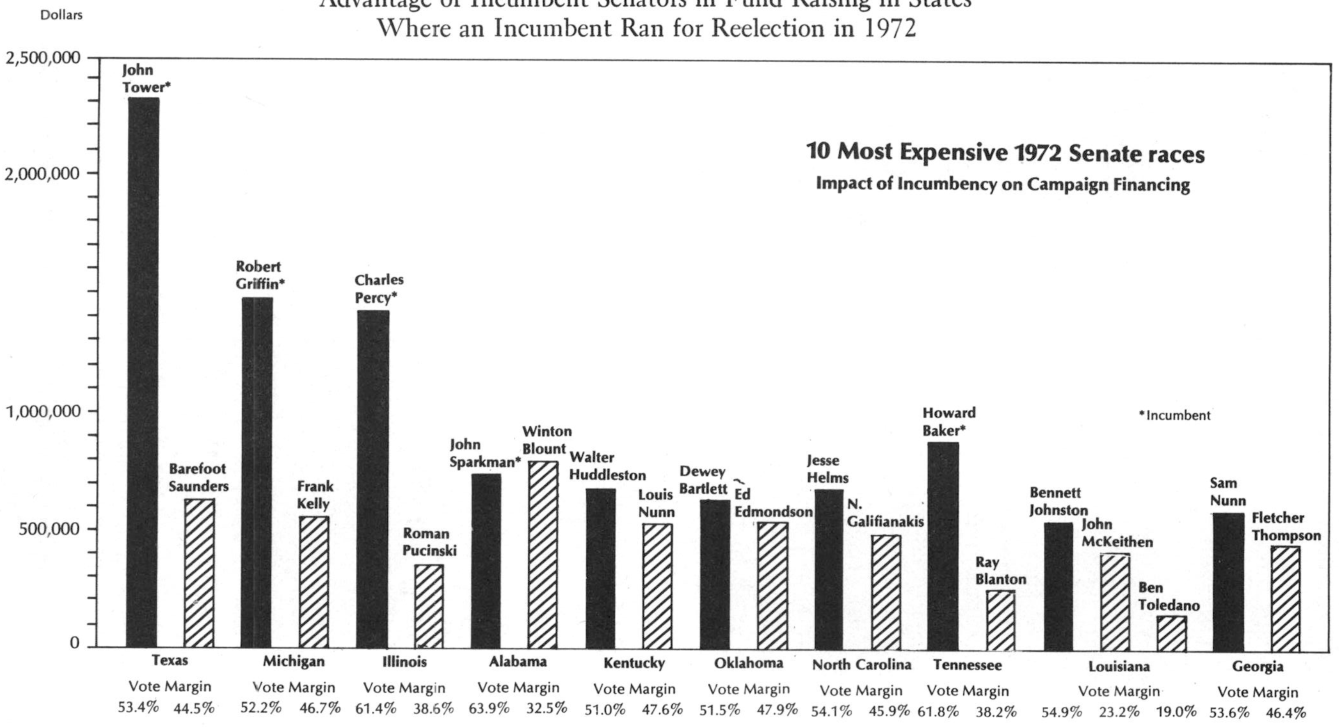

10 Most Expensive 1972 Senate races
Impact of Incumbency on Campaign Financing

*Incumbent

SOURCE   Washington Post, *September 14, 1973.*

private funds. They have a track record of help to certain interest groups and individuals, and most contributors know that incumbents are seldom beaten. To add insult to injury, most of the money raised by the Democratic and GOP Congressional campaign committees goes to incumbents.[54]

The challenger, either for the House or Senate, usually has great difficulty in even making his name known around the district. Many candidates and campaign managers are convinced that extensive television advertising is the only way to achieve name recognition. The cost is enormous, particularly for candidates in the large urbanized states, where a House candidate can only reach his district by paying thousands of dollars a minute to television stations blanketing the whole region. Even back in the mid-1960s, Senator Charles Percy (R-Ill.) recalls, "It took $1 million in my State to wage a losing campaign, just to try to pull name identification up from zero to somewhere into 50 or 60 percent, and still be battling a name recognition of 80 or 90 percent."[55]

Campaign costs were astronomical by the late 1960s. Senate races often cost a million dollars, and House races hundreds of thousands. In several cases rich men had used vast amounts of their own money to overcome the recognition barrier and capture nominations or elections. In 1970, for instance, hugely expensive primary campaigns won Democratic Senate nominations in New York and Ohio for two underdog challengers.

The problem was sufficiently serious to spur a 1970 Congressional drive to set some limits. Congress passed the 1970 Political Broadcast Act, sharply cutting back permissible levels of media spending. After the President vetoed the bill to protect the GOP's campaign finance advantage, Congress tried again in 1971 and 1972. The result was a partial reform, limiting spending on future television campaigns and restricting a candidate's use of his personal fortune.

While the reforms limited some of the grossest abuses and imposed new reporting requirements on candidates, the basic system remained largely untouched. Some dubbed the legislation the "incumbent protection act," since one consequence was to make it far more difficult for a wealthy amateur to take on an incumbent in a primary or general election. Even with the new law, campaigns were very expensive and the incumbent's advantages enormous.

As the disclosures of the Watergate scandal dramatized the corrupting influence of large-scale fund-raising, interest in basic

Figure 13-3

Indexes of Direct Campaign Expenditures by National-Level Committees, Consumer Prices, and Number of Votes Cast, 1912-1968

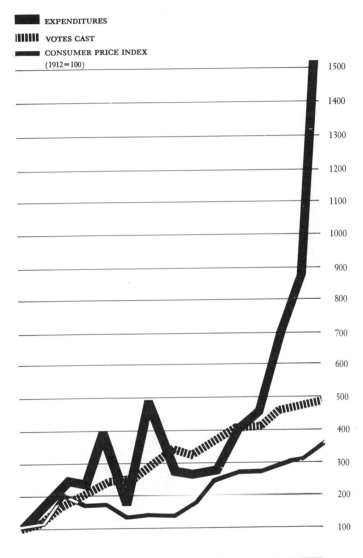

■ EXPENDITURES

|||||| VOTES CAST

■ CONSUMER PRICE INDEX
(1912=100)

1500
1400
1300
1200
1100
1000
900
800
700
600
500
400
300
200
100

1912 1916 1920 1924 1928 1932 1936 1940 1944 1948 1952 1956 1960 1964 1968

SOURCE *Robert L. Peabody, Jeffrey M. Berry, William G. Frasure, and Jerry Goldman,* To Enact A Law: Congress and Campaign Financing *(New York: Praeger, 1972), p. 11.*

311

reform grew. Senator Joe Biden (D-Del.) testified about the corrupting influence of massive fund-raising:

> . . . it's the most degrading damn thing in the world to go out and have to raise money unless you happen to be in a position where you are so strong you don't have to ask. . . . As a practical matter, we know what it takes to go out and raise money . . . with our hat in our hand whether it be to a labor union . . . or whether it be to big business interests.

Biden told how large contributors tried to exact commitments from him on defense contracts, tax reforms, and other issues.

> We politicians are put in a position where at least there is a great deal of pressure . . . to prostitute our ideas, if not our integrity. . . . At least to compromise. . . . I know I said to myself, time and again, "Well it's much better that I get elected with 80 per cent of my ideas intact . . . so maybe I should go ahead and do it."[56]

Concern was sufficiently widespread by late 1973 that a bipartisan group of Senators worked together to add a reform amendment to the Administration's bill raising the national debt ceiling. The amendment provided for public financing of both Congressional and Presidential campaigns. Powerful members of the House opposed using the emergency bill to suddenly transform Congressional campaigns, but agreed to the reform of the Presidential election process. When the compromise came to the Senate floor, however, it was blocked by a White House–supported filibuster. The White House also undermined support with threats of a veto if the bill were enacted. The reformers chose the debt-ceiling measure as a vehicle because the government would be unable to pay its bills unless the measure was rapidly enacted. The President's support of the filibuster indicated that he considered the issue of such importance that he was prepared to take the risk.[57]

Stability in a Landslide The circumstances of the 1972 Congressional elections seemed almost ideal for a large turnover of seats. The year saw the party with the Congressional minority win one of the largest Presidential landslides in American history. At the same time reapportionment after the 1970 census brought the first simultaneous redistricting of the entire country in American history. The changes appeared to favor the Republicans:

. . . more than a dozen entirely new districts were created, and others had major changes in their boundary lines. Many of the changes tended to favor the Republicans because many of the new districts were placed in fast-growing Republican suburbs and because legislatures in several states drew the lines to partisan Republican advantage.[58]

If there was to be a weakening in the recent semipermanent Democratic control of Congress, or in the domination of elections by incumbents, this should have been the time.

Although the national election found the Democratic Party in profound disarray, with a very weak national ticket and unpopular positions on several issues, little in fact changed. In spite of the historic Presidential landslide, the Congressional results were a bleak disappointment to those hoping for more turnover. Congress was virtually unaltered. In the House the GOP gained only thirteen seats, a number of which came from the South and represented no real ideological change. Over 90 percent of the House incumbents running for reelection won. In the Senate the Republicans actually lost two seats. The shift in partisan alignment was less than half the size of the usual swing in the past thirteen elections. Even when the number of resigning members was added in, the turnover was very close to normal.[59] A calculation of the ideological meaning of the election by the widely respected National Committee for an Effective Congress concluded that "progressive forces in Congress were strengthened . . . by at least 3 in the Senate and 14 in the House."[60]

The 1972 election results suggest, if anything, that the Congressional system of frozen incumbencies is intensifying. There will not be another reapportionment until 1982, at which time relaxed Supreme Court standards will permit even more leeway for protection of incumbents. The failure of the GOP to score real gains in 1972 suggests a long extension of the period of domination of Congress by elderly Democrats. The 1972 experience shows that only a very severe political or economic crisis is likely to significantly curtail the longevity of incumbents.

The Persistence of Abuses The rarity of real competition and the nature of the current system of raising campaign funds introduce some important biases into Congressional representation. Since campaigns require vast amounts of money and the great bulk of money comes from large donors, the corporate and union interests that generate directly or indirectly a great

Table 13-3

Incumbents Reelected to Congress, 1956–1972

	Total number of incumbents—				Percentage of incumbents running in general election, elected
	Defeated in primary	Running in general election	Elected in general election	Defeated in general election	
1956:					
House	6	404	389	15	96.29
Senate	0	28	25	3	89.29
1958:					
House	3	393	355	38	90.33
Senate	0	31	20	11	64.52
1960:					
House	6	400	374	26	93.50
Senate	0	29	28	1	96.55
1962:					
House	12	396	389	22	98.23
Senate	1	34	29	5	85.29
1964:					
House	44	389	344	45	88.43
Senate	4	32	38	4	87.50
1966:					
House	11	402	362	40	90.05
Senate	3	29	28	1	96.55
1968:					
House	3	401	396	5	98.75
Senate	4	24	20	4	83.33
1970:					
House	7	391	379	12	96.93
Senate	1	29	23	6	79.31
1972:					
House	13	380	367	13	96.58
Senate	2	25	20	5	79.31

	Total number of incumbents—		Percentage of incumbents running in general election, elected 1956–72
	Running in general election 1956–72	Elected in general elections 1956–72	
House	3,551	3,350	94.34
Senate	261	221	84.67

SOURCE *Library of Congress calculations, printed in* Congressional Record, *October 10, 1973, p. E6372.*

deal of the resources enjoy easy access to decision-makers and powerful influence upon them. They also possess considerable influence over the launching of Congressional careers, since the availability of these vital funds can often influence both decisions to run and success in the primaries. The nature of this system tends to make it very difficult for Congress to alter any of the major prerogatives and privileges of these central economic institutions, even when obvious abuses exist.[61] A second form of bias is that against newer political movements. Although the movement against the Vietnam War, for example, claimed the support of a large fraction of the Democratic Party, it was long almost without representation in the House of Representatives, except for a few recently elected "peace" candidates and a handful of more senior members.

The stagnant membership of the House is probably a principal reason for the ossification of Congressional leadership and the intensification of a system of leadership by inheritance that contributes little to the development of new national policies, and often exercises only a fraction of its potential power.

While reforms have been proposed to eliminate some of the distorting effects of campaign financing, they may have the unplanned consequence of intensifying the problem of institutional rigidity. If a ceiling is placed on campaign spending, for example, or each candidate given an equal amount of public funds, the interests of the economic pressure groups would be diminished, but incumbents might become even more difficult to defeat. Challengers often feel that they must spend more to overcome the dual problems of their own low name recognition by the public, and the built-in subsidy that goes to the incumbent. Nowhere, in the early 1970s, was there a serious movement to reform the process of creating safe one-party districts, or to seriously diminish the advantages of incumbents, to limit terms or enforce a retirement age.

Some very serious difficulties lie in the path of basic change. The evidence that we have suggests that most people don't even know the names of their Congressional representatives, let alone their positions on the major issues. Most candidates for Congress are happy if they can even get their name widely known in the constituency. This is why they usually concentrate their campaign funds on the mass media. Reform is possible, however, because the local party organizations that decide endorsements are open in most areas. There is also substantial evidence that a large-scale volunteer campaign effort, built around personal contact and identifying and turning out supportive voters, can make a dramatic difference at the polls.[62] If there is a sufficiently coherent and persistent drive for representation, it can be won through local political work. Given the extreme localization of the structure of political power in the United States, this is probably the only way to significantly change the character of Congressional representation in the long run, barring a very serious national crisis.

NOTES

[1] Fenno, pp. 450–53.

[2] The statistics come from summaries prepared at the end of Congressional sessions by the House Appropriations Committee and reported in the following issues of the *Congressional Record:* December 23, 1969, p. 40981; December 31, 1970, p. 44300; December 17, 1971, p. H12749; October 18, 1972, p. H10403.

[3] *Setting National Priorities:* The 1973 Budget, p. 75.

[4] *Congressional Quarterly, Congress and the Nation,* Vol. 2 (Washington: Congressional Quarterly, Inc., 1969), pp. 86–87, 107.

[5] *Congressional Quarterly Almanac,* 1971, p. 737.

[6] Reports of the House Appropriations Committee, cited in footnote 27.

[7] *Congressional Quarterly,* October 28, 1972, p. 2879; November 4, 1972, pp. 2911–13.

[8] *Congressional Record,* March 1, 1973, p. H1270.

[9] *New York Times,* December 7, 1972.

[10] *Washington Post,* January 29, 1973.

[11] *Congressional Record,* April 30, 1973, pp. S7886–92.

[12] Edward R. Fried, Alice M. Rivlin, Charles L. Schultze, and Nancy H. Teeters, *Setting National Priorities: The 1974 Budget* (Washington: Brookings Institution, 1973), pp. 1, 17, 409–10.

[13] *Congressional Record,* March 7, 1973, p. E1366.

[14] Gallup Poll cited in *Congressional Record,* April 30, 1973, p. S7891; Harris Survey reported in *Washington Post,* February 26, 1973.

[15] *Congressional Quarterly,* April 7, 1973, p. 795.

[16] *Ibid.*

[17] *Congressional Quarterly,* November 10, 1973, pp. 2943–44.

[18] *Ibid.*

[19] *Ibid.,* pp. 2969–72.

[20] Louis Fisher, *President and Congress* (New York: Free Press, 1972), pp. 122–27.

[21] *New York Times,* February 28, 1971.

[22] *Washington Post,* March 4, 1971.

[23] *Congressional Record,* March 29, 1971, p. S3961; *Washington Post,* April 5, 1971.

[24] *Congressional Record,* October 17, 1972, p. S18515.

[25] *Ibid.,* p. S18523.

[26] *Congressional Quarterly,* February 3, 1973, p. 213.

[27] Louis Fisher, "Impoundment Relies on Weak Arguments," *Washington Star-News,* February 25, 1973.

[28] This was discussed during an open meeting of the House Committee on Education and Labor on June 6, 1973, which the author attended.

[29] *Congressional Quarterly*, July 28, 1973, pp. 2065–67.

[30] *Ibid.*, September 1, 1973, pp. 2344–51.

[31] For an account sympathetic to the President, written by his former domestic policy advisor, see Daniel P. Moynihan, *The Politics of a Guaranteed Income* (New York: Vintage, 1973).

[32] *Congressional Record*, February 8, 1964, p. 2577.

[33] *Ibid.*, p. 2578.

[34] *Ibid.*, pp. 2581–82.

[35] *Ibid.*, pp. 2578–80, 2583–84.

[36] Richard P. Nathan, *Jobs and Civil Rights* (Washington: U.S. Commission on Civil Rights, 1969), pp. 50–51.

[37] Barbara A. Brown, Thomas I. Emerson, Gail Falk, and Ann E. Freedman, "The Equal Rights Amendment: A Constitutional Basis for Equal Rights for Women," *Yale Law Journal*, LXXX (April 1971), pp. 886–87.

[38] *Congressional Quarterly Almanac*, 1970, p. 707.

[39] *Ibid.*, p. 706.

[40] *Congressional Quarterly Almanac*, 1971, pp. 656–58.

[41] William Watts and Lloyd A. Free, *State of the Nation* (New York: Universe Books, 1973), pp. 61–62.

[42] Dennis R. Young and Richard R. Nelson, "Public Policy for Day Care of Young Children: Organization, Finance, and Planning" (Washington: Urban Institute, 1972), p. 18.

[43] *Ibid.*, p. 28; Senate Committee on Labor and Public Welfare, Subcommittee on Employment, Manpower, and Poverty, and Subcommittee on Children and Youth, Hearings, *Comprehensive Child Development Act of 1971*, 92d Cong., 1st Sess., 1971, p. 435.

[44] Senate Committee on Labor and Public Welfare, Subcommittee . . . Hearings, pp. 758–64.

[45] *Washington Post*, November 1, 1971.

[46] *New York Times*, November 21, 1971.

[47] Veto message, *Congressional Quarterly*, December 11, 1971, p. 2533.

[48] *Congressional Record*, June 20, 1972, p. S9759.

[49] *Ibid.*, pp. S9682–9759.

[50] Young and Nelson, pp. 36–37.

[51] Charles S. Bullock, "House Careerists: Changing Patterns of Longevity and Attrition," *American Political Science Review* LXVI (December 1972), pp. 1295–98.

[52] *Ibid.*, p. 1298.

[53] David W. Brady, "A Research Note on the Impact of Interparty Competition on Congressional Voting in a Competitive Era," *American Political Science Review* LXVII (March 1973), pp. 153–55.

[54] David Rosenbloom, *Electing Congress: The Financial Dilemma* (New York: Twentieth Century Fund, 1970), p. 36.

[55] Robert Peabody, Jeffrey M. Berry, William G. Frasure, and Jerry Goldman, *To Enact a Law: Congress and Campaign Financing* (New York: Praeger, 1972), p. 17.

[56] *Washington Post*, October 1, 1973.

[57] *Washington Post*, December 3 and December 4, 1973.

[58] Congressional Quarterly, *Congressional Districts in the 1970s* (Washington: Congressional Quarterly, Inc., 1973), p. 1.

[59] *Congressional Quarterly*, January 6, 1973, p. 13.

60 National Committee for an Effective Congress, "What If . . . ? NCEC 1972 Election Report."

61 The nature of contemporary union power is discussed in a series of 1972 *Washington Post* articles by Haynes Johnson and Nick Kotz, reprinted in the *Congressional Record*, May 3, 1972, pp. E4642–60. Among the many discussions of business influence, see Philip M. Stern's *The Rape of the Taxpayer* (New York: Random House, 1973), or Robert Engler's *The Politics of Oil* (New York: Macmillan, 1961).

62 William T. Murphy, Jr., and Edward N. Schneier, *Vote Power* (New York: Doubleday-Anchor, 1974), chapter 2.

CONGRESS and SOCIAL POLICY: A SKETCH in SUMMARY

The United States has been passing through a period of massive social and economic change during the past decade. Congress has played an extremely important role in shaping the uneven governmental responses to those changes. Contrary to popular clichés, the nation has not entered a period of an imperial Presidency and a passive Congress, nor has deadlock totally paralyzed action in most areas of policy.

The past decade has brought profound changes in the position of blacks, women, and young people in the social and political system. The major civil rights laws were a powerful response to the central shame of American democracy, governmental enforcement of the racial caste system of the South. After decades of resistance, Congress not only passed these laws, but strengthened them and then protected them from a hostile President. Congressional action has been crucial to the women's movement's attack on concepts of female status ingrained in Western culture. Congressional action making eighteen-year-olds full citizens has had little visible immediate impact, but will surely make the political system more open and responsive to young people.

After Congress approved the vast expansion of the federal role in domestic programs in the 1960s, the determined efforts of a conservative President to reverse the trend tested the real dispositions of the Democratic Congress. The period found even the more conservative elements of the legislative branch operating more progressively than the President. This was very apparent, for example, in the massive Social Security boosts approved by the Ways and Means and the Senate Finance committees, and in the continual rejection of the President's meager education and health budgets by both Appropriations committees. In most cases Congress led the executive branch in responding to new ecological issues and in creating new tools for control of the economy.

The period of the late 1960s and early 1970s witnessed simultaneously the advance of sweeping claims of Presidential powers, and the decline of the real strength of the Presidency. During the period between the end of the Second World War and the late 1960s, Presidents enjoyed great latitude in the conduct of foreign policy and military affairs. This freedom of action, and the bipartisan Congressional support that sustained it, began to erode when rising opposition to the Vietnam War destroyed the Johnson Presidency. At first it affected the margins of international power, such as foreign military assistance, but by the early 1970s it had produced serious Congressional pressures to restrain the military apparatus and to subject Presidential action to legislative control. War powers legislation—passed over a Presidential veto—and some reductions in the defense and foreign aid budgets began to cut into the muscle of executive leadership; 1973 saw the extraordinary spectacle of Congress forcing the end of military action in Cambodia by cutting off funds, and Congress rejecting trade legislation central to the policy of détente with the U.S.S.R.

The Nixon period witnessed the resurgence of some long-neglected legislative powers in domestic affairs, and the most striking Congressional rejection of a President's domestic program in decades. In the major Supreme Court nomination fights, Congress resumed an active role in the constitution of the highest Court, a power that had lain dormant for most of the twentieth century. When the early phases of the Watergate scandal indicated grave improprieties in the executive branch, Congress acted both through a massive investigation and through insistence on an independent special prosecutor to force revelation of the most serious corruption in American history. When the investigation came under Administration at-

320

tack, very heavy Congressional pressure persuaded the President to retreat. Eventually he was forced to leave office.

The success of the legislators in resisting a sustained, intense White House fight against serious investigation of the scandals and in helping the press educate the public, and forcing the President to yield unprecedented personal records was a tribute to the vitality of Congress. The experience seemed certain to increase both Congressional power and Congressional vigilance for some time to come. Anyone who doubts the continuing reality of Congressional power need only read the transcripts of the extraordinary White House tapes that President Nixon was forced to release by pressure from the House Judiciary Committee. Amid all the plots and the bitter, candid criticisms of men and institutions, it is evident that President Nixon and his chief advisors retained a fear of Congressional power. While their discussions are full of plans to thwart the independence and manipulate the operations of various governmental institutions, the mass media, and the criminal justice system, there is a continual recognition of the limited power the White House can exercise over Congress.

In 1974 the House Judiciary Committee began the impeachment process for the second time in American history. The process had been virtually forgotten since Congress failed to impeach Andrew Johnson after the Civil War, but now it worked. Only when impeachment and conviction seemed certain did the President resign. The revival of Congress's ultimate weapon surely lends strength to the legislative branch, and diminishes the power and autonomy of future Presidents.

Presidential power rests to a substantial degree on the sense of respect and legitimacy accorded to the office of President. One certain effect of the Watergate scandal and the President's resignation has been to weaken that respect for some time to come, thus increasing the relative power of Congress.

While the Watergate disaster dramatized Congress's investigatory power and resurrected the idea of impeachment, its drama often obscured more mundane facts about the period. In the long and often unpublicized domestic policy struggles of the period, Congress responded to intense and single-minded White House pressure without yielding its role.

The period of Presidential reaction on social policy under President Nixon showed that the close tie between Congress and various organized constituencies could have liberal as well as conservative consequences. Coming to office with the belief that he had a mandate to reverse many of the domestic innova- **321** tions of the Great Society, the President encountered determined resistance from Congress. Congress responded by rejecting a higher portion of Nixon legislative proposals than those of any recent President, even though Nixon presented a relatively slim set of innovations. Only by stretching executive powers and spending his political authority in bitter confrontations with Congress over vetoes and impoundments was the President able to slow the momentum of those programs. Eventually, the price to be paid was strong Congressional attempts to cut back on the powers of the executive branch.

In arguing that Congress possesses a substantial capacity to initiate new national policies, and that those policies may well be more "progressive" or "responsive" than positions taken by a President, this book certainly does not mean to support another false view of Congress. While Congress may be *relatively* more activist than a conservative President, it can hardly be described as a liberal institution. The major liberal force in American politics is the Northern and Western wing of the Democratic Party. Only when political circumstances give that wing of the party an operating majority in Congress (a rare circumstance) or predominant influence in the executive branch (a more common occurrence) does that institution become the primary focus for policy innovation.

During the Nixon Administration Congress succeeded in putting a few major new social issues on the national agenda, and in protecting much of the Great Society framework. On many other issues, however, its record was far more mixed. Design of new housing policies, for example, was long stalled by a stalemate within Congress, as well as by one between Congress and the White House. Congress delegated vast powers over the economy to the executive branch without making basic policy decisions. Congress preserved existing civil rights laws, aimed primarily at the classic Southern forms of discrimination, but proved incapable of developing policies to cope with the intensifying racial separation of the urban North. There were few significant new ideas in education policy in the legislation of the early 1970s, and the intense national discussion of health care needs yielded little on Capitol Hill. Efforts to reform the tax structure or to alter the basic assumptions of welfare policy were largely barren. The list goes on and on.

Judged against the national goals of activist liberal groups, or even against the Democratic Party platform, the record of Congress was fundamentally inadequate. Congress has not responded forcefully to a number of evident social needs. The

322

obstacle has been sometimes the President, and sometimes Congress itself.

The important thing to remember is that the failings criticized by activists are usually not failings produced by the structure or procedures of Congress, but by the vision of its members. The shortcomings—and many of the achievements—result from reasonably effective Congressional representation of widely held and often contradictory values of the public and of the members' active and important constituents. The unwillingness to move forward in some significant areas of social policy reflects far less the inadequacies of Congress as an organization than the failure of middle-class Americans to recognize that any social crisis exists. The basic reason why neither Congress nor the President is truly liberal is that liberalism normally represents a minority position in the United States—a fact often obscured by the assumption that the Democratic Party is a liberal party, rather than an exceedingly broad coalition.

Much of the national movement for extensive Congressional reform is based on false assumptions. Reform and rationalization of committee jurisdiction, chairmen's powers, the budget process, Congressional staff capacity, etc., may produce a more efficient legislative body, more equitable to individual members, and perhaps better able to compete with the executive branch. These are worthwhile goals, but they are not likely to transform the substance of Congressional decisions. Reformers who promise an institutional answer to a political question are likely to be disappointed. There are no shortcuts. Probably the only way to build a new Congress is to undertake the hard political work necessary to send new men and women to Capitol Hill.

Although Congress is neither the liberal institution some would wish, nor the conservative institution many believe it to be, it is a powerful force in the construction of national policy. While the political circumstances of depression, wars and international crises, and a burgeoning executive branch have often served to magnify the Presidency, the remarkable fact is that Congress has preserved the Constitutional model of fragmented power through an era of serious parliamentary decline in most Western nations. If anything, the political scandals of the early 1970s have only reinforced this model, increasing public support for the assertion of Congressional authority.

The difficulty of weighing the role of Congress in the policy process is magnified by the complex and often obscurely indirect nature of Congressional influence. Fortunately for this 323 analysis, the rare circumstance of clear and frequently harsh ideological and partisan differences between the President and Congress during the Nixon Administration brought out into the open much of the continuing but often subliminal contest for power. This makes possible a more accurate perception of the policy process, and a growing awareness of the largely unused reservoirs of Congressional authority that can be drawn upon when a President neglects the tradition of consultation and compromise with the legislative branch.

In a society experiencing rapid social and political change, the major democratic institutions reflect shifting constituencies and evolving political alliances. At the present time these forces tend to be moving Congress away from its very conservative past, and the Presidency away from the historical circumstances that once made the White House the powerful spokesman for urban minorities. The very heavy dependence of GOP Presidential candidates on Southern support and the growing power in the House of liberal Democrats from safe one-party urban seats are two signs of these changes. Nothing suggests, however, that there is anything permanent or historically inevitable about these changes. The time has come for students of American politics to recognize the limits of institutional generalizations based on the political circumstances of the recent past.

The abuses of Presidential power revealed by the Watergate scandals have tended to replace the popular image of the beneficence of Presidential power with a popular fear of the abuse of executive authority. The long-established tendency of progressives to look to the White House for responsive leadership is being replaced by a judgment that the President is excessively powerful, and by a tendency to look to Congress for salvation. Both images assume that the President possesses vast, even excessive, powers. While this is surely true in the fields of foreign policy, military affairs, and national security, it is not true in the development of the nation's social policy. Thus, for example, institutional changes intended to reduce the power of a corrupt executive branch may have the consequence of constricting the already limited power of a future liberal President to initiate and implement major social reforms.

It has been a disservice—and one currently conducive to a crushing disillusionment with politics—for academics to spread the belief that Presidential power is better than Congressional power. (What they actually meant was that during the period between the early 1930s and the mid-1960s, the Presidency was usually controlled by the Democratic Party, and that the President tended to respond to a more liberal constituency than that of the Congressional leadership.) It would, of course, be equally misleading to assume that Congressional power is better, more progressive, or less corrupt.

It is vital to realize that the making of national domestic policy takes place in a context of genuinely divided power, and that the Congress as well as the President possesses both the ability to initiate and the power to veto major policy changes. The system works well when there is a clear consensus in the country, or clear control of both branches by the dominant wing of either party. Usually these conditions are not present and the system is biased either toward compromise and incremental change, or toward confrontation and inaction. The Nixon period clearly shows that the modern Presidency can be quite as efficient an engine of negative social policy as was Congress during certain earlier progressive Administrations.

It is only fair to recognize that much of the criticism that has been aimed at Congress has been misdirected. It is really criticism of the inefficiencies and delays built into the American Constitutional system, and of the nebulous and often contradictory ideological bases of the alliances that constitute the national political parties. Failure to correctly identify these underlying causes leads one to misjudge the solutions.

The people of the United States generally have the kind of legislative body they want and deserve. It is a Congress that has the power to take decisive action, but most of whose members rarely believe the public demands such change. It is an evolving institution and an increasingly representative one. It has great power but rarely selects leaders who use that power with energy, skill, and imagination. With a few significant exceptions, the altering of its internal rules will not change its decisions much. Congress is likely to be a moderately progressive institution in the next years. If it is to be much more than that —or less—its membership must be significantly changed.

INDEX

and Emergency Employment Act, 212–14, 217–28
and impoundment, 292–96
and job discrimination, 80–90
manpower goal, 201–03
massive use of veto, 286–92
1973 attack on public jobs, 243–45
opposition to civil rights, 71–73
opposition to new domestic programs, 266
postelection budget offensive, 160–64
and public works, 235–42
revenue-sharing counterproposal, 165–71
Schlesinger on, 256
Southern strategy, 71–72, 108
Supreme Court nominations, 103–16
veto of emergency employment program, 212–14
and welfare reform, 51, 229–33

O Congress (Donald Riegle), 26
Office of Economic Opportunity, 197
Office of Education, U.S., 128, 130–32, 139, 147, 148
Office of Management and Budget, 37, 267, 295
O'Hara, James G., 158, 203, 204, 209, 212–13, 220, 224
O'Neill, Thomas P., Jr., 28, 157, 276
Operation Mainstream, 192, 196
Osborne, John, 173–74

Parker, John, 104
Parliamentary system, English, 13
Panetta, Leon, 74
Pastore, John O., 158

Patman, Wright, 291–92
Payroll tax, 275–76
see also Taxation
Peabody, Robert, 53
Pell, Claiborne, 168
Percy, Charles H., 8, 158, 159, 163, 310
Perkins, Carl D., 134, 138, 155, 156, 161, 166, 168–69, 178, 183, 200, 227
Philadelphia Plan (for ending job discrimination), 62, 84–88, 117
Phillips, Kevin P., 7
Polarization
desegregation aid and, 173–88
Policy
domestic, Congressional leadership in, 45
foreign, see Foreign policy
racial, 269–70
regulatory, 268–78
Policy-making, 253–325
misconceptions about, 253–58
Political Broadcast Act (1970), 310
Political science, 5, 13–14
behaviorist, 5, 23
traditional, 5, 13, 23
Pollak, Louis, 112
Pollution-control legislation, 284
see also Environmental programs
Poverty
programs, 36, 47, 49, 53
amid prosperity, 193–94
see also specific measures
Powell, Adam Clayton, 127, 128
Power, Congressional
Constitutional basis of, 14
fear of, 13–15, 253–54, 321
Power, Presidential, 5, 6, 10, 20–21, 40, 254–57, 261, 293, 320, 321, 324–25
Presidency
changing, in Nixon era, 5–7

335

337

A 4
B 5
C 6
D 7
E 8
F 9
G 0
H 1
I 2
J 3